'I love Dan's insight from his beginnings as an everyday guy, who pushes himself into operating in a very, very non-everyday environment. A fascinating account of what it is like to go into battle, and the unseen mental battles that arise from the experience. Honest and inspiring. I loved it.'

HAMISH BLAKE

'Dr Pronk walks us to the very gates of hell and points to the nightmare that is modern warfare. The thrall of combat, the dread of buried mines, and the shattered bodies of his mates all feature in this parallel universe that was Australia's war in Afghanistan. This is not some well-worn trope of heroism in war – it brings to life the ghosts of Australia's best fighters: their grit, their humour, and their final moments. These fallen sons both haunted and inspired Dan to live a complete life. A searing story: unforgettable and important.'

MARK WALES

'Dan gives us an uncensored look into the darkest sides of combat and a raw, personal account of events that have become legend in the Special Forces world. An open, frank look into the mind of the doctor you want by your side when the unthinkable happens.'

DAMIEN THOMLINSON

'Dr Dan Pronk transports the reader into the boots and under the combat helmet of Special Forces in a way few writers can. The idea of a fully armed doctor engaging with an enemy to potentially take life and then within seconds fighting to save one is an incredibly unique perspective. Dan's memoir of his time as a combat doctor, saving lives and at times losing them in the midst of battle, offers a rare, heartfelt perspective of the best, bravest and worst of humanity – but one we all benefit from hearing.'

MERRICK WATTS

'Beyond the headlines, popular imagery and mythology of SAS and Commandos, are stories of duty and devotion to one another. *The Combat Doctor* is both a participant and an observer – of skill, courage, death and growth from the traumatic aftermath of war. Step out of your comfort zone, accept the challenge to be a better person.'

HON DR BRENDAN NELSON AO

Dr Dan Pronk resigned himself to studying medicine on an army scholarship after failing dismally in his first career dream of being a professional triathlete. Upon qualifying as an army doctor Dan completed SAS selection and moved into special operations, where he served for five years, including four tours of Afghanistan. He was awarded a Commendation for Distinguished Service for his conduct in combat on his second tour.

Upon discharge from the army, Dan completed an MBA and moved into medical leadership roles, including as deputy medical director of a regional hospital and medical director for a state prison health service, before moving into emergency department work.

Dan regularly presents to a wide range of audiences on resilience and has co-authored a book on the topic, *The Resilience Shield*. He is also 'Dr Dan' on the hit TV show *SAS Australia*. In his spare time he can often be found driving his vintage Lamborghini in the Adelaide Hills (or standing next to it on the side of the road awaiting yet another tow truck!). Dan is married to a very tolerant wife and has three sons.

Also by Dr Dan Pronk

The Resilience Shield
(with Ben Pronk DSC and Tim Curtis)

THE COMBAT DOCTOR

DR DAN PRONK

MACMILLAN
Pan Macmillan Australia

Some of the people in this book have had their names changed to
protect their identities.

Pan Macmillan acknowledges the Traditional Custodians of country throughout
Australia and their connections to lands, waters and communities.
We pay our respect to Elders past and present and extend that respect
to all Aboriginal and Torres Strait Islander peoples today.
We honour more than sixty thousand years of storytelling, art and culture.

First published 2022 in Macmillan by Pan Macmillan Australia Pty Ltd
1 Market Street, Sydney, New South Wales, Australia, 2000

 A catalogue record for this
book is available from the
National Library of Australia

Typeset in 11.7/16 pt Sabon by Midland Typesetters, Australia

Printed by IVE

Any health or medical content contained in this book is not intended as health or medical
advice. The publishers and their respective employees, agents and authors are not liable
for injuries or damage occasioned to any person as a result of reading or following any
health or medical content contained in this book.

The author and the publisher have made every effort to contact copyright holders
for material used in this book. Any person or organisation that may have been
overlooked should contact the publisher.

Aboriginal and Torres Strait Islander people should be aware that
this book may contain images or names of people now deceased.

 The paper in this book is FSC® certified.
FSC® promotes environmentally responsible,
socially beneficial and economically viable
management of the world's forests.

First and foremost, this book is dedicated to the Voodoo Medics of Australia's Special Operations Command, and specifically for those who repeatedly put their own lives at risk in order to save their comrades in dire circumstances. You know who you are, and I have served with many of you. To have walked among you was humbling; to have led you was the greatest privilege.

To my wife Kristy, my best friend and the love of my life. I will be forever indebted to you for your unconditional support in allowing me to pursue my dreams, and for being there when those dreams turned to nightmares. Every day I thank the higher power that allowed me to return to you, while denying others the same opportunity to return to their loved ones.

Finally, to the warriors of Australia's Special Air Service Regiment and 2nd Commando Regiment. Thank you for accepting me into your worlds. I have the utmost professional respect for all who wear the sandy or green berets of your respective units. You are a breed apart and few equal your stoicism. My time with you will never be forgotten.

CONTENTS

This book contains detailed descriptions of the application of battlefield medicine, including on some patients who did not survive the ordeal. These passages may be triggering for some veterans. Reader discretion is advised.

It is not the critic who counts; not the man who points out how the strong man stumbles, or where the doer of the deeds could have done better. The credit belongs to the man who is actually in the arena, whose face is marred by dust and sweat and blood; who strives valiantly; who errs, who comes short again and again, because there is no effort without error and shortcoming; but who does actually strive to do the deeds; who knows the great enthusiasms, the great devotions; who spends himself in a worthy cause; who at best knows in the end the triumph of high achievement, and who at worst, if he fails, at least fails whilst daring greatly, so that his place shall never be with those cold and timid souls who knew neither victory nor defeat.

—THEODORE ROOSEVELT

PROLOGUE

'STOP WHAT YOU'RE DOING – HE'S GONE.'

The sound of the surgeon's voice, coupled with the expression on his face, portrayed the frustration he felt. The resuscitation team stopped their actions and fell silent, waiting for what came next.

'Time of death ten forty-seven hours,' the surgeon continued, stripping his bloodied gloves from his hands and flicking them into a nearby contaminated waste bin.

A scribe dutifully scribbled down the time and date, 2 July 2012, on the casualty's formal documentation, while the rest of the team looked grave.

I felt nothing, despite the fact that the heavily tattooed SASR operator lying dead before me was a friend of mine. My intimate involvement with three more just like him during my previous tour of Afghanistan had stripped me of the human

1

emotion required to register what was occurring at the time. I had become robotic in my response to death, and viewed it simply as a series of forms that would need to be completed, and hoops that would have to be jumped through, to get the body home to Australia.

I had not always been that way. Just a few years earlier I would have responded to the situation as a normal person might, with grief and tears. You see, I was a general practitioner, no different on paper from the friendly, balding, slightly overweight doctor you might consult when your kids have an ear infection, brimming with sympathy and empathy. But I had swapped my stethoscope for an M4 carbine rifle; now my consulting rooms were the dusty battlefields of Afghanistan. I had become something different, and I wasn't sure if I liked it.

The surgeon gestured for me to come to the casualty's side, pointing out the devastating damage the enemy bullet had done to the SAS operator's vital organs. An aperture had been created between the ribs of his left chest wall in a desperate attempt to identify and rectify the injuries that had claimed his life. I could immediately see the extent of the damage and take solace in the fact that death would have been near instantaneous. After a brief moment of contemplation, I stepped back from my friend's body as the mortuary affairs team arrived to begin their processes.

Making my way out of the resuscitation room at the multinational hospital on our base in Tarin Kowt, Afghanistan, I was met by a small crowd of the dead operator's mates. I stood with them as the body was wheeled out of the resuscitation bay, and together we followed it to the morgue. After a short ceremony led by the Special Operations Task Group padre in the confines of the refrigerated mortuary shipping container, the door to the morgue was shut and bolted, our dead friend within, the lives of his family and loved ones irreversibly altered.

I left the hospital and made my way back to the Australian special operations base. As I walked, I replayed the day's events in my mind, as well as the events of my previous tour, and the deaths of my three teammates. The task group had not lost anyone since, but here I was, back in Afghanistan less than one year later, and the SOTG had suffered another fatality. The way I saw it, my presence was the common factor in the deaths, a jinx of sorts. I could not blame fate for my circumstances; the fault was all mine. A series of calculated and very deliberate life choices had brought me here.

Voodoo Medicine was the umbrella term used by the medical elements from the units of the Australian Army's Special Operations Command (SOCOMD). Its origins stemmed from one of the fraternity's most highly decorated medics who, while on deployment in Afghanistan in 2007, first drew a small voodoo doll logo and married it with the phrase *Dominating the Dark Arts* to describe the act of providing medical support to the unique establishment that is Australian SOCOMD. Voodoo Medicine encompassed the full spectrum of medical support required by the special operator, from the day-to-day management of their coughs, colds and sore holes to the frontline application of dressings to bullet wounds or tourniquets to amputated limbs. Voodoo Medicine was delivered by day or night, by land, air, sea or sub-surface, and in peacetime as well as at war, because that was what SOCOMD demanded.

During the five-year period between 2009 and 2013, I had the privilege of serving as a regimental medical officer with the Australian Army's two premier special operations combat units – the 2nd Commando Regiment (2 CDO) and the Special Air Service Regiment (SASR) – and became one of the leaders of the Voodoo Medics. It was a busy time for Australian SOCOMD, with the conflict in Afghanistan in full swing, and during my time in the command I completed four operational tours of that theatre of war. When I think back on my SOCOMD career – more than a hundred missions in Afghanistan, including a spectrum of special operations missions and forward aero-medical evacuations – I remember spending a lot of time cold, hungry, hot, wet, thirsty, exhausted, filthy, nauseated, seasick, airsick, frustrated, busting for a piss or shit, laughing until I cried and, on one occasion, crying until I laughed. I experienced soaring highs – including passing the gruelling SASR selection course and being decorated for my conduct in action – as well as the gut-wrenching lows of watching friends die on the battlefield, helpless to save them. I felt the exhilaration of combat, and walked away from a helicopter crash unscathed (albeit a minor one).

Strangely, I don't ever recall feeling scared. Disgusted and repulsed, yes, but never scared. This has nothing to do with being brave; I spent a lot of time around bravery and I know what that looks like. I put it down to being too stupid to register when I should have been scared, so that by the time it occurred to me that my life had been in danger, the moment for fear had passed.

Prior to joining SOCOMD I viewed the organisation through rose-coloured glasses, everything go-fast and shiny. That illusion stayed intact during my regular army career, my time training up for SASR selection, my time with the commandos and throughout my first rotation of Afghanistan. I left that first tour wanting more: more action, more combat, more dead enemy and more casualties to treat. It proved to be a case of be careful what you wish for, as on my subsequent tours I got all of that and then some. The glossy veneer of special operations gradually wore off, and I had glimpses of the horror of what can exist underneath.

During my cumulative time in Afghanistan the SOTG lost four soldiers, three of whom I was on the ground with at the time they were killed. Seldom a day passes when I don't think of the sacrifice made by these four soldiers. I certainly appreciate that across the coalition there are thousands of others who made the same sacrifice and unquestionably deserve the same respect, but having not been there for their deaths I simply cannot feel the same about them. I know exactly what it felt, sounded and smelled like when the men I knew died; the memories are etched into my mind and played for years on loop during sleepless nights.

This book started as a means of excavating these memories: an attempt to exorcise my mind of them and trap them in the hard drive of a computer that I could turn off at night when I needed to sleep. It was not until I began to write it all down that I started to truly appreciate the exceptional nature of the people around me during my years with SOCOMD, and especially during my time on special operations in Afghanistan. Through immersion in the special operations culture I had become desensitised to the bravery and heroics of the members of the 2nd Commando Regiment, the SASR and the Special Operations Engineer Regiment. Events in which Australian soldiers gave their lives and others risked their own to try to help them didn't strike me as remarkable at the time. They do now.

This is the story of how it all came about. How I went from a directionless teenager to an army officer and doctor. How I then traded the practice of regular medicine for Voodoo Medicine, and the profound consequences of that choice. It is a cautionary tale for those contemplating a similar path: the psychological injuries you suffer might be as severe as the physical wounds you treat, and the battle to reintegrate into society may prove as fierce as any gunfight you encounter in the field.

It is also a story of hope for veterans struggling with the demons of war. There is a pathway out of the shadows, although in the darkness that path can be hard to see. The same resilience that you subconsciously built in becoming an instrument of war can be rebuilt in the aftermath of your service. Through the finding of new purpose and integration into a new tribe, the chrysalis of a new identity can begin to form, from which the evolution of yourself can emerge. It is not only possible to recover from the wounds of war but to thrive because of them. I know this because I have done it. Ultimately, this is a story of post-traumatic growth.

I

AN UNLIKELY SOLDIER

I HAVE NO CLEAR RECOLLECTION OF WHEN I BECAME AWARE of the concept of special operations, and I certainly had absolutely no desire to join a special operations unit, or the military at all, until well into my early twenties.

Military service was in my blood, though. I was born in 1977 in Townsville, Queensland, where my dad, Hendrik – Henk for short – was posted as an army helicopter pilot. Dad had been named after his uncle, a Royal Air Force Spitfire pilot in World War II who was killed in an air-to-air collision around the time of the Battle of Britain. During my youth and early adulthood, Dad rose through the ranks to command an army aviation regiment. My mum, Eliza, was a speech therapist. In between raising kids she would pick up work, only to be uprooted a couple of years later with the army's next posting cycle and have to re-establish herself all over again.

My brother Ben, fifteen months my elder, seemed destined to follow in the family footsteps. In the photo albums from our youth, it is rare to find Ben without his trusty plastic M16 rifle in hand. He joined school cadets as soon as he was old enough and never looked back.

Despite these influences, or perhaps because of them, I headed in a different direction.

My memories of my primary school years are mostly positive ones of barefoot camping expeditions, barbecues with my dad's army mates and their families, and open days on the army bases he was posted to. Dad's postings during my pre and primary school years included a brief stint in the UK, Canberra, Toowoomba, Sydney, and eventually Brisbane at the time of my transition into high school. Starting afresh at a new school every two or three years as we relocated meant I never established a group of close friends, and I suspect this intensified my natural tendency towards introversion. I was a deep-thinking kid but an average student, achieving comfortable passes in all subjects but never shining. I could hold my own across a range of sports without excelling, and stayed chubby until my mid-teens, drawing the attention of the occasional bully.

As I progressed through high school my future didn't seem to hold any special promise. There was no indication that I'd end up in a career such as medicine, special forces or – heaven forbid – both. However, with the benefit of hindsight some of the personality traits that would draw me towards the pursuit of excellence, and the 'tip of the spear', were apparent.

One such trait, later labelled a *sensation-seeking personality type* by a special operations psychologist, began to emerge by early high school, facilitated in no small part by my best mate at the time, Trevor.

Trevor was a South African emigrant who had lived a significantly less sheltered life than me. He had been put back a year in school when he moved to Australia, while I had been put up a year due to a move and the misalignment of interstate school curriculums, meaning Trevor was a full two years my senior as we entered high school. We bonded over a shared love of Run DMC and became thick as thieves.

By the time I was twelve, Trevor had mentored me in the fine art of rolling my own cigarettes and smoking them without coughing my lungs up, as well as introducing me to the joys of alcohol on a night when I was sleeping over at his house. Trevor's mum cooked us a big feed of spaghetti bolognaise and then she and Trevor's dad went out, leaving us boys in the care of Trevor's sultry teenage sister, who gave zero fucks about us. Letting us know that she was not to be bothered under any circumstances, she locked herself in her bedroom downstairs and turned the music up high.

Left to our own devices, Trevor and I zeroed in on the liquor cabinet. Trevor, who unlike me had some experience with alcohol, retrieved a full bottle of gin from the back of the cabinet, cracked the seal and took a huge slug before passing it my way and gesturing for me to follow suit. I fought the urge to gag as the searing liquid flowed down my gullet, my face contorting into what I imagine a bulldog's might look like when licking piss off a thistle. The effect was near instantaneous and profound. I felt brilliant. In my naivety, I had no idea that the amount-of-alcohol versus feeling-of-goodness curve was not linear, but took a steep downward turn past a certain point. I would learn that important life lesson about an hour later. After handing the bottle back and forth until it was empty, Trevor and I ran riot through the living room as Run DMC's *Tougher Than Leather* pumped from his cassette player at a volume rivalling the Seattle grunge coming from Trevor's sister's stereo downstairs.

Trevor was the first to turn a little green from the half-bottle of gin in his guts, and leaving me to party on alone he retreated to his bedroom to lie down. Around fifteen minutes later, and still feeling great myself, I stumbled down the hallway to check on Trevor, finding him incoherent on his bed in a pool of his own vomit. Despite my inebriated state, I registered on some level that this would certainly give our game away when his parents got home, so I wandered back out to the kitchen to fetch a bowl of water and a cloth to try to clean up Trevor's mess. It was only when I returned to the bedroom and started trying to clean the vomit that the first waves of nausea struck me. The pungent smell of Trevor's regurgitated spaghetti bolognaise filled my nostrils and precipitated a violent reaction in my stomach. Having the presence of mind to seek a more appropriate place to hurl up my own innards, I was running down the hallway towards the kitchen when the first torrent of acidic fluid rushed up my food pipe. As I clutched my mouth in a futile attempt to prevent its exit, the regurgitate sprayed with force from my nose, painting the walls and floor of the hallway, and leaving a single strand of spaghetti dangling from my left nostril.

I kept running and made it through the kitchen door onto the back verandah in time for the second wave of emesis, delivering what seemed like litres of pureed pasta and meat sauce onto the back garden. Then, struggling for balance in my vertiginous state, I stumbled down the stairs to the yard and lay on my back staring at the spinning night sky, wishing for the experience to be over and vowing that I would never touch alcohol again.

That vow would last all of one week. This introduction to the joys of intoxication was the first of many drinking sessions with Trevor, and led somewhat predictably to a less-than-stellar academic performance in my first year of high school. Perhaps fortuitously, my dad posted to the Oakey Army Aviation Centre at the end of the year and we relocated back to the nearby city of Toowoomba.

Without the influence of Trevor in my life I managed to conform to my new high school, although I never quite fit in. It was an old English-style boys private school with a proud tradition in rugby union and academic excellence, neither of which I could contribute to.

I managed to keep my rebellious streak at bay for several years, but as the hormones kicked in it came to the forefront once more. I would receive the cane on a near weekly basis and, in the absence of any other strong personal identity, became known as the kid who goaded the teachers until they hit him. My new partner in crime, another Dan, picked up where Trevor had left off, and we continued together down the same destructive path. I started growing my hair long, wearing an earring and ditching school to hang out with Dan, and it came as no surprise when I was asked to leave the school one term into year eleven. It transpired that *asked to leave* was a euphemism for expulsion that looked better on my school record. Thankfully, it allowed me to enrol at another private school across town, one far more accommodating of my personality and interests, and which had the added bonus of being co-ed.

By that stage I had developed a penchant for aerosol art, which led to my first forays into clandestine missions. Pre-mission planning would begin at the start of a school week, with lesson after lesson spent sketching what I intended to spray-paint rather than learning physics, maths and biology. As the week progressed a target would be determined, mostly in the form of a parked coal train in the local shunting yard or a set of public toilets. Coordination conferences would be held with any other operatives involved and, this being an era before mobile phones, a marry-up time and point would be decided upon for team missions. Insertion plat-forms consisted of skateboards or BMX bikes, which were pre-positioned in the bushes out the front of my house, along with my backpack full of paint and sketches. On the night in question, I would wait up until my parents were asleep before stealthily removing the flyscreen from my bedroom window and lowering myself to the ground below. I would make my way to the designated target, decorate it with my pre-drawn mural, which often took four or five hours to complete, and then exfiltrate back home just prior to dawn. After stashing my insertion platform and backpack in the garden, I would heave myself as quietly as possible through my bedroom window, replace the flyscreen and sleep until midday.

During one such sleep-in following a night mission to graffiti two walls of a public toilet in a park near my house, I was rudely awoken by a loud banging on our front door followed by the sound of my mum's voice.

'Good morning, officer.'

Fuck. I strained to hear the other half of the conversation but couldn't.

'Yes, Dan Pronk does live here – I'll just go and get him.'

Fuck, fuck. I leaped out of bed and was pulling on some clothes when Mum burst into my room.

'Dan, there's a police officer at the front door asking questions about some new graffiti on the public toilets at the park.' She fixed me with an accusing look. 'Was it you?'

Figuring that the game was up, I confessed. 'Yeah, that was me. I did it last night.'

I headed down the hall towards the front door to face the music.

Mum followed. 'Who else was involved?' she asked, continuing her interrogation.

'No-one, it was just me,' I replied truthfully; it had been a solo mission.

When I got to the door, there was no sign of a police officer. I peered out into the street. Maybe the cop had gone to get something in the car – handcuffs, perhaps. But there was nothing. Confused, I looked back at Mum, who had now been joined by my dad. The pair of them, who were grinning smugly from ear to ear, burst into hysterical laughter at the look on my face. There had been no police officer at the door; Mum and Dad had gone for a walk in the park that morning and saw murals that were a dead ringer for the drawings I had been dumb enough to stick up on my bedroom wall. My operational security definitely needed some work! That debacle led to the flyscreen in my window being permanently fixed in place, making it exponentially harder to sneak out of the house at night – but not impossible.

Academia was not my forte during high school, although looking back I realise my teachers had caught glimpses of what might be. *Dan shows potential, however he is not working to the best of his ability* was repeated on my report card year after year.

My early career aspirations included commercial art and panel beating. As I progressed through my final years of school, and motivated primarily by the desire to lose weight to make myself more attractive to girls, I began to run. I was particularly drawn to middle-distance and cross-country running, and very quickly started to show promise, winning school and regional championships in 1500-metre races. From there I started competing in triathlons, and soon found myself on the podium for my age group in state titles. At a time when my friends were graduating from drinking alcohol and smoking cigarettes to popping pills and smoking weed, I had transformed my life-style into a healthy one, giving up all the smoking and drinking, and even going vegetarian for a year. My new drug of choice was competitive sport, and not only was it a brilliant outlet for my teenage frustrations, it was also socially acceptable, and for the first time in my life I earned accolades from my school.

I fumbled through my senior high school studies, just managing to pass maths and physics, and graduating with results good enough to get me into university, but nowhere near good enough for me to have my pick of courses. It didn't matter; by that point I was convinced I had a future as a professional triathlete.

Strongly encouraged by my parents to further my educa-tion, after high school I moved to the Gold Coast, where I enrolled in a part-time degree in exercise science and joined an elite training squad for triathlon.

Meanwhile, Ben, who had finished school with the highest possible scores, had been awarded a scholarship to the Australian Defence Force Academy and was on the road to becoming an army officer. Parades were held to mark significant milestones along the way, and my parents and I would pile into the car and drive to Canberra to attend.

I recall watching with bemusement as the clean-cut officer cadets marched around the finely manicured grass parade grounds in perfect unison, while I stood on the sidelines with my earring and shoulder-length wavy hair. I have a vivid memory of one of my dad's army friends asking me whether I would be joining up as well. My response was something along the lines of: 'Look at me – what do you reckon?', believing that never in my wildest dreams would I join the military. (The irony was not lost on me when, about five years later, I found myself clean-cut, formed up and in uniform on that very same parade ground as part of my own army officer training.)

It was around the time that my brother was at ADFA that my interest in special operations was first piqued. I had stumbled upon *Bravo Two Zero*, Andy McNab's book about his SAS team's compromised mission in Iraq during the First Gulf War, and with a week to kill between triathlon races in Sydney and Canberra, I started reading. Like others before me, I found the story astonishing and devoured the book in a matter of days, followed a few months later by Chris Ryan's *The One That Got Away*, which covered the same subject. I could never have guessed that some fifteen years later I would hear the story first-hand when I encountered one of the other members of that ill-fated patrol during a combined training activity with the British SAS. At the time, I simply thought of the two books as good reads, and they certainly didn't inspire me to pursue a similar career. I was hell-bent on becoming a professional triathlete, and so I continued on with my life of shaved legs, lycra, hours of training and part-time study.

* * *

I graduated university after four years, during which time I had slugged away at my triathlon regime with limited success. Despite doing the exact same training as the best in the world, I was simply making up numbers in the professional field, with the occasional podium finish here and there at carefully chosen smaller races on weekends when the top pros were racing elsewhere. Short of resorting to performance-enhancing drugs, I could see no plausible way of becoming the athlete I had dreamed of being. I saw my life playing out for another decade or so in much the same way before trying to scrape together enough money to open a bike shop.

After finishing university I allowed myself a year in which to give professional triathlon a final go, but I sustained an Achilles tendon injury early in the season, which hammered the final nail into the coffin of my athletic aspirations. I drifted around the Gold Coast aimlessly for the remainder of that year, working behind the bar at a local restaurant and making up for time lost during my years of training, drinking great quantities of beer and eating copious amounts of fast food. I played a lot of mediocre golf, stacked on the weight, and was completely directionless.

On a positive note, I had done quite well at university, graduating in the top percentile of my class with a Bachelor of Exercise Science. As a standalone degree it didn't open many doors, but as a launch pad for further studies it was quite handy. Encouraged by my girlfriend at the time, and on a bit of a whim, I sat the Graduate Australian Medical School Admission Test for postgraduate medical studies, never truly believing that I had the smarts to get into med school.

It came as a genuine shock when my results arrived in the mail and were high enough to apply to study medicine. I began to view myself as smart. For the first time in my life,

I *had* worked to the best of my ability and achieved some of the potential my high school teachers had seen in me years prior. It was an epiphany. Having seen the benefit of consistent effort, and realising that I had some smarts, my perception of what was possible in life expanded dramatically.

Around the same time, my mum made me aware of a military scholarship scheme that sponsored medical students through university in return for them signing up for a period of service. Seeing the massive flashing sign that read FREE MONEY, I cut my hair, had a shave, lost weight and interviewed with the army. I was successful in my applications for both medical school and the scholarship, and on 21 January 2001 I became Lieutenant Dan Pronk, first-year medical student at Flinders University, Adelaide.

By the time I was starting my military career and medical degree, Ben had finished his army officer training, served as a lieutenant in an infantry battalion (including a tour of East Timor) and successfully completed selection and reinforcement training to qualify with the Special Air Service Regiment.

In August of 2001 the SASR hit the front page of Australian newspapers when they seized the Norwegian freighter the *Tampa* in the seas off Christmas Island, and it was only through Ben's involvement in the incident that I had taken any interest at all. In September of the same year I watched from my lounge room in disbelief as footage of the Twin Towers burning in New York City was broadcast on the TV screens of the world. The dramatic impact that event would have on the trajectory of my life could not have been anticipated. One month later, the Australian government announced that it would be sending special operations to Afghanistan, and in November 2001 the first SASR elements were deployed. Ben was gearing up to deploy with SASR's second push to Afghanistan in early 2002, and during the Christmas holidays following my first year of medical school I travelled to Perth to visit him before he deployed. This trip would have a profound effect on me, as from this point on the sole focus of my life became joining the Australian Special Air Service Regiment.

I arrived in Perth late on a Saturday afternoon, and after my brother picked me up from the airport we went straight to a barbecue at one of his mate's houses. The party was a final gathering of members of my brother's SASR troop, the elite warriors he would be commanding at war, before they all went their separate ways for a brief period of leave prior to departing for Afghanistan. With wives and girlfriends included, there were around twenty people in total, and it was much like any other Australian backyard gathering but for a few subtle differences. First, while plenty of beer was being consumed, this crew did not resemble the average beer-drinking Aussie barbecue-goers. There was not a beer gut among them; to a man they were lean, muscular and for the most part heavily tattooed. The second anomaly was their tendency to leap up onto a metal bar spanning two brick columns on the host's back patio and knock out inhuman numbers of chin-ups in between beers. The final thing that struck me about the group was their complete lack of machismo and attitude. It was as if they were so confident and comfortable with themselves, and so sure of their own abilities, that they had no need to dick-measure.

I was on to my third or fourth beer and engaged in conversation with an operator named Keith Fennell, who has since written two books about his experiences with SASR – *Warrior Brothers* and *Warrior Training* – when another operator, Dave, joined the conversation. When I mentioned that I was studying medicine on an army scholarship, his response ignited a flame inside me that would still be burning a decade later.

'You should do selection and come across to the unit, mate.'

'Nah,' I replied. 'I'm studying to be a doctor with the army.'

'That's what I'm saying: do selection and come across as a beret-qualified doctor.'

'Yeah, you should do that,' Fenno chimed in.

The cogs in my head started turning, slowly initially but then gaining momentum.

Until that night, most of the little I knew about special operations had come from the two books I had read, which had depicted a kind of life that seemed beyond the realm of possibility for an ordinary person. Sure, my brother had joined the SAS, but that seemed different. For him it seemed preordained, and he had told me little about his experiences, and certainly offered no encouragement to follow suit. Yet there I was, with two real-life special operators in front of me, urging me to join their unit, as if giving me the permission to try. Operators who, in a few weeks' time, would be conducting clandestine operations against al-Qaeda in the mountains of Afghanistan.

I recalled the buzz of my teenage graffiti missions, and imagined how that would be amplified by the life-and-death consequences of SAS operations, backed by a purpose of international significance. I imagined kinship with a tribe who would kill or die for each other. A switch flicked in my head. Yes: I would become a doctor with SASR.

There were only a few small issues with the plan, not least of which was the requirement that I complete three more years of medical school, an internship year and a further year as a junior doctor before I would even pull on an army uniform for posting to my first unit. But I wasn't deterred. During the remainder of my visit to Perth I met several more of my brother's workmates and spent time touring around Campbell Barracks, home of the regiment, getting some exposure to what went on behind the fortified front gates. By the end of my visit, I was determined to make my SASR dream a reality.

As my brother deployed on his first rotation to Afghanistan, I commenced my second year of medical school with a newfound direction in life. While I found medical school intellectually challenging, I craved something more. Since relinquishing my triathlon dreams I had missed the self-accomplishment and physical rigour of elite sport. Training for service with SASR was the perfect thing to fill this void.

Before I left Perth my brother had given me a recruiting pamphlet for the regiment which outlined in broad-brush the selection process and some skill sets and attributes that could be developed to improve an individual's chances of succeeding. It was somewhat dated but served as an excellent starting point for my journey. I studied every last detail of that pamphlet. It said that scuba diving experience might prove useful; I joined the university dive club and started logging dive time. Language skills were a plus; I enrolled in a Modern Standard Arabic course. (As it turned out, the only time I would use those language skills was to order coffee in Kuwait City on my way home from my first trip to Afghanistan.) Navigation skills were essential; I took up rogaining, a sport involving long-distance, cross-country orienteering. Rock climbing was recommended; I started to climb.

Physical fitness was obviously going to play a huge part in the selection process, but not the kind of fitness I was used to, so while I continued my running and cycling I also added pack-marching – or stomping, as it is known in military circles – in nearby national parks to my training regime to toughen my feet and shoulders.

Shooting skills were a must, so I contacted the local Army Reserve unit and, wearing uniforms and equipment borrowed from my brother and dad (I hadn't yet been issued my own), worked to get qualified in the standard weapons of the regular army. These interactions led me to meet the local RAAF airfield defence guards, who put me through further qualifications in several weapons, including machine and handguns. I joined a local pistol club and qualified for a semi-automatic handgun licence, then I purchased a Glock 17 9 mm pistol and began competing in International Practical Shooting Confederation events.

I also began reading up on special operations, learning the history and function of all the significant units from around the world and their hallmark moments, both good and bad. I came across an excellent book by British Army surgeon Richard Villar, who had been the doctor with the British 22 SAS at the time of the Falklands War. Villar had passed the infamous British SAS selection course, and his book *Knife Edge* was hugely inspirational to me as it was precisely what I hoped to achieve with the Australian SASR. I reread the book many times in the following years and even emailed Villar. He replied promptly wishing me the best of luck in my endeavours. I printed that email out and carried it with me for the years of training that followed, often referring back to it for motivation in tough times.

* * *

It was during this period that I had another life-altering moment. In 2002, during my second year of medical school, my flatmate and I got part-time jobs tutoring science students in human physiology. About ten minutes into my first tutoring session, as I was explaining a concept using a diagram on a whiteboard, my class was interrupted by a late arrival. I turned to greet the young woman, who introduced herself as Kristy and apologised for her tardiness. She was inconveniently beautiful to have as a student, with bright blue eyes, shoulder-length dark hair and a subtle nose stud. She wore figure-hugging jeans, a long-sleeved t-shirt and Converse sneakers. The first awkward words I would utter to my future wife were: 'That's okay, these sessions aren't mandatory, so you don't have to be here at all.' But I was infinitely glad that she was. I tried to return my focus to the subject at hand, but my train of thought had been derailed by the girl.

Debriefing with my flatmate later that evening, I knew I was in trouble. But we agreed that trying to spark up a relationship with a student was inappropriate. So, I waited. Inventing a feeble excuse to stay in touch with Kristy after the semester had finished, I eventually managed to wangle an invite to her house for dinner shortly before I was due to head off on an army course for a few weeks. Not wanting to miss the opportunity to formalise our relationship before I departed, at the appropriate time and with the nerves of a teenager I leaned in and kissed her. The kiss was reciprocated, and what would become the most important relationship of my life began. Kristy would become the epicentre of my universe, the mother of my children, my North Star when the world became indecipherable, and the only person who would know the true me over the decades to come.

* * *

I told very few people about my military aspirations as I continued my medical schooling, partly for fear of ridicule, but mostly because I was reluctant to share the dream, as if that would somehow sap the energy from it.

It was during my second year of medical school that I first worked up the courage to contact the Special Forces Training Centre, which at the time managed the applications of candidates wishing to attempt special operations selection in Australia. The SASR representative I spoke with was highly supportive of my aspirations, but informed me it would be at least five years before they would consider allowing me to attempt selection; I would need to be well established within a military unit first. Undeterred, I continued the regime I had established for myself, logging dive time, pack-marching thousands of kilometres, and undertaking hundreds of hours of language and medical studies. By the time I graduated medicine in December 2004 I had managed to complete Tasmania's 82-kilometre Overland Track in 27 hours straight, in the middle of winter, carrying a 40-kilogram pack; I had lost a diving acquaintance to a great white shark attack; I had reached intermediate level in Arabic; and I had recovered from a rock-climbing fall in which I broke both ankles, my left forearm and three ribs.

On reflection, little of what I was doing corresponded with the requirements of my subsequent special operations career, but that mattered not at the time. I was convinced I was tempering myself for the rigors of selection and, with each session logged, was improving my suitability and edging closer to achieving my dream.

* * *

My medical internship year was highly demanding and required long hours of work in the hospital, leaving me with little time to train. To ensure I maintained adequate fitness, I would pack-march the 6 kilometres to and from work daily. There was a children's playground near my house, and I would stop at the monkey bars to do sets of chin-ups with my pack on for upper body strength. Walking home after a night shift, by which time I would have been awake for 30 or more hours, was perfect training for the sleep deprivation and physical stress that I would surely endure on SASR selection. Stomping through the national park after one particularly arduous shift, I succumbed to my fatigue and decided to sit down to rest for a few minutes before continuing. What seemed like a second later, I jolted awake to find the sun high in the sky and the sound of other people in the park. Fortunately, Kristy, who I was living with by that stage, was working days and wasn't home when I arrived four hours late, saving me the embarrassment of having to explain to her what had happened.

Internship came and went, and I began my first year as a medical resident in the hospital system. The following year I would be posted to a military unit to commence work as a regimental medical officer (RMO). My army career progression required me to become qualified as a general practitioner and so, despite my original intention to become a surgeon, I applied for and was accepted into the training program for the Royal Australian College of General Practitioners.

It was also time to start jockeying for an appropriate first military posting to give me the best possible chance of lining myself up for service with special operations. Through my brother, I had been in contact with the RMO at SASR, and with his guidance I had devised a career path that would set me up perfectly.

The first posting I was required to do was to an army hospital or one of the large Combat Services Support Battalions (CSSB), filling a supernumerary RMO position that would allow me to spend much of the year away on army induction training courses. Once that suite of courses was complete, I would be considered deployable and could then be posted to one of the combat units where, after a period of one to two years minimum, I could be considered for SOCOMD. My plan was to post to the army hospital in Holsworthy, Sydney, which at that time shared a base with the paratroopers of the 3rd Battalion, Royal Australian Regiment, known as 3 RAR, and the commandos of the 4 RAR (CDO), which was later to become the 2nd Commando Regiment, or 2 CDO. The plan was to progress through these three units respectively before attempting to make the move west to Perth and service with SASR. I had discussed this with my various army career advisers many times throughout my years of medical schooling and junior doctoring, and I had been assured it was locked in place.

My residency year drew to a close and my first posting order came in the mail. Having been assured that I was Holsworthy-bound, I opened the letter to find myself posted not to Sydney but to Darwin. I was fucking furious.

Conveniently, army career advisers go on a moratorium period which renders them uncontactable around the time of posting orders being disseminated in order to prevent livid soldiers from tracking them down and giving them a piece of their mind, or worse. I stewed on the posting order for the duration of the moratorium period, and the second my career adviser came back online I phoned him and let him have it as best I could given that he significantly outranked me.

He shut me down unceremoniously and fed me the usual bullshit I would become all too familiar with in the years to come about Darwin being a great career move, and the need to have a well-rounded career, and so on and so forth. It was at that point I realised that if I was going to realise my SOCOMD ambitions, I would have to force the army's hand rather than wait for a career adviser to line up the ducks to get me there. This further strengthened my resolve to complete SASR selection and, setting my sights on the 2008 course, I drew up a training program and dared to mark a calendar with a date. It was becoming real.

Before leaving Adelaide for Darwin, Kristy and I were married. It was a perfect summer's day, and we tied the knot in front of an intimate crowd of our closest friends and relatives, in the same gardens overlooking the sea where I had proposed to her. Our reception was held at a local winery where we ate, drank and laughed, and my new bride and I performed a choreographed and well-rehearsed dance to an acoustic version of Lifehouse's 'Hanging by a Moment'. The following day we took off to the idyllic South Australian beachside town of Robe for our honeymoon, with Kristy's extended family in tow. As many of them had travelled halfway around the world from England for our nuptials, Kristy had felt terrible at the thought of leaving them in Adelaide while we honeymooned. Such is her love and loyalty to her family that they were extended an invite. Initially, and I feel somewhat justifiably, I was lukewarm on having Kristy's relatives in the cabins immediately either side of ours on our honeymoon, however, that attitude quickly changed. Our time together as a group was brilliant, and on more than one occasion the manager of the cabins had to tell us off late in the night when other guests complained we were keeping them awake with our laughter.

The photos from our wedding and honeymoon show Kristy and me with the carefree, genuine, joyous smiles of a youthful couple full of optimism. While smiles still feature in our photo albums, in the years since, they have never been quite the same. We had strapped in for an emotional rollercoaster ride that was just about to start.

II

THROWING ON
THE UNIFORM

Australia Day 2007 found Kristy and I sweating it out in the uncomfortable humidity of the Darwin wet season. The temporary accommodation we were living in while awaiting Defence housing was less than stellar, and we shared it with a family of the largest cockroaches I had ever seen. Aggravating the situation was a broken air conditioning unit. Kristy, by that time two months pregnant with our first child and horribly morning sick, was having a miserable time. She had left her job and social support system in Adelaide to join me, and while we had regularly discussed my aspirations for an army career, we were now beginning to experience the stark reality. It was the very first indication that the road ahead would be a rocky one for us as a couple.

By the winter of 2007, I found myself in a neatly pressed uniform at the Royal Military College at Duntroon, marching around the same frosty parade ground I'd watched Ben on all those years ago. I was there to complete the basic officer training afforded to doctors and other army specialists. While some of the students on the course hated it with a passion and rebelled at every opportunity, I thought it was fantastic and relished the opportunity to learn all I could about operational planning processes and the like. I had begun the seemingly unlikely metamorphosis from civilian life to the military and was surprisingly happy to be on the ride.

Completing my Duntroon training, I returned to Darwin. I was living about 10 kilometres from the army base, and I maintained the practice of pack-marching to and from work, performing upper body workouts during my lunch hour and when I got home at night. The march between my house and work could be done almost exclusively on dirt tracks through scrubland, which minimised the impact on my body when compared to training on harder surfaces, and thankfully minimised the strange looks from passing motorists and homeowners. During the wet season, the torrential rain turned stretches of the tracks into a knee-deep quagmire. I would often get caught in the deluges at the start or end of the day, forcing me to dig deep into my mind's hate bank for motivation. I stuck rigidly to my training regime, consistently logging more than 100 kilometres of pack-marching a week, and I had instructed Kristy to ridicule me if I showed signs of slacking off.

She did so spectacularly on one particular morning. It was bucketing rain when my alarm went off at 0430 hours for me to get up and stomp to work. Exhausted from the cumulative fatigue of my training program, I silenced the alarm and rolled over to go back to sleep, resigning myself to driving to work a couple of hours later. As I was drifting off, I was jolted awake by a swift kick to my ribs.

'Get up and train,' Kristy ordered.

'Nah, baby, I need the rest. I'll drive to work today.'

'You told me to call you a pussy if you didn't train, so you're a pussy. *Get up.*' Another kick, this time in the bum.

I rolled out of bed, got dressed, hauled my heavy pack onto aching shoulders and wearily trudged to work through the mud, soaked to the core by the heavy rain. I know that deep down Kristy resented the hours I spent training for selection, and although I would like to think that her kicking me out of bed that morning was a motivational gesture to keep me focused on my goal, I suspect she enjoyed the opportunity to give me some grief. That said, while she didn't love the idea of my serving with special operations, she would prove to be a pillar of strength for me throughout my career, for which I am forever indebted to her.

By August 2007 I had completed the courses necessary to be considered deployable as an army doctor, and at my request had been embedded with the 5 RAR infantry battalion. Experience with an infantry unit would put me one step closer to my special forces goal.

The next month, on the morning of 6 September 2007, Kristy and I went to the Darwin Private Hospital for a caesarean section to deliver our baby boy. A combination of big-headed Pronk genes and Kristy's petite pelvis meant that bubs was never going to enter the world the conventional way, and even at the 40-week mark his head was yet to move into position. It was intensely exciting but somewhat odd to enter the hospital knowing that, in a few hours, we would have a small human of our own making to take home and care for.

The C-section went without complication and to our delight our little man came out screaming and kicking. He was a perfect, chubby, blue-eyed baby boy we named Hendrik, or Henk for short, in honour of his Pronk forebears.

It was around the same time of Henk's birth that I once again harassed the Special Forces Training Centre about the SASR selection course. The representative I spoke to at the SFTC recommended that I wait at least one more year but agreed that I could apply now, telling me they might consider allowing me on the course. That was good enough for me. I started the application process for selection, booking the prerequisite medical and psychological screening for special operations suitability, and approaching my commanding officer to ask him to release me for the selection course.

The CO of 5 RAR at the time was a good man, and although supportive of my goals, he faced the dilemma of his unit preparing for deployment to Timor-Leste (formerly known as East Timor) at the end of that year, for which he would require an RMO. He agreed to release me for SASR selection on the proviso that even if I was successful on the course, I would return to 5 RAR and deploy with them if he couldn't find another RMO for the trip. That seemed fair to me, as he would have been well within his rights to shut me down altogether, so we shook hands on it and he signed my application form.

What followed was a maelstrom of paperwork, and medical and psychological screenings, that resulted in a completed SASR selection application. I sent it off with that *holy fuck* feeling you get when you've done something significant but you aren't quite sure it was a good idea.

While I awaited a response from SFTC, I continued my newly established routine as the RMO with 5 RAR. The average day would commence with unit physical training, followed by a shower and change into uniform, and then the conduct of 'sick parade' for any acutely unwell or injured soldiers in the unit. Next up were routine medical appointments and military meetings to fill out most days. The weekly schedule was varied and interesting, with regular sessions of weapons training and stints out in the field exercising infantry warfighting tactics. It was all new and exciting, and I loved every moment of it.

A couple of months after sending my application, I received a letter from SFTC confirming they had panelled me on the 2008 SASR selection course, and including a preparation package for the tactical theory component of the course's officer module. My excitement on receiving the package soon turned to dread as I flicked through the pages of assumed knowledge and recommended preparation exercises. It might as well have been written in a different language; I had no idea how to even begin approaching the tactical scenarios.

My saviour came in the form of a selfless 5 RAR infantry officer who devoted many hours to tutoring me until I reached a point where I felt competent enough to bluff my way through.

Meanwhile, I also had a lot to learn from a practical skill perspective. One of the other Darwin guys who was attempting selection had a contact in the Territory Response Group, the tactical unit within the Northern Territory Police, and we would periodically go to their compound to practise weapon drills, and stripping and assembling M4 carbine rifles and Heckler and Koch MP5 submachine guns. The only weapon I couldn't manage to get my hands on, but was pretty sure I'd need to know about, was the AK-47. Although 5 RAR had a supply of them, they were rendered inert and had all their working parts welded in place, making them useless to practise with. In the end, I resorted to good old YouTube, where I found a plethora of videos demonstrating strip and assemble procedure and drills for the rifle. God bless the internet!

As I prepared for the selection course, my dream of becoming a beret-qualified doctor with the SASR had further morphed into a desire to jump ship from medicine altogether and attempt to become a troop commander with the unit. I had learned of an air force F/A-18 Hornet pilot and a navy submariner who had successfully completed selection and reinforcement training to become troop commanders with the unit, and I decided I would attempt to add a doctor to that list of unorthodox backgrounds for the job.

It was with this mindset that I approached my army career interview in April 2008. The guy who'd shafted me with the Darwin posting was no longer my adviser, and by all reports the new guy was a good bloke, if a little rough around the edges.

It was just on lunchtime when I entered the room for my interview and found my career adviser slumped in a chair behind a large desk, eating his lunch with gusto. He didn't rise from his chair to greet me as I braced up and introduced myself, which was hardly encouraging, but I plugged on, trying to make a favourable impression. Things took a fairly dramatic turn for the worse, though, when he asked about my future plans.

'I've applied to do SASR selection this year, and if I'm successful, my intent is to become a troop commander with the unit,' I informed him confidently.

His reaction was slightly delayed while he sucked in enough air to laugh with appropriate condescension, and in the process he inhaled a small remnant of food, which sparked a violent coughing fit. His face reddened and then transitioned to purple, the veins in his neck bulging to near rupture. I couldn't look away.

Once he had recovered, he delivered a ten-minute *you're shit* speech, warning me that my SASR pipedream was never going to become a reality, and I was sacrificing the chance to build a real career as an RMO by chasing it.

Looking back now, I can certainly see things from his perspective. The army had just spent hundreds of thousands of dollars on my education, only for me to declare that I wanted to cast medicine aside and attempt to become a troop commander. The career adviser must have found this infuriating. At the time I simply thought he was a dickhead.

After his tirade wound down, there was a brief pause in proceedings when he seemed to register that he hadn't ticked all the boxes required for the interview.

'So . . . you married?' he enquired awkwardly.

'Yep.' My response was curt; I was in no mood to talk.

'Any kids?'

'One boy.'

And so it went on until he had completed his paperwork and I was dismissed. I left that interview completely gutted and close to tears, but with another hefty deposit in my hate bank to motivate me to train. I was now more fired up than ever to pass selection, if for no other reason than to stick it up the arse of that career adviser.

With selection fast approaching I found myself spending a lot of time heading up a field resuscitation team in support of training at a military range a few hours' drive from Darwin. Mt Bundey was a desolate shithole surrounded in all directions by scrubland, which made it perfect for military training and, in particular, the use of the armoured vehicles and tanks from the Darwin units. During my time out at Mt Bundey I would routinely log more than 150 kilometres of pack-marching a week, and would often do more than 1000 push-ups a day, as well as circuit training and sets of heaves to the point of exhaustion.

When the units we were medically supporting were finished training for the day, they would radio through to us that we could stand down to a lower level of readiness. I would take those opportunities to practise my night navigation skills, setting off into the dark scrub surrounding the training ground for hours on end with my pack and compass, bouncing around pre-determined checkpoints that I had generated on the map.

On one such evening my resuscitation team had decided that they would get some takeaway burgers from the nearest truck stop, some 20 kilometres back up the highway from the training facility towards Darwin. I saw this as the perfect opportunity to do a cross-country night navigation exercise from the truck stop back to Mt Bundey. Grabbing my map, and cramming 40 kilos of kit into my pack, I hopped into the ambulance bound for the truck stop, planning my navigation route back as we drove. To avoid being seen by truck stop patrons, I got dropped off 100 metres short of our destination, and after jumping a small fence into the scrub paralleling the highway I commenced my stomp back to the training ground.

I had intended on doing the navigation exercise without using any light, but within an hour of setting off it was pitch-black, forcing me to use a head torch. Fearing an encounter with a shotgun-wielding farmer as I moved across private property, I flicked across the red lens of my head torch to avoid projecting white light that might highlight my presence.

The going was extremely tough and the route was littered with obstacles in the form of large rocks covered in thick lantana, making it extremely physically taxing to force my way through the vegetation and very difficult to assess how far I had travelled. I had become highly competent at judging my distance travelled on a flat route through counting my paces, and when using a GPS to confirm my location I would consistently find myself within a whisker of where I'd thought I was on the map. On that particular night, I couldn't gauge how far I had travelled by counting my paces, and my GPS was telling me that I was making poor distance and at my rate of movement I wouldn't be back in time to support the start of the military training exercise the following morning. I kept going as fast as I could, clambering gracelessly over the rocks, often on my hands and knees.

I hauled myself up onto one such rock and went to stand when my face struck a tree branch immediately in front of me that I hadn't seen owing to the limited red light coming from my head torch. Slightly dazed from the blow, I staggered backwards. I recall my arms flailing wildly in a futile attempt to counter the weight of my pack before I fell heavily off the rock and was knocked unconscious.

I have no way of knowing how long I lay there, out cold. When I did come around, it took me quite some time to work out where I was and what had just happened. My head torch was gone, no doubt having been flung off by the fall, and the light must have been smashed by the impact because it was now back to pitch black. I was wedged between rocks, my heavy pack and the lack of visual cues making it difficult to right myself.

Surveying my face with my hand, I felt the warm, stickiness of blood coming from both my nose and the back of my head. This was not good. There I was, literally in the middle of nowhere, injured, disoriented, having lost my only torch, and with no choice but to get back to the training ground to support the activity the following morning.

I lay there thinking for a good ten minutes, mostly about how lucky I was that I'd regained consciousness at all; it would have taken a few days of searching to find my body otherwise. I estimated I had covered about 5 of the 20 kilometres back to the training ground, but there was no way I was going to make it the remaining 15 cross-country. I concluded that my only option was to backtrack along the route I had taken until I reached the highway, and then stomp along the road. This would add about 7 kilometres to my distance, but it would require no navigation and was my only chance of making it back to Mt Bundey in time.

Remembering that I had a stash of Cyalume chemical light sticks in my pack, I struggled out of my position in the rocks, took out a Cyalume and cracked it. I checked my GPS and map, plotted a route back to the highway and set off.

It was a demoralising experience, and painfully slow going through the scrub. My head throbbed from the hit I had taken, but the bleeding from both my nose and scalp had stopped. I reached the highway a little after 0100 hours and, head down, began the trudge back to Mt Bundey. Every time a car or truck came by I scampered off the bitumen and hid in the ditch on the side of the road in order to avoid any weird interactions with motorists should they stop to see why some idiot was pack-marching along the highway in the middle of the night.

I made it back to the training ground, blistered and exhausted, just as dawn broke and was greeted by one of the other members of the resuscitation team. He had woken in the night to go for a piss and, realising that I wasn't back, had been on the verge of hitting the panic button to get a search party out to look for me. Thankfully he hadn't done that, saving me the embarrassment, and I had a quick shower before collapsing into my bed to sleep most of the day away.

The whole exercise was a debacle, no question, but rather than discouraging me I viewed the experience in a positive light. I had set a goal, met with adversity, and managed to pivot my plan and devise a solution. It had been a tough night, but I had been equal to it.

When I was within two months of selection, and despite my training going excellently, I became increasingly paranoid about coming down with an illness that might cost me training time or potentially jeopardise my chances of starting the course at all. To decrease the likelihood of falling ill I had started taking a throatful of vitamins and supplements every morning before training. This was all fine and beaut leading up to the course, but obviously wouldn't be possible once on selection, where our kit would be searched for such contraband. If found, it would be confiscated and would likely result in severe consequences – possibly even removal from the course.

Ben, who had otherwise been spectacularly unhelpful in providing training tips for selection, had at least warned me of the potential for infection on the course, particularly in blistered, unwashed feet. He himself had developed cellulitis in one of his feet at the end of his selection course, which may have forced his medical withdrawal if it had occurred earlier. Having thought long and hard about this prospect, and how disappointing it would be to have to withdraw from a course I had waited six years to attempt, I devised a cunning plan to minimise my chance of infection.

During my internship I had spent three months working at a health centre in Central Australia, where we had frequently injected intramuscular boluses of the long-acting penicillin Benzylpenicillin into patients to treat specific infections, and sometimes as a prophylaxis against certain other diseases. The patients universally hated the injections, often crying out in pain as the thick, milky antibiotic was forced into their buttocks through a massive needle, but the alternative was for them to take multiple pills daily for periods of months to years; at least with the needle there would be no compliance issues.

As the long-acting penicillin stayed at therapeutic levels in the system for up to a month, I viewed it as the perfect means to render myself infection-proof for selection; I just needed to convince a doctor to prescribe me some.

Not wanting to go to an army medical officer, I made an appointment with a local private GP for the consultation. After a loose explanation of what I wanted and why, the GP agreed to write me a prescription. Not knowing how I would react to the drug, I decided to test-drive it two months out from the course, with a top-up planned just prior if I tolerated the drug without side effects. I filled my script for two doses of the antibiotic and, knowing Kristy would not approve of what I was doing, chose to inject it on an afternoon when she was working late.

Stripped completely naked, I stood at the bathroom sink of our Darwin home and swabbed my right buttock clean with an alcohol wipe before drawing up the thick, white antibiotic into a large syringe. Standing with my feet shoulder-width apart I leaned forward over the sink, supporting my weight on my left arm, with the syringe in my right hand. Eyeballing myself in the mirror above the sink, I sucked in a few deep breaths to pump myself up, and then swiftly rammed the needle into my arse cheek. *Not so bad*, I thought to myself, maintaining eye contact with my reflection in the mirror and wondering why all the patients I had jabbed with the same drug complained so much.

This mental query was answered immediately as I attempted to depress the plunger of the syringe with the thumb of my right hand. The muscle fibres of my bum had locked up around the needle and were resisting the infusion of the drug with all their might. I pressed as hard as I could on the plunger, sending a searing pain through my right buttock.

It was absolutely excruciating, as if a scalding-hot golf ball was being squeezed through the syringe into my tissues, and I watched in the mirror as all the colour drained from my face and beads of cold sweat formed on my forehead. As I continued forcing the plunger of the syringe my ears began to ring and my peripheral vision began to draw in to a narrow tunnel with my reflection at its far end. I was going to faint.

I felt the plunger of the syringe hit home against the body of the device, indicating that it was empty and my job was done. Withdrawing the needle, I collapsed back onto the toilet in the bathroom, barely clinging to consciousness. It had been a dreadful experience, and as I recuperated I silently apologised to all the patients I had thought weak for complaining about the injections.

The sound of Kristy's car pulling up in the driveway startled me back into action. I quickly pulled on my clothes, hid the needle, and went out to greet her, hoping she wouldn't notice my slight limp.

My right buttock hurt like a son of a bitch for days after the injection, but after an uncomfortable fortnight of training post-injection the pain settled – just in time for my next ailment.

I hadn't heard from my right Achilles tendon since it ended my triathlon aspirations all those years prior, but sensing a good opportunity to shit on my dreams again it flared with exactly six weeks to go until selection. Doubling to twice its thickness with inflammation, the pain from the tendon started to severely limit my training to the point where pack-marching became almost unbearable. Seeing the potential for my dream to slip away, I scoured my medical texts for a solution to the injury. Physiotherapy had little to offer other than a few weeks rest followed by months of eccentric strengthening exercises to rehabilitate it, which I obviously didn't have the time for. The only intervention that looked even remotely like a solution to the inflammation was a cortisone injection – the problem being that most references I consulted advised strongly against injecting cortisone into an Achilles tendon for fear that the drug would weaken the structure and make it more prone to rupture.

Running short on other options, I once again found myself in the GP's office pleading my unorthodox case for another prescription of injectable medication. Comfortable that I clearly understood the risks and was prepared to take full responsibility for any adverse outcomes, the GP agreed, administering an injection of a potent anti-inflammatory medication into the sheath surrounding my Achilles. Within a week the swelling settled and the pain resolved, and I was back out pounding the pavement again.

Owing to my high volume of training I had lost a considerable amount of weight and was the leanest I had been since my triathlon days. While I found this aesthetically pleasing, it wasn't going to do me any good on the selection course, during which I was likely to drop significant further weight due to the extreme physical exertion coupled with periods of food deprivation. I therefore started making a concerted effort to put weight on, indulging in high-calorie foods at every opportunity.

I had been looking forward to this process and thought it would be one of the few fun things associated with preparation for selection. I gorged on pizza, chocolate and KFC on top of my normal diet, but instead of feeling like a treat it was horrible. I felt bloated when training, and on more than one occasion I ended up vomiting the extra calories straight back up. I did achieve my goal to a limited degree, putting on about 3 kilograms of weight before the course began.

Three weeks before selection, my body made one last-ditch attempt to stop me from attempting the course. It was my right leg once again, but not my Achilles tendon this time; it was my calf. To compensate for the injured Achilles, I had been favouring the leg by loading it differently, which had led to a calf strain. Pack-marching didn't seem to irritate it, but any effort to run at pace, or to cover more than a few kilometres, would send the calf into spasm. I was at my wits' end by this point; once again, it looked as if my dream might slip through my fingers at the last moment.

I hit the physiotherapist on base. He thought that dry-needling might be the answer, so he used my calf as a pin cushion daily for those last three weeks. He even taught me the needling technique and gave me a box of needles so I could repeat the process every night at home. It was extremely painful, but it did seem to loosen up the calf muscle.

I did very little running or pack-marching in those final weeks, owing to my calf, and instead concentrated on my push-ups, heaves and clothed swimming, which would be required on the course. I brushed up again on the limited military tactical skills that I had, my YouTube AK-47 videos and my knot-tying, all the while scoffing down buckets of fried chicken and litres of chocolate thickshakes. With one week to go it was time to ante up again and inject myself with Benzylpenicillin. It was as excruciating as I remembered.

And then, finally, it was time to hop on the plane to Perth for the selection course. I kissed Kristy and little Henk goodbye at the airport, cleared security and took a seat at the departure gate to wait for the plane to board. My stomach churned with nervous anticipation. I had waited six years for this opportunity and had invested a herculean amount of emotional and physical energy just to get to the starting line. I hoped I wasn't going to fuck it up.

III

SELECTION

'GET OFF THE FUCKING BUS AND FORM UP IN ONE RANK BEHIND THE WITCH'S HATS, GO, GO, GO.'

The instruction delivered by the PTI, or physical training instructor, was simple and unambiguous. In the manner I imagine a burning aircraft would be evacuated we hauled arse off the bus, which had stopped at a military base halfway between Perth and our ultimate destination for the selection course. The other two buses in our convoy were being emptied in a similar fashion. Being seated near the front, I was one of the first to pile out. *Off to a good start*, I congratulated myself briefly, before making the sickening realisation that everyone except me was holding a garbage bag.

I turned to the candidate next to me and, trying to conceal the note of desperation, asked, 'Hey, mate, what's in the bag?'

'A set of cams for the swim and a dry set to put on

afterwards,' he replied. We were dressed in physical training outfits comprising shorts, t-shirts and runners, but of course we would need to change back into camouflage uniforms at some point.

Fuck, fuck, fuck, fuck. How had I missed that? By that time most of the other candidates had already formed up, but I had to go back for my gear; there was no other choice. I dashed back across the road and hauled open the luggage compartment of the bus. The list of equipment to bring on selection was fairly specific, so I was confronted with 40 or so sets of packs and dive bags that looked identical to mine. Shit.

I began frantically pulling out packs and dive bags, leaving them strewn on the ground around me, before finally locating my own. Ripping out a couple of sets of cams, I hastily stuffed them into a garbage bag then piss-bolted back across the road to be the very last candidate to form up. Naturally this drew the unwanted attention of one of the PTIs, and although I can't recall the exact content of the monologue he delivered two inches from my face, of the twenty or so words that he offered me at least ten of them were *fuck*.

Once formed up, we were instructed to drop our garbage bags and follow the PTIs for a half-hour workout, which consisted of uncomfortably fast running, punctuated with ballistic sets of push-ups, sit-ups and burpees. By about the two-minute mark of the first activity I got the coppery taste in the back of my mouth that comes from doing high-intensity exercise without an appropriate warm-up, and with it came my first moments of self-doubt. What on earth had I got myself into? I looked around at the other candidates on the course, all of whom looked stronger, fitter and better suited for the SAS than I was. This was a bad habit I had developed in my triathlon days, when I would psyche myself out at the start line of races. Despite not suffering from this negative thought spiral since my time as a triathlete, it crept back into my mind at that moment.

The workout ended abruptly and we were force-marched to an empty parking lot, where there was a freestanding chin-up beam, a series of mats on the ground and more witch's hats. It was time for our push-up, sit-up and chin-up assessments. One of the PTIs had his car there and we did the activities to a regular beeping cadence played the car's stereo. Fortunately I had been given a heads-up that the assessments would be done to a cadence and had trained accordingly. Many of the candidates clearly hadn't, and about a quarter of the guys in my group failed to get out the requisite 60 push-ups to pass. I managed to get out 72, which gave me a huge morale boost. As horrible as it sounds, I viewed it as me versus the other candidates, and I had to take any chance I could get to beat them.

I managed 17 on the heave test with the pass mark being 10, and I placed third in my group for the 2.4-kilometre run, coming in at a time of 8 minutes 24 seconds. It felt brilliant to be underway and I had managed to put some solid, if not excellent, scores on the board.

It was difficult to tell exactly how much effort needed to be put in to any given activity on the course. Naturally the directing staff would be looking for 110 per cent on everything, but I figured that this rate of effort would be unsustainable over a three-week course and I would need to pace myself.

I had come across the theory of the 'Grey Man' on several occasions when reading books referring to special operations selection courses. The Grey Man was the guy who was never at the very front or the very back of the pack and therefore drifted through selection, making the grade but going largely unnoticed. I ascribed to this theory to some degree, however I felt the better option was to aim for a sustainable 90–95 per cent effort, with a view to finishing in the top few whenever I was physically capable of doing so. I had achieved that on the very first assessment criteria of the course and was quietly pleased with myself.

An icy swim test followed, which I passed comfortably, and once all candidates had completed the preliminary physical testing, we loaded back onto the buses to continue our trip to the SAS Regiment's field training ground in the remote Western Australian town of Bindoon.

It was well after dark when the buses made a right-hand turn off the highway and pulled over on the side of the road. It had started raining lightly as we were ordered off and told to fetch our equipment from the cargo hold and begin marching. The buses did U-turns behind us and began the return trip to Perth, leaving us in complete darkness and with no lifeline back to civilisation. We were committed.

After a good couple of hours stomping we drew close to a large, well-lit shed brimming with directing staff. We were stopped 100 metres short and formed up in single file. When it was my turn, I moved forward to a reception area where a DS sat behind a desk covered by a large printed spreadsheet.

'Name?' No eye contact was made.

'Pronk.'

'You are no longer Pronk – you are now Candidate Eighteen. Do you understand?'

'Yes, sir.' I was pretty sure I outranked the guy, however I had decided to call everyone *sir* until instructed to do otherwise.

My photograph was taken and I was ushered into the main area of the shed, where numbered piles of military equipment were laid out in rows on the cold concrete floor.

Officers made up the lower numbers in the front rows, and other ranks were behind. I found the pile numbered 18 and stood behind it, surveying its contents. The kit included a Steyr rifle, five magazines, a rifle-cleaning kit and a bag of blank rounds. Also in the pile was an extra dive bag, a radio and associated equipment, a fluorescent orange panel marker for our packs, a compass, Cyalume sticks, a pace counter, a map cover, a strobe light and five one-day ration packs. Rounding out the pile was a small first-aid kit and several pieces of paperwork, including a Withdraw at Own Request form, and copies of the song lyrics for 'Happy Wanderer' and 'Lili Marlene' (being the SASR's fast and slow march songs respectively), as well as both verses of the Australian national anthem.

The remaining candidates filed into the shed to be processed, the whole procedure taking well over an hour to complete for the entirety of the 160-strong course. Standing in the open shed, soaked from sweat and the rain, I began to chill down and shiver uncontrollably. The weather had been hot in Darwin leading up to the course, and with no time to acclimatise to the Perth weather the cold was knocking me around. To distract myself, I took the opportunity to take in my surroundings, trying to avoid eye contact with the DS who prowled up and down our ranks staring daggers at us. It was intimidation at its best, with most wearing the coveted sandy beret of the SAS Regiment and some done up in full combat order, wearing body armour brimming with high-speed equipment. One DS in armour had a leashed military working dog that he paraded around the shed, well within range of the candidates.

After the last group of candidates had been processed, we were instructed to unpack all the kit we had brought with us onto the ground. One DS read out the list of required equipment, and we had to hold up each piece for inspection by the other DS who were patrolling among us. Following a subsequent kit search, we were instructed to strip off our clothing. I interpreted this as stripping naked, but others behind me must have interpreted the order differently, as the DS yelled, 'THAT MEANS STRIP FUCKING NAKED – NOW,' which clarified things nicely. So there we stood, 160 fit, young men, nude, in a freezing-cold shed well after midnight.

The kitted-up DS with the military working dog made his way towards me and I noted out of the corner of my eye that the dog's head was at precisely the same height as my genitals. I took solace in the thought that, given the frigid temperature and my petrified state, my shrivelled manhood probably wasn't presenting as an appealing snack, even to a hungry hound. In fact, my testicles had retreated so far north to avoid the cold that I may as well have been wearing them for earrings.

The dog moved on, and the next DS to parade past was a petite, attractive brunette from the unit. Pausing briefly in front of me, she looked down, smirked, then moved on to humiliate the next candidate in line. I was completely unfazed by this, as I was there to try to join the SASR, not to impress any ladies. Besides, I was pretty sure it wasn't the first time a girl had laughed at the sight of my naked form. (The young lady on genital inspection duty that night would end up being my next-door neighbour for three years, which was nowhere near as awkward as you might expect!)

I would later learn that one of the candidates lined up behind me had stripped off to reveal a fully waxed body with a perfect head-to-toe solarium tan completely devoid of tan lines. Apparently this drew unwanted attention from the DS, and the candidate withdrew at own request very early in the course. When it came to personal grooming, it was definitely a good idea to be the Grey Man rather than the bronzed man.

After standing naked for fifteen minutes we were instructed to dress. Clear direction was provided as to exactly where our equipment was to be located in our packs, webbing and pockets, as well as which items were to be dumped in the spare dive bag provided. This kit would be left behind, only to be retrieved on withdrawal or at the end of the course. Included in the items prohibited on the selection course were our watches – a final quick glance at mine showed it to be 0230 hours by the time we were done with the initial administration.

We were then formed up on the road outside the shed with our packs and webbing on and marched a short distance to a small camp. Here we were briefed on the rules of the selection course and told in no uncertain terms that most of us would not complete it. Of those that did, not all would be selected for service with the SASR.

To illustrate the point, the DS addressing us had one out of every three candidates stand while the rest of us remained seating. 'This is how many of you will make it to the end of the course.' He paused for effect, then instructed half of them to sit, leaving around 25 candidates standing. 'This is how many of you will be selected for service with the Special Air Service Regiment.' Another pause, then all but five of the candidates were instructed to sit. 'Officers, take a good look. Statistically, this is how many of you will be selected at the end of this course.' I looked around the sea of seated candidates, with the five men standing self-consciously among us, and felt exactly as demoralised as the DS had intended. The inspirational speech was enough to convince one candidate that selection was not for him, and he produced his Withdraw at Own Request form and signed himself off the course then and there. *One down, one hundred and fifty-nine to go,* I thought at the time.

Up until that point, the majority of my academic and sporting pursuits had been competitive and objectively categorisable with regard to achievement. Either you passed the test or you didn't, and you were ranked in line with your score. Either you won the race or you didn't, and if you didn't, you knew exactly where you came in the field and who beat you. My aim then had been to study or train harder in order to climb higher in the ranking next time. As I had gravitated towards individual sports, the concept of a team effort was somewhat foreign to me, and so I approached selection with a 'me versus them' attitude towards other candidates. I had failed to understand that the question the DS were asking themselves about me wasn't: 'Did he beat the other candidates?' but: 'Would I want this person on my team at war?' In the three weeks that followed, it would dawn on me that the others on the course were my teammates, not my competition, and I would be unable to finish the course without their support. On that first night, however, I had little sympathy for my fellow candidates. I took out my own withdrawal form and, when I was sure no-one was looking, I chewed it up and swallowed every last piece. I reasoned that having to ask a DS for a new form, which would no doubt entail explaining what had happened to the old one, would be a powerful disincentive to withdraw.

The first 48 hours of the course passed in a blur of fatigue and physical exertion, relieved only by a slightly more sedate navigation exercise designed to ensure we all had a minimum level of competence in the craft ahead of activities to come.

On the evening of the second day we were moved from the temporary camp location into a nondescript building on the Bindoon complex, which was part of a large urban training facility used by the regiment. The red-brick perimeter fence was topped with razor wire and pocked with bullet holes from live-fire training at the complex. The concrete floors and walls inside the cold, leaky building were charred from the use of live munitions, and splashes of brightly coloured paint gave away the use of Simunition non-lethal training ammunition. A crude set of steel-grated stairs joined the various levels.

The course was allocated the open third floor. We were packed in like sardines, the folding stretchers we used for beds almost hard up against one another with little room in between for our equipment. After being instructed on how our kit was to be laid out and where we could and couldn't go within the building, we were at long last told to get some sleep. By that stage it must have been approaching the early hours of the third morning of the course, but as none of us had watches it was impossible to tell. We had been awake for well over 40 hours straight and the nervous energy of the first couple of days had worn off. I collapsed into bed and was instantly out like a light.

I had no idea if I had slept for five minutes or five hours when I was woken with a start by a terrifying cacophony. In my dazed state, I had no idea what the fuck was going on.

It turned out the song 'Dig', by death metal band Mudvayne, was blaring at an impossibly loud volume from large speakers all around us. It sounded like a migraine had somehow been converted into audio format. DS and PTIs burst into the dark room, screaming at us to get our PT kit on and form up out the front of the building. The military working dog from two nights prior added to the chaos by barking ferociously and straining against its leash. We frantically got dressed and packed away our bed spaces in the prescribed manner before filing down the staircase and bolting outside. Thus began the barracks phase of selection, with its relentless barrage of rushed lessons on a range of complex military-related concepts interspersed with nauseating PT sessions and hurried meals.

Sometime in the very early hours of the following morning, after a particularly brutal PT session in an icy drizzle, we were instructed to prepare our packs and webbing for the 20-kilometre pack-march assessment that would be taking place within a few short hours. The 'twenty clicker' was one of the well-publicised assessments on selection, and we all knew it needed to be completed within 3 hours and 15 minutes, carrying a minimum load of 27 kilograms in order to pass. Packs and webbing would be weighed at the start and end of the activity, with an underweight load at the end constituting a fail. This meant that water for consumption during the stomp would need to be additional to the starting weight of the equipment. Complicating matters was the fact that we had no watches with which to pace ourselves.

A set of scales was made available and once my pack and webbing were finally prepared and weighed, I returned to the communal sleeping area. As I walked back to my stretcher, I noticed that the place wasn't quite as crowded as it had been the day before. It turned out that ten or so candidates had quietly withdrawn that day and had been whisked away without the rest of us knowing.

The stereo system that had delivered the barrage of death metal that morning was now pumping out 'Happy Wanderer' on loop at a medium volume. I crawled into bed and, despite the music, the lights and flurry of activity around me, was immediately asleep.

* * *

'*RAAAAAAAAAAAAAAAAAAAAAH!*' The blood-curdling scream of Mudvayne's lead singer assaulted my eardrums, reefing me from a deep sleep and plunging me into an equally deep state of panic. When I came to my senses, the scene was a sickening replay of the previous morning, except this time the dress for the day was cams and boots, and thankfully the military working dog must have been sleeping in, its absence reducing the chaos a fraction from the day prior.

We grabbed our webbing, packs and rifles and made our way downstairs and out into the freezing cold, pre-dawn darkness, where we were loaded into the cargo trays of waiting Unimog trucks. Once we were aboard, canvas flaps were pulled down to completely obscure our view. We sat silently in the dark as the trucks drove for about twenty minutes before coming to a halt. The cover was flung open and a screaming DS ordered us off the truck and directed us to form up.

All that covered my torso was my camouflage uniform with a t-shirt underneath. I stood there shivering and watching my breath make mist in front of my face as we waited for all the candidates to assemble at the start line for the assessment. Then, moving as a group, we set off along a muddy dirt road through the scrub. It must have rained heavily overnight, as the ground underfoot was boggy. Thick mud immediately caked the bottom of my boots and slowed my progress. Large puddles had accumulated in the low points of the road, and to keep my feet dry for as long as possible I skirted around them, adding to my distance travelled. I plugged on doggedly, though I was struggling to find a rhythm. Others around me were clearly suffering too, with some dropping significantly off the pace very early in the march.

By the time dawn broke, the group was stretched out over several kilometres, and I was sitting somewhere towards the front of the pack. On the long, straight stretches of dirt road I could still see the orange panel marker on the top of the leader's pack out in front, with about twenty candidates scattered between him and me. Knowing that I needed to cover roughly six kilometres every hour, I tried to pace myself, walking the uphill sections, running the downhills and shuffling along the flats. DS in vehicles patrolled the course, eyeballing candidates and periodically jumping out to walk beside us, firing questions and abuse.

At what I assessed to be about the halfway point I noticed a commotion a few hundred metres ahead where a gaggle of candidates had stopped by the side of the road. Shortly after, one of the DS vehicles came roaring past, horn blaring for me to get out of the way. It screeched to a halt where the crowd had gathered and the DS piled out of the car to assess the situation. As I drew closer I saw they were attending to an unconscious candidate. I offered to stop and help but was waved on my way along with the rest of the onlookers and informed that an ambulance would be there shortly. The course appeared to have claimed another victim.

I ploughed on, but the going was slow. By what I reckoned to be the two-hour mark, my boots and socks had long been soaked through, and I was starting to get hot spots on the friction points of my feet where blisters were forming and popping. My shoulders and lower back ached from the weight of the equipment, and the skin on both of my hips had been chafed raw by my webbing rubbing over wet clothing as I marched. This was the exact purpose of the assessment: to push candidates to a point of significant discomfort to see who could press on and who would quit. The activity had transitioned from a physical exercise to a psychological one. I tried to steer my mind away from the pain and increase my rate of effort, knowing that I was well past the halfway point.

The course seemed never-ending, with constant bends and short, sharp inclines slowing my progress to a near crawl and causing my lungs and legs to burn. Finally, after what had felt more like five hours than three, the dense scrub around the dirt road opened up and I saw three Unimog trucks waiting at the end of a long, straight stretch of road. Focusing on the trucks, I powered my way home, pouring all my remaining effort into the final stretch. On the downhill sections I ran as fast as my tired legs would let me. *Not long now*, I told myself as the distance shrank to 300 metres, 200 metres . . . I broke into a jog going up the slight incline towards the DS holding a stopwatch.

'Three twenty-seven – fail,' were the shattering words he spat at me as I crossed the finish line.

I stumbled to the side of the road and collapsed, exhausted. Sitting there, resting against my pack and staring out into the bush, it took a moment for the DS's words to properly register in my glucose-depleted brain. I had failed. And not by a minute or two – by *twelve fucking minutes*.

As that reality sank in, I felt absolutely devastated. Tears welled in my eyes. All those years of effort had amounted to nothing: I had fucked it. After another couple of minutes, a DS approached and instructed me to go get my kit reweighed. I hauled myself up on cramping legs and limped over to the scales for the post-activity kit weigh-in. As a small consolation, my equipment was still above the minimum weight, so while I had failed to meet the time for the activity, at least I wasn't a cheat as well.

Looking around, I did a rough count of the candidates who had finished before me. There were about twenty of them, and given that I had flunked by such a margin at least half of those guys must have failed as well. Dozens of candidates were still finishing, all of whom had failed too, leaving only ten or so to have passed, by my calculations. This realisation lifted my spirits a little. They couldn't fail all but ten of us, could they?

When the last of the candidates had finished and were done weighing their packs, we were ordered back onto the Unimogs and for the return trip to the accommodation building, where we were formed up and addressed as a group. Our collective performance on the twenty clicker was shit, the DS informed us, but there would be an opportunity to redo the test in several days' time. Though I wasn't exactly thrilled by the prospect of going through it again, especially given I was guaranteed to be even more fatigued a few days from now, it was the opportunity I was hoping for. I would have a chance to redeem myself.

After a hurried lunch we were thrust back into the round-robin lessons, however between my exhaustion and preoccupation with having failed the pack march very little was sinking in.

When we were finally released back to our sleeping area, the pile of folded stretchers along the wall indicated there had been more withdrawals. Yet to develop empathy for my fellow candidates, I drew great inspiration from watching the numbers thin out while knowing that I was still hanging in there.

Music was once again pumping through the audio system, this time alternating between the national anthem and 'Lili Marlene'. After we'd spent an hour or so stretching our legs and tending to blistered feet, a DS entered our area and informed us sombrely that we were required out the front of the accommodation building where the unit RMO would speak to us. There had been a great deal of conjecture about the candidate who had fallen unconscious during the pack march that morning, and the demeanour of the DS suggested we were going to hear some bad news.

The DS indicated that there was no need to dress for the talk with the RMO; the attire we had on was fine. Many of the candidates were getting around in thongs to air out their feet, and I slipped on a set of sneakers then joined the group heading down the stairs and out into the cool night. The RMO was leaning against the side of a parked ambulance van, its closed sliding door facing us. When we were all assembled, the RMO asked that anyone who had witnessed the collapse of the candidate during the pack march make their way over to him, and he quietly consulted with the small group out of earshot of the rest of us. *Fucking hell, the guy's dead*, I thought to myself, secretly a bit excited to be a part of a selection course hardcore enough to claim a life.

The RMO wrapped up his talk with the witnesses and then addressed the group again as a whole. 'I've got some good news and some bad news,' he told us. He had our undivided attention; you could have heard a pin drop as he continued. 'The good news is that candidate one hundred and thirty-six is recovering well in hospital and sends his regards to all of you. The bad news is . . .' His words hung in the cold night air for a fraction of a second before the door of the ambulance slid open and two screaming PTIs exploded from within. It scared the absolute piss and pick handles out of me!

'*FORM UP ON THE FUCKING ROAD IN TWO FUCKING FILES RIGHT FUCKING NOW!*' The PTIs circled our group at a jog, bellowing instructions.

We formed up and commenced our after-dinner PT torture, some of the candidates having to complete the session in flip flops.

Once the short but extremely sharp session was complete, we were once again formed up and introduced to the torturer who would play the intimidating role of Corporal Punishment for our selection course, responsible for disciplining the group when required.

As we stood in the cold night, light rain falling, the towering figure of Corporal Punishment made his way out of the accommodation building towards us. Careful not to make eye contact, I darted occasional glances his way to assess what we would be dealing with. It was not good. Corporal Punishment stood a shade over 2 metres tall and was built like a tank. He was dressed in camouflage uniform and boots, with his sandy beret draped casually over the top of his right eye. His piercing stare suggested that he would make us suffer for the honour of joining *his* regiment. (I didn't know it at the time, but Corporal Punishment was a well-known figure in the regiment who had been decorated for gallantry on the battlefield and would be further decorated in the coming years.)

He stared the course down for an eternity before he spoke. After laying down a few more ground rules, he ordered us to do several sets of excruciatingly slow push-ups on our knuckles before finally releasing us.

What followed was a days-long montage of suffering, interspersed with more rapid-fire lessons in novel skills at a pace that made retention improbable, though we were told to be prepared for subsequent testing. Bolstering my confidence during this period of the course was a pass in both the mandatory 3.2-kilometre webbing and rifle run, as well as the redo of 20-kilometre pack march.

Also memorable was the briefest of interactions with my brother Ben. While he was a squadron commander at the unit, and a DS on the course, every effort had been made to ensure that our paths didn't cross. But one night, just before lights out, I was making a mad dash to the toilets located across a court-yard from the accommodation building just as Ben happened to be walking in the opposite direction. Our eyes met, but no words were spoken. As implausible as it might sound, despite us both serving the next five years in army special operations, that was the one and only in-person professional interaction I had with Ben. As fate would have it, we would never find ourselves in the same unit, or on the same deployment, at the same time.

As the second week of selection progressed, our group was split by rank structure, with me and the other officers commencing a module designed to assess our suitability to lead in the special operations environment. By that stage of the course there were 30 officers remaining, and after allocation into groups we were immediately sent off to rooms within a previously desig-nated out-of-bounds areas of the accommodation building.

In the days that followed we undertook a relentless series of cerebral activities including debating, essay-writing and generating time-pressured solutions to tactical scenarios with incomplete information.

One of the activities of the officer module was known as Circle of Friends. As ever, the benign-sounding name masked the overwhelmingly intimidating nature of what was involved.

The Circle of Friends was an opportunity for existing officers serving within the regiment, from the commanding officer down, to grill officer candidates and assess how they functioned under pressure. I knew in principle what I was in for, but I couldn't possibly have prepared for what the activity entailed.

Dressed in cams and webbing, and clutching my rifle, the only instruction I was given by the DS in the dim corridor outside the room was to march in, salute the CO and then follow direction. The DS then opened the door and through I went.

I was instantly blinded by floodlights. As my eyes struggled to adjust, I could just make out the CO of the regiment sitting behind a large desk at the back of the room. He was flanked by seated officers to both sides, extending across the back of the room and down my left and right sides. Behind the seated officers, another row of officers was standing. A single child-sized seat was positioned in the very centre of the room; this was obviously intended for me. I made my way towards the comically small chair and, doing my best to appear calm, braced up and saluted the CO. He ordered me to sit, and when I did I discovered that one leg of my tiny chair was shorter than the other three, causing it to rock wildly so that I almost slid onto the floor. While I was still regaining my composure, the CO hit me with a barrage of questions. He opened with the standard *What makes you think you're good enough for my regiment?* to which I responded with a prepared answer containing words like *competent* and *confident*. The inter-rogation continued for several minutes along the same line, with other officers around the room chiming in. Each of my answers was followed by a long period of awkward silence as the crowd scrutinised me.

My eyes had adjusted to the bright environment, and I began to take in more of my surroundings. Squinting against the floodlights, I darted quick looks up to the top corners of the room, where several video cameras were mounted, their flashing red lights indicating that I was being recorded. I was processing that thought when I was blindsided by a question from my immediate left.

'What's your opinion on Iran's nuclear program?'

To be perfectly honest, I didn't give a single fuck about Iran's nuclear program and had nothing sensible to say about it. Squirming in my seat, I attempted to justify my ignorance by explaining that every spare hour was spent trying to stay at the cutting edge of medicine and that left me little time in which to stay up to date on current affairs. I had been wrong-footed by the question, as intended, and the follow-up from the CO was equally unnerving.

'On page three of your essay on transnational terrorism in [redacted] you've suggested that pre-emptive strikes against [redacted] might be a viable option to reduce the terrorist threat to Australia. Justify this position.'

Fuck me, I thought. A few nights prior we had been woken in the middle of the night and had a pencil and pad thrust at us with instruction to write 3000 words on one of several topics. Anticipating something like this, before selection I had brushed up on a few global terrorist organisations, as well as the situation at the time in both Iraq and Afghanistan. As luck would have it, one of the topics was something I had studied and I regurgitated what I knew, being sure to include some impressive-sounding wank-words like *transnational terrorism*. I had assumed that the exercise was primarily aimed at depriving our group of sleep; it hadn't occurred to me that anyone would read my essay, let alone pick it apart and ask me to justify my position on a throwaway statement made a couple of thousand words in. And yet there I was, tap-dancing through a response, hoping the beads of sweat on my forehead would be put down to an effect of the hot lights. I fumbled through another ten or so minutes of this before I was released.

It was a huge relief to step back into the darkened corridor and close the door behind me.

I would learn later that a fellow officer candidate had become disorientated on being dismissed from the Circle of Friends and, instead of exiting into the hallway, he had inadvertently walked into a broom closet, shutting the door behind him. He then had the nauseating realisation that there was no way out other than the door he had entered through. He waited around 30 seconds before sheepishly re-entering the room of smirking officers and leaving through the correct door.

Once all officers had completed the Circle of Friends we were split into groups, with mine ushered to the next activity, which involved a 'foreign agent' who looked suspiciously like an SAS operator in disguise and had a highly questionable accent.

What ensued was a wild-goose chase in the scrub surrounding our accommodation building stretching into the early hours of the morning to find a buried deposit of 'radioactive isotope'. After finally locating and digging it up, the next task was to carry the impossibly heavy box containing it several kilometres to a designated checkpoint. Struggling through the darkness, we eventually encountered the other officer candidates, who had been scattered around the area getting beasted in a similar fashion.

Upon our reunion as a group, the foreign agent became quite agitated and began to insinuate that we were in danger and needed to move back to our quarters in a hurry. He herded us through the main entrance of the building, but instead of going up the stairs to our accommodation level we were ushered through a trapdoor and down a set of stairs into a series of underground cells. As soon as the last man of our group had reached the bottom of the stairs, the trapdoor at the top was slammed shut behind us with an almighty clang of steel on concrete. This was followed by the unmistakable sound of a bolt being slammed home.

We had done the night activity with our packs on, so we had our sleeping gear with us. After waiting half an hour to make sure no-one was coming back for us, we spread out our sleeping kit in the pitch-dark to get some rest.

I recall being fairly pleased with the situation as I found myself a spot in a corner of one of the cells and stretched out on the damp, cold concrete floor. Within a few minutes the cells fell quiet. I couldn't say for certain, but I'm pretty sure that I could hear the muffled noise of someone crying as I drifted off to sleep. Everyone has their phobias, I guess, and perhaps being locked in a dark cell was more than someone could bear that night. But to be warm, comfortable and have no-one yelling at me for a while? I was stoked.

The same metallic clang I'd heard the night before woke me sometime later. I had no idea how long we had been allowed to sleep, but I felt refreshed. I climbed out of my sleeping bag and was stuffing it back into my pack when a DS opened the trapdoor and descended the stairs to the cells. We were instructed to drop our packs at our accommodation then form up out the front of the building in cams, running shoes and webbing with two full water bottles. It was PT time.

There is one PT session on every selection course which is designed to assess just how determined a candidate is to be a part of the unit. This was to be ours.

As soon as all 30 officer candidates were accounted for, the DS running the session addressed us. 'Candidate Eighteen, front and centre,' he bellowed.

Fuck, that's me. My mind raced as I tried to recall what mistakes I had made recently that might have led to me being singled out. I ran to the front of the assembled candidates and reported to the DS. He produced a piece of grip-strengthening exercise equipment with two handles and a spring in between. The idea was to hold the device in one hand and squeeze it together between your thumb and fingers. Handing me the device he announced to the group that if I could close it fully we would be exempt from the PT session.

Challenge accepted. I took the device in my right hand and, sucking in a big breath, went to work on closing it. Gripping it with all my might, I huffed and puffed and doubled over trying to move that fucking thing but it didn't budge even a fraction of an inch. Not being one to quit, and with such high stakes, I wrestled with it until I could feel my face going purple and the veins in my forehead throbbing. On the verge of a stroke, I finally gave in and sentenced the entire officer module to the PT session.

I had assumed subsequently that the DS was a mate of my brother and had wanted to see me struggle in front of the other candidates for a laugh. Not so. I met him properly five years later, and – still addressing me as Candidate 18 – he explained in front of a group of government agents we were training at the time that I had been singled out because I was the smallest in the group and he'd thought I would have no chance of closing the device. As it turned out, he was quite correct, though I've always suspected it was welded open, or at a minimum had been borrowed from Arnold Schwarzenegger's personal collection!

After a punishingly paced warm-up run, the first activity of our epic PT session was tyre flipping, conducted on a gently sloping gravel area next to a road. I watched as the DS made their way among us offering words of 'encouragement' at top volume from an uncomfortably close range. It wasn't long before it was my turn.

'Candidate Eighteen, it has been noted that you are very cool under pressure,' the DS announced.

That's a weird thing to say, I thought. It almost sounded like he was complimenting me.

He continued, 'From now on, whenever you are spoken to you will respond. Are we clear?'

I responded that we were, and with that the other DS unleashed a verbal spray.

'I think you're a piece of shit and a pretender, Candidate Eighteen,' he snarled.

Under strict orders to respond, I replied, 'I'm sorry you think that I'm a piece of shit and a pretender, sir.'

The DS looked unhappy with my response. 'There's no room for another Pronk in the regiment,' he told me. 'But you're going to fail anyway, so I suppose it doesn't matter.'

I had been completely unaware of a Pronk quota at SASR and briefly entertained the thought of enquiring about it before dismissing the idea.

'I'm sorry, sir, I'll try harder,' I said, refusing to be baited.

Getting no satisfaction from my submissive answers, the angry DS moved away to try it on with another candidate and I went back to flipping my tyre.

Eventually the tyre flipping ended, and in pairs we were allocated a tyre to roll with us as we moved away at a run down a nearby dirt road. There had been heavy rain the preceding night and the dirt road was muddy in sections, making rolling the massive tyres a challenge. We toiled with them over the undulating track for several kilometres before reaching a knee-deep creek crossing at the base of a short but very steep incline. The following hours were filled with hill sprints, demoralising upper-body sessions with 15-kilogram steel bars, push-ups and plank holds in the icy waters of the creek.

The hill session finally ended and we once again grabbed our tyres in pairs, rolling them up the huge hill and moving on at a run along the dirt track. Shortly after cresting the hill it occurred to me that I hadn't had a single mouthful of water in the hours since the PT session had begun. Bucketing sweat, I knew I would be dehydrating at a dangerous rate, so in coordination with my partner candidate I moved away from the tyre, withdrew a water bottle from my webbing and slowed down slightly to take a long slug. With my neck craned back to drink, I didn't notice the furious DS encroaching on my personal space until he erupted.

'*CANDIDATE EIGHTEEN, HOW FUCKING DARE YOU LOOK AFTER YOUR OWN PERSONAL COMFORT WHILE YOUR PARTNER ROLLS THE TYRE BY HIMSELF!*'

Startled, I spilled more water down my front than I had managed to drink. I quickly screwed the cap back on my water bottle, replaced it in its pouch and sprinted to catch up to my tyre.

After an eternity, we reached a bitumen road that I recognised as being the turn-off leading back to the accommodation building. My mood lifted at the thought that the session might be nearing a close.

My partner and I had fallen to the very back of the pack (and were copping a predictable amount of DS attention as a result) when I noticed that the front pairs had stopped and appeared to be huddled around something on the ground. Drawing closer, I saw a candidate lying on the bitumen, only semi-conscious. Corporal Punishment was standing over him and, as we drew to a halt, he addressed us as a group.

'This is what weakness looks like,' he thundered, gesturing at the twitching, incoherent form in front of him. 'There is no room for weakness in this regiment.' He then retrieved two completely full water bottles from the candidate's webbing and pointed out that the candidate hadn't had a single sip of water during the session, proving he was incapable of looking after himself.

It was damned if you do, damned if you don't, I realised, as my own attempt to take a drink had also been met with a tirade of abuse.

Fucking hell, shouldn't someone be helping this guy? I remember thinking at the time. Now, having medically supported several selection courses in the years since, I know that there would have been a medical team in an ambulance hovering very close by, ready to swoop in and intervene if required. Corporal Punishment's current performance was an act calculated to drive home the point that failure was not an option for an officer with the SASR and wouldn't be tolerated by the operators of the unit.

At long last we were allowed to make our way back to the accommodation building. I was absolutely spent, but far from shattered. I had no way of knowing how long that session lasted for, though if I had to wager a guess I'd say it was a good five hours. Before I could relax, I was accosted by a DS who ordered me to sing 'Happy Wanderer'. Despite having been given the lyric sheet at the start of the course and the fact the goddamn song had been playing on loop in our accommodation most nights, I was still struggling with the words. But I had to commit, and so I belted out a loud, tone-deaf rendition of random lyrics with such conviction that I could see the DS questioning his own familiarity with the song. I finished to the stunned silence of the other candidates, who no doubt were bracing themselves for the inevitable physical punishment that would be coming due to me not knowing the words. I watched the DS's face, a confused look etched on it as he wondered if perhaps *he* was the one who'd been singing incorrect lyrics. In the end, our next session commenced without punishment. It was interesting to observe and it's a technique I have fallen back on many times since that incident. Most people will believe anything you say as long as you say it with absolute confidence!

After my solo choir practice, the next activity was a Rate Your Mates session in which we were instructed to rank ourselves from 1–30 in order of perceived competence and suitability to be an SASR officer. This was an uncomfortable exercise for me, as I'd always preferred to let my actions speak for themselves rather than talking myself up. I watched as the alpha males of the group jockeyed for the top few spots, literally using their elbows to physically assert themselves into position. I opted to sit on the fence and put myself plumb in the middle, at number 15. The DS then moved from candidate to candidate asking each of us to justify why we had positioned ourselves where we had. They made a big deal out of the fact that only five or so officers from the course would be selected for service with the SASR, pointing out that if we hadn't put ourselves in the top five then we mustn't really believe we should be there. I listened to the arguments put forward by some of the candidates who thought they should be ranked higher than they'd ended up. I couldn't believe some of the things they said. I guess they saw it as an opportunity to self-promote, but it seemed to me they were digging big holes for themselves.

Looking around the room, it was interesting to note the physical stature of those who had positioned themselves in the top ten versus those in the bottom ten. The top ten consisted of the tall, physically impressive specimens that the general public might envisage a special forces soldier to look like. The bottom ten, however, were almost exclusively short, wiry soldiers, with a few pairs of glasses scattered among them for good measure. If subsequent experience has taught me anything, it is that this bottom ten is where you will find most of your successful candidates. It is the wiry, tough little bugger who will still be standing at the end of the course for the simple fact that he is *not* as physically capable as the natural athlete and therefore had to want it more and work harder to be there. He is generally the one who has strengthened his resolve to the point where he will literally die before signing a Withdraw at Own Request form. As Mark Twain said, it's not the size of the dog in the fight, it's the size of the fight in the dog.

My aspirations of being a troop commander had waned since my career adviser interview the year before, and I had started selection with the intention of getting into the SASR as a qualified doctor, as per my original ambition. When my turn came to justify my position in the group, I thus told the DS that I was there to be the doctor and as such wasn't competing directly with anyone in the room.

The DS studied me for a moment before saying, 'Candidate Eighteen, you are the most educated person in this room and probably the smartest.'

Compliments from this guy, and in front of everyone else? What the fuck is going on? He then continued dismissively,

'But clearly you have no confidence in your own abilities if you've rated yourself number fifteen in the group.' And with that he moved on.

I felt my face redden and disappointment welled inside of me. I'd just missed a huge opportunity to prove myself. Maybe I should have jockeyed for a higher position, but that just wasn't in my nature. The session ended and I left the room feeling absolutely gutted. The DS had temporarily achieved their objective of making me feel as though I was failing the course, and I knew I needed to let go of my disappointment and focus on the task at hand. The toughest components of the course, Happy Wanderer and Lucky Dip, were still ahead, and I couldn't afford to burn a single ounce of emotional energy on the past if I was going to endure what was coming.

IV

LUCKY DIP

I NOTICED A CAR IN THE DISTANCE, HEADING IN MY DIRECTION. Figuring that it was likely to be DS checking on us, I made my way to the side of the road and upped my pace a little to make myself look as impressive as possible.

As the car got closer, I peered at it through the rain and saw it was being driven not by a DS but by an elderly lady who pulled up next to me and got out. I could see that she was distraught. I must have been a pathetic sight judging by the way she looked at me.

'You poor darling,' she said. 'Look at what they're making you do.'

As she spoke, she moved around to open the boot of her car. I wasn't quite sure what was going on and thought for a second that this might be a test set up by the DS. We had been instructed not to interact with civilians and certainly not to take anything from them. But something about this woman's sincerity told me she was legitimate. I had no idea what she thought was being *done* to us, or who the *doers* were, but I decided I'd play along.

'How long have you been out here?' she asked.

'Three days,' I replied, adding for good measure, 'with a few more to go.'

The lady returned with a handful of Tim Tams and a mandarin. 'I'm so sorry, but this is all I can offer you.'

I thanked her and she muttered something further about how horrible it was what *they* were doing to us before she got back in her car and drove off. I devoured the Tim Tams and mandarin, making sure to throw the mandarin peel well into the bush, so it wouldn't be spotted by any passing DS, before setting off again.

The Happy Wanderer phase of selection was well under-way, and I found myself in the heart of the Stirling Range National Park, in the far south of Western Australia. Lugging a 50-kilogram pack and navigating from checkpoint to check-point, often located on the peaks of mountains, the preceding 72 hours had been brutal on my body. I was burning calories well in excess of those being replaced by our daily ration pack. As well as losing a significant amount of weight, I had also started to accumulate injuries. First came a quadriceps strain while negotiating a particularly steep descent from a mountain checkpoint, then an abdominal muscle injury.

One consolation of this stage of the course, however, was the strict instruction not to move after dark or before first light, which equated to full nights of uninterrupted sleep. Despite this, my body was beginning to break down and the final and hardest component of the selection course, the famed Lucky Dip, was still days away.

* * *

First light dawned on the fifth and final day of Happy Wanderer and it was harder than ever before to get up and moving. My emaciated body ached from head to toe and the pain in my right thigh was agonising. I completed my usual morning routine of packing away my sleeping kit and making a coffee, and then checked my map before setting off for my final day of stomping. I had covered a little more than 100 kilometres to that point and had a 20-kilometre undulating transit to the base of the next climb, at the top of which was my final check-point. If I could make it before nightfall, I would have covered 120 kilometres and climbed five peaks, which, according to rumour, was the minimum required to pass the activity and progress on the course.

Normally there would have been nothing particularly challenging about covering 20 kilometres and a climb in a day, but given my physical state at the time I was struggling. I set out but going was slow. Our strict instruction to stay on formed roads and tracks had made the navigation component of the activity pretty simple. As such, I had been bumbling along all morning down a dirt track my map told me would be intersected by a service road I would need to take. In my zombie-like state, the sun was well overhead by the time it registered that I had passed the point where the service road should have been. A shot of cold adrenaline cleared my thoughts, but frantic backtracking to find the turn-off revealed nothing. Using a navigation technique known as a resection, I confirmed my position on the ground and came to the reali-sation the service road simply wasn't there. Fuck.

I began to get a little panicked. There was no time for me to stay on the tracks and still make it to my checkpoint by last light, but being caught by DS moving cross-country would have consequences. After a few moments' thought, I decided I would plot the shortest possible cross-country distance to the road I needed to be on and make a dash for it.

The route would be about a kilometre, and before I set off I took the day-glo orange panel marker off the top of my pack and stuffed it in my pocket. The excitement of the situation boosted my spirits, and the requirement to move fast would force me to cover some good ground. I did a final check of my compass bearing and then set off into the bush towards my destination. Movement through the light scrub was easy and I began to wonder why I hadn't thought of cutting some corners like this over the previous few days. It certainly would have saved me some time.

As I approached the point where I needed to pop out again on the destination dirt track I could hear the sound of a motorbike in the distance. The area had a short, dead-end dirt road that I would need to leg it along before getting back on the track to the base of my final climb. While it was not against the rules to be on the dead-end track, I had no plausible reason for being there, and being spotted would certainly give away the fact that I had gone cross-country. I got within 100 metres of the dead-end road and hid in the bush, watching for the motorbike. Before long it came into sight, and sure enough it was a DS on one of the unit's four-wheelers. I waited for him to turn and ride off then put my panel marker back on my pack and piss-bolted out onto the track and towards the intersection I needed to reach before I was seen.

I made it to the intersection then propped on the side of the road to catch my breath just as a white ute screamed around a nearby bend. The car screeched to a halt in the dirt in front of me.

'Where the fuck did you come from?' demanded the DS in the passenger's seat.

'Just up that road,' I lied, pointing.

'Bullshit, we just came from there,' the DS snapped.

'I know – I saw you drive past.' I was committed to my lie, so I might as well play it out and see what happened.

'We didn't fucking see you.'

'Yeah, I'd moved off the track to take a shit.'

The look on the DS's face told me he was pretty sure I was bullshitting, but he had no way of proving it. He wound up the window and the car pulled away at pace, the resultant shower of dirt doing nothing to dampen my spirits after getting away with my cross-country dash and fabricated story.

After a short rest I picked up and continued on my way to the base of the final peak.

The route to the climb took me along a paved road with steeply cambered dirt shoulders on either side. After four and a half days of pack-marching, my feet were a bit the worse for wear, and the impact of walking on the bitumen was giving me hell. At long last, and just on sunset, I reached the turn-off to a small side road leading to a car park at the base of my final climb.

By that time I was mentally defeated and had resigned myself to the fact that I wasn't going to make it up the final peak before last light. I had decided that I would set up camp at the bottom of the climb and settle for four peaks. My mood was low, and I was completely exhausted.

As I trudged up the short road to the car park another candidate drew level with me, snapping me out of my self-defeatist wallow. We had a quick chat about how long we thought the climb would take, and both agreed that we couldn't make it before last light. That said, he was going to go for it anyway, stating that he didn't want to leave any stone unturned on the course and he would rather face the wrath of the DS for moving after dark than finish Happy Wanderer with one less peak. His positive attitude made me feel even worse about my resolve not to attempt the climb.

As we reached the car park, he peeled off down the path to the start of the climb, and I went in the other direction to look for a suitable spot to set up camp for the night.

Finding a flat piece of dirt, I dropped my pack and sat down on it in time to watch the other candidate disappearing up the track at the base of the climb. As I sat there, I thought back to the brief discussion I'd had with a candidate I had crossed paths with the day before, and his 'inside info' that we needed five peaks and 120 kilometres to pass. I was sitting on about 120 kilometres, but only four peaks. My fifth was right there in front of me but there was no way I could make it to the top before dark.

My body was in bad shape and my mind was trying to quit on me. I went to take out my sleeping kit to set up camp, but something inside wouldn't let me. I'd trained too hard for this course to not give this final climb a crack. *Fuck it*, I thought, and instead of unpacking my kit I threw it back on my shoulders and jogged towards the base of the climb, cursing myself for burning a good twenty minutes of stomping time while I sat suffering from what I perceived to be a mild case of weakness.

I attacked the climb with everything I had, figuring it could well be the last thing I did on the course if I failed Happy Wanderer, and not wanting to leave anything in the tank if that was to be the case. As I neared the summit, the sun had well and truly set, making the path difficult to see and leaving me stumbling over every small rock underfoot. I was frantic.

Sweat was pouring off me, my legs and lungs were imploring me to stop. The narrow track cut through thick foliage that grabbed at my pack and webbing with bony fingers, slowing my progress. The gradient finally flattened out into an expanse of rock that signified the top of the climb. I paused and scanned the darkened area for the checkpoint, making out a small light glowing in a one-man tent. I approached it with caution, still weighing up the pros and cons of checking in with the DS, and risking being reprimanded for moving after last light. As I drew closer, I realised that the DS who was manning the checkpoint was none other than Corporal Punishment himself! I was there, I told myself, so I might as well roll the dice. It was going to be either a triumph or a spectacular failure.

I declared myself to Corporal Punishment and in the near-complete darkness checked in. To my overwhelming relief, he acted as if nothing was out of order and gave me instruction on the pick-up procedure for the following morning. He then suggested that I set up camp next to him on the flat rock, an invitation I politely declined before making my way a few hundred metres back down the track to find a good spot for the night.

I went about my night routine, quietly pleased with myself for manning up and doing the final climb. Whether or not I had done enough to pass the activity I couldn't be sure, but at least I could honestly say that I had given it everything I had. Now the final component of the selection course loomed: Lucky Dip.

While it might have sounded like a children's game, Lucky Dip was rumoured to be a living hell and it had been looming over all of us like the blade of a guillotine waiting to drop. I knew relatively little about the activity other than that it was five days of pretty much complete food and sleep deprivation, during which time the daily routine consisted of carrying impossibly heavy items over great distances while being yelled at by DS, and then being kept awake all night. The concept sounded simple enough, and in my naivety I remember thinking: *How hard could it possibly be? It's only five days.* I would soon find out.

There are no words to describe just how dreadful Lucky Dip is, and I fear that my attempt here will not do it justice. Try as I might, I have never been able to come close to conveying how nightmarish the activity is to those who haven't experienced it. Certainly as I commenced the first activity of day one, I had no existing mental reference point to even begin to process what was about to unfold.

We were split into five groups, or 'sections', of ten, indicating to me that over two-thirds of the candidates who had commenced the course were gone. Each group was force-marched in a different direction. The pace of the march was uncomfortable, and wearing our packs and webbing, and loaded with water, we were each lugging around 30 kilograms. Trying to keep up with the unladen DS was impossible, and our group fell behind, its members strung out in a line behind him. The DS would periodically stop and rip into us for not keeping up, and not staying together as a group. Predictably, the punishment was push-ups, before the march would resume at the same pace. When we finally reached our first activity location, known as a 'stand', we were already close to the point of collapse.

Waiting for us was a massive pile of stores, comprising full ammunition boxes, jerry cans and .50-calibre machine guns with tripods, which of course had to be moved over an impossible distance, in an impossible timeframe. Since there were more stores than we could physically carry at one time, we would have to move forward with some of the stores, dump them 50 or so metres towards our objective, and then return to get the remainder. Naturally we didn't do this fast enough for the liking of the DS, and we were punished accordingly. Timings to reach checkpoints came and went and we never met them. It was, by design, demoralising.

The gruelling stores carry continued non-stop from dawn until mid-afternoon, at which point we were given a brief respite while we got a new DS. One of the candidates in our group took the opportunity to whip out his Withdraw at Own Request form and sign himself off the course. We tried to talk him out of it, but he would not be dissuaded. Immediately after he handed his form in, a second member of the group quit as well. I could see where they were coming from; the day had been an absolute living hell already and it was only mid-afternoon. And there were still four and a half seemingly insurmountable days of Lucky Dip remaining.

The daylight was fading as we approached our second-night stand. As had been the case the night before, the activity was far less physically taxing than the daytime activity and was primarily designed to deprive us of sleep. We were in a camp of sorts, but we were required to remain tactical and that meant no fire. Our task was to build a comprehensive series of defensive positions at strategic points around the perimeter of the camp using pieces of wood gathered from the surrounding area. As we completed one structure and moved on to the next, a DS would come along behind us and tear them down, making for a Sisyphean cycle of perpetual rebuilding.

At some stage during the night I became aware that the back of my right ankle was particularly painful. The rest of my body was screaming at me too, but the back of my ankle felt different. Waiting for a time when I was meant to be off collecting wood for the umpteenth rebuild of our defensive position, I ducked behind a large tree and hastily removed my right boot to investigate the source of the pain. I found my sock crusted onto the back of my right ankle by what appeared to be a combination of dry blood and pus. I ripped the sock off and in the dim red light of my head torch inspected the ulcerated lesion. It did not look good. A gentle squeeze of the surrounding area sent a gush of pus down the back of my ankle and a lightning bolt of pain up my leg. What had clearly started as a simple blister was now badly infected and in desperate need of a good clean and dressing. The infection appeared to be spreading into the adjacent tissues, and the whole area around my ankle and heel was swollen and hot to touch. I had cracked out my small medical kit and was getting out some iodine to clean the wound when I was interrupted.

'What the fuck are you doing?'

The DS's voice snapped me out of my concentrated state. I had been completely absorbed in what I was doing and hadn't heard him approach. Fucking phantoms of the jungle.

'Ah . . . sorry, sir, just dressing a blister,' I mumbled.

'Sitting here looking after yourself while the rest are out working, hey? What's your number?'

'Eighteen, sir,' I replied.

The DS noted it down. 'An officer, huh? Typical. What unit are you from?'

'5 RAR, sir.'

'A fucking infantry officer! Fuck me.' His rage was escalating.

'No, sir. I'm the medical officer there, sir.'

My response obviously confused him, because he didn't pursue the matter.

'Right, well get the fuck up and do some work,' the DS concluded. He stood over me as I scrambled to get my putrid sock and boot back on. I grabbed my rifle and made off into the night to continue gathering wood, mentally kicking myself. First, I'd been caught before I'd managed to get my wound cleaned, and second, I'd suffered through those excruciating antibiotic injections and *still* got a fucking infection!

In the very early hours of the following morning we were gathered up as a group and briefed on a mission to meet a friendly agent who would provide us with food. I assumed – rightly, as it turned out – that the mission would be a set-up and I adjusted my expectations accordingly. Stomping through the darkness, our patrol made it to the rendezvous point in the allocated time, and after we'd set up a defensive perimeter a couple of candidates from the group moved forward to meet the agent. Predictably, everything went wrong, and instead of an agent we were met with hundreds of blank rounds fired at us from three directions, causing us to hightail it back to our camp. We arrived just as dawn began to, exhausted and hungry. It had been over 48 hours since we'd had food, and the cumulative sleep deprivation and fatigue brought on by the unrelenting challenges we'd faced over the last couple of weeks on the course was causing cracks to start to show in some of the candidates. One of the guys from our group began cooking off about how we had fucked it, insisting that if we had arrived at the RV sooner, and been more careful, we would have got the promised food. In his tired, hypoglycaemic state he simply couldn't comprehend that even if we had been there an hour prior and approached the RV with ninja stealth, the outcome would have been the same. He had been sucked in exactly as intended.

We shouldered our packs and were once again force-marched to the next stand. By that time the pain in my right ankle was constant, and with every step the friction of my boot rubbing on it was electric.

We arrived at our stand for the third day of Lucky Dip to be greeted by an animated DS playing the role of a friendly foreign fighter in need of our help. In this scenario, the fighter's brother was on a petrol-powered life-support machine and a delivery of fuel was urgently needed to keep the machine going. There was a truck full of jerry cans parked nearby and we were ordered to grab a full one each. I put the jerry in my pack, which brought the weight of my combined load to about 55 kilograms. It was certainly heavy, but it was a snap compared to the loads of the previous two days, and I couldn't believe that this was all we would need to carry for the day. My morale soared as we headed off into the scrub towards the undisclosed location of the brother in need.

Naturally, when something on selection seemed too good to be true, it probably was, and about half an hour into the journey our animated leader stopped. Doing some calculations aloud, he determined that we didn't have enough fuel and ordered us to lug our loads back to the truck so we could get another jerry can each.

With our individual burdens now approaching 80 kilograms, we set off back down the path we had already covered that morning.

The weight was overwhelming, and I was struggling. In the absence of food my body was wasting away, and I was racked with the pain of my torn abdominal and quadriceps muscles as well as the spreading infection in my right ankle. Looking around, I realised everyone else in my section was suffering too. There was little talk among us; everyone was retreating into their own personal space to fight the mental battle against their failing bodies.

We trudged on. By mid-morning our progress had slowed to a crawl, the lack of urgency infuriating our foreign leader.

During one of our many stops I was applying some Chapstick to my cracked, sunburned lips when it occurred to me that it might contain some calories. Doing a quick check to ensure no-one was watching, I ate the whole thing. It was chewy and delicious but left me with a slightly queasy feeling in my guts and a waxy coating on my teeth.

We suffered on until mid-afternoon, when we arrived at our 'complex reasoning' stand for the day and were finally allowed to drop our packs. The activity was a water crossing, and our task was to get all of our section, along with our kit and jerry cans, to the other side of an 80-metre-wide dam. Lying at the water's edge were half-a-dozen 44-gallon drums, some lengths of wood and some rope. A crowd of DS onlookers, including the man who was special operations commander of Australia at the time, was gathered to observe our performance. I'm not sure if my performance on that activity was actually shit or if he was just joking, but every time I saw that particular commander after selection, he would bring up my dismal performance on the water crossing.

We fumbled through creating a raft and slowly but surely moved our section and all our kit across the dam. Most ended up somewhat soaked, and those of us who'd managed to remain dry were required to wade back into the water up to our waists to ensure we all suffered equally when night fell and the temperature dropped.

In the early hours of the following morning, with no sign of the DS, we formed a large huddle in an attempt to stay warm. It must have looked quite a sight: a small group of skinny, dirty soldiers hugging one another in the middle of the bush. We would take turns being in the centre of the huddle, where it was the warmest, and discussed in whispers the first meal we were going to eat when the course ended. I remember one candidate describing in detail a dish of his own invention that he dubbed a pizza hoagie, which involved rolling up a whole loaf of garlic bread in a large pizza and then eating it all like a sub sandwich. My meal of choice was going to be sushi.

By day four the screws were being tightened further to try to push more of us to withdraw, but no-one in our group was going to quit at this late stage. We had all dug our claws in and were hanging on for the ride to end.

In a monotonous repeat of the theme of previous days, this time a loaded Zodiac boat had to be carried cross-country for most of the day, being swapped in the early afternoon for a smallish box that we were ordered to pick up and continue on our way. We had been supplied with some lengths of wood and ropes, and we used the rope to lash the wood to the box in order to carry it. The size of the box dictated that we could only get four members of the group around it at any given time, leaving three to walk alongside and provide security for the move.

Once ready, we attempted to haul the box up onto our shoulders, but literally could not move the thing. I was perplexed, wondering how on earth the DS had managed to fix the box to the ground. We drew in the three guys on perimeter defence and with a haemorrhoid-inducing effort heaved the box up and onto our shoulders.

The weight of the box was extraordinary. It felt as though my spine was compressing just standing there; the idea of moving with the load was unthinkable. It was without question *the* hardest thing I had done in my life to that point. With the only other option being to withdraw from the course, we edged forward at a painfully slow shuffle under the massive weight. We would move somewhere in the order of 50 metres at a time before our bodies would start to buckle and we would be forced to lower the box, rotate members to our mobile perimeter defence, and go again.

Upon being loaded up with the box on one occasion, I felt a sharp shooting pain in the centre of my upper back and immediately felt myself collapsing under the weight. For fear of dropping the box unexpectedly and potentially injuring the other guys carrying the load, I yelled out to them that I was failing and that I needed to lower the load. All the surrounding DS zeroed in on me, berating me for being weak and letting the team down. It was a low moment for me. My condition was deteriorating by the hour, and I wasn't sure how much longer my mind could continue to drive my body. I gritted my teeth and once again shouldered the ridiculous load for another short shuffle forward. My upper back lit up like a hot knife was being wedged between my shoulder blades but there was no way I was going to drop that box again.

That afternoon, and for no apparent reason, my nose began to bleed uncontrollably. I did my best to hide it from the DS for fear of being medically reviewed and potentially withdrawn, but it was no use. Blood had soaked through the front of my shirt and my attempts to wedge tissues up my nostrils to stop the bleeding proved ineffective. When approached by a DS about my condition, I lied and told him that I had hit my nose on a low branch. I figured if I could offer a tangible reason for bleeding, rather than confessing the truth – that my head was inexplicably leaking blood – the DS would be less likely to make an issue of it. I was right. The DS seemed happy to permit me to continue bleeding and we moved on with our activity.

Late in the afternoon we stumbled upon a clearing in the scrub where a DS acting as a village elder met us. He seemed friendly and urged us to join him for a meal. My suspicions were aroused – it was too good to be true – and I remained on my guard as we dropped the box and followed the man into the village area. There he produced two large stainless-steel trays covered with aluminium foil. I still wasn't convinced we would be fed, but I was becoming increasingly interested. I had heard rumours that there would be a feed at some point during Lucky Dip but it would be decidedly unpalatable. Having already resorted to eating my Chapstick, I was willing to give almost anything a go.

We were ordered to form a perimeter defence, and then one by one were allowed to quickly dart into the village centre and grab a scoop of whatever was on the trays.

My turn came and as I hastily approached the tray I made out what looked like chunks of dark matter suspended in blue jelly. On first glance it appeared to be some sort of delicious-looking dessert, and in my mind I convinced myself that's what it was. Oh, how disappointed I was when I returned to my defensive position and realised it was actually a combination of eyeballs, testicles, tongues, kidneys and stomach lining, suspended in a tasteless, cold blue gelatine. It was utterly disgusting. A DS had been assigned to stand over each of us and monitor whether we ate the offering or not. I choked down a chunk of stomach lining before starting on a tongue. I tried to think of steak as I chewed but it was no good. I began to gag, only just managing to stop myself from vomiting on my DS observer's feet. Thankfully he moved away for a brief period, and I hastily dug a small hole in the dirt with the heel of my boot and buried the remainder of my horrid meal. When the DS returned he noted my empty cup and enquired if I wanted more.

'Couldn't fit another thing in, sir,' I replied, then watched on as others in my group went back for seconds and even thirds, until the trays were empty.

The mealtime had provided a welcome respite from lugging the box, but once the trays were empty it was back to the grind.

While leaving an awful taste in my mouth, I could feel the energy from the food surging through my body, and the load didn't seem as heavy as it had that morning. We continued our epic struggle with the box until nightfall, when we were finally permitted to dump it on a waiting truck. Bidding the box good riddance, we commenced our march to what we had calculated would be our final night stand.

The night stand involved collecting wood and constructing a shelter large enough for the entire section to sleep in. Once it was completed, a DS came and inspected it and then ordered us to dismantle the shelter and return the wood, instructing us to ensure there was no evidence that the area had been disturbed.

Several hours later we achieved that task to the satisfaction of the DS and we were allowed to sleep.

One hour later I was awoken by a foot in my ribs and opened my eyes to see a DS standing over me. He informed me that I would be the section commander allocated to lead our team of candidates for the day, and ordered me to get the guys ready to move.

I woke the remainder of our group and, after we'd packed up our sleeping kit, drew them in for a brief. We all thought it would be the final day of the course, but I recommended that we should keep our guard up in case this assumption was wrong.

Our march to the day stand was the longest yet and as torturous as usual. Eventually we reached a series of Unimog trucks and saw other groups of candidates milling around them. The course was coming back together as a whole. Surely that was a good sign.

Once all the groups had assembled at the start point, we were each allocated a stretcher with a simulated casualty on it: the activity for the day would be a casualty evacuation exercise. The simulated casualties were 80-kilogram mannequins and ours had been decorated with a gut wound made of raw steak with tomato sauce for blood. I eyed off the steak; the second our group's DS looked away I would eat it, I decided. However, the DS had other ideas.

'Hey, Eighteen, aren't you meant to be some kind of doctor?'

'Yes, sir.'

'WELL, DRESS THAT FUCKING WOUND, FOR FUCK'S SAKE!' he bellowed.

Leaping into action, I ripped a field dressing out of my webbing and began to wrap the tasty-looking steak. (I did manage to sneak a lick of the tomato sauce, but that only left me refluxing tomato-flavoured acid for the rest of the day.) Then the groups lifted their individual stretchers and we took off at a fast walk down an undulating dirt track. It was the stereotypical SAS selection stand that I had read about in books over the years. The extraction trucks would wait at the top of a distant hill, and the moment we reached them they would fire up their engines and drive to the top of the next hill. Or, just when we were getting close, we would be ambushed and forced to drop our stretchers and establish all-round defences as the trucks drove away.

As the day progressed, my physical state deteriorated to the point where I was stumbling and collapsing every 50 or so metres. I was no longer able to shoulder the weight of the stretcher and was struggling even under the 30 kilograms of my individual load. Unable to walk in a straight line, I zigzagged along the road, battling to keep pace with my stretcher-bearing colleagues. I was in real trouble; my mind was still willing, but my body was giving up on me.

I felt ghastly; my body was refusing to do what my mind was telling it to. I was losing control. At one point, I collapsed next to one of the trucks. The medical officer supporting the course (who would years later become a mentor and close friend) offered me a ride in the ambulance, but there was no fucking way I was quitting. The trucks kicked over again and drove off to the next hill. Another candidate hauled me to my feet and, supporting me with one arm, helped me to continue.

Things were desperate. We frantically scrambled the few hundred metres to the trucks' new position, expecting them to pull away once again – but they didn't. I was physically incapable of climbing onto the back of the nearest truck and had to be pulled up by candidates who were already aboard. Could this be it? I grew teary at the thought, and began apologising profusely to the other members of my section for being unable to help carry the stretcher for the last hour of the activity. Just a few weeks earlier I would have revelled in the failure of these other candidates; now, they had not only shouldered my share of the stretcher carry, they had refused to leave me behind in the dirt. I had been humbled.

The trucks pulled away and drove a short distance back to the accommodation building. There we were ordered off the trucks and instructed to change into our cleanest set of cams and assemble back out the front with all our belongings. *It must be over*, I kept thinking, but I hardly dared to believe it.

I was on my way back to the sleeping area when I was suddenly doubled over by a pain in my gut. I had to shit – *immediately*. I hobbled at best pace to a nearby portable toilet and, without a second to spare, dropped my strides and unleashed a horrendous, jet-black, liquid torrent, the smell of which caused me to gag. The stench within the confines of the small cubicle was unbearable, so I reached for the lock, thinking I might crack the door open a little for some fresh air. But the toilet was situated on a slight slope, and the weight of the door caused it to fling wide open the second I unlocked it. Unable to reach it again from my seated position, I finished my business in full view of the rest of the candidates, who were moving back and forth from the accommodation building with their kit. I should have been humiliated, but after everything I'd been through I was way beyond caring.

I finished up, changed into my cleanest set of cams, collected my kit and joined the others.

The same buses that had taken us to the Stirling Range pulled up, and we loaded onto them to find piles of food waiting for us on the seats. *This fucking thing must be over,* I thought again, but still there was no official word. We were ordered to pull the curtains of the bus shut and told not to look out as we drove. I was ravenously hungry, but only managed to eat a single chocolate biscuit and half a banana before I was uncomfortably full. Despite my brain screaming at me to eat more, I stopped at that.

Sneaking a few peeks out the window as we drove, I could tell we were returning to Perth, and by late afternoon we were back where it had all begun: Campbell Barracks. As we debussed, Corporal Punishment addressed us, and for the first time his tone was amicable. 'In case you were wondering, the course is over.'

His words lifted the world's weight off my shoulders. The personal belongings that had been taken from us on the first night of the course were returned, and I immediately took out my camera and snapped a photo of myself for prosperity. My second order of business was to phone Kristy. She answered on the third ring and I tried to talk but burst into tears instead. Years of emotional investment had been poured into getting to this point, and at exactly that moment it boiled over.

I wouldn't learn until the following day if I had passed or failed the course, but either way selection was finally over and I was still standing. Just.

V

THE SCENIC ROUTE TO THE SAS

In the immediate aftermath of selection we were required to clean and hand back all the kit we had been issued for the course. We spread out in the sun on a large grassed area on Campbell Barracks and cleaned our rifles and radios. The DS moved among us, shaking our hands and sharing a laugh about things that had happened over the last three weeks. It was nice to see that they were human after all.

When I was content that all my kit was ready to be handed back, I approached a small table manned by Q-store guys and began checking things off our issued equipment list.

We had been issued a chocolate ration prior to Lucky Dip, with strict instruction to only eat it in extremis. As I went to return mine I was informed that no-one was keeping track of the chocolate at all and that most candidates had eaten theirs. I felt ripped-off and approached a nearby candidate.

'Hey mate, did you eat your chocolate ration?'

'Yeah, of course. Didn't you?'

I couldn't believe it. I was feeling dumber by the second.

'Nah, I thought it was only for emergencies,' I offered in a lame attempt to validate my stupidity for not having eaten the chocolate.

'It was an emergency, I was fucking starving to death!' the candidate replied. It was hard to argue with his logic.

Once our kit was returned, we were issued keys to rooms in a nearby accommodation block and released to settle in. I dumped my belongings in the room I was sharing with three other candidates and then took a long, hot shower. It was the first chance I'd had for about a week to really inspect myself. I was covered in ticks and deep bruises and my shoulder blades and ribs were sticking out due to my weight loss. My cheeks were hollow and when I looked in the mirror I hardly recognised my own reflection. Selection had been particularly cruel to me. When I stood on the scales I weighed in at 58 kilograms; I'd started the course weighing 73 kilos. My right leg was grossly swollen from the foot all the way to my groin, and it was red, hot and painful with infection.

We were left alone for that first night, and although we were fed well at dinnertime, we were all hungry again a couple of hours later so we ordered a bunch of pizzas (they came pre-sliced, so our colleague wasn't able to indulge in his fantasy pizza hoagie), but my stomach had shrunk so much I couldn't eat more than a few mouthfuls without feeling sick.

After eating I tried to sleep but couldn't. The other guys in my room were out like lights but I found myself wired. I did eventually drift off, only to wake a short time later having had a nightmare that I was back on the course.

The following day we were ordered to dress in a clean set

of ironed cams and a beret. It was time to find out whether or not we had passed selection. Of the 160 who'd started the course, only 38 of us had finished, and we knew that not all of us would be selected. I had no idea whether I was among the best of the candidates or the worst.

The eight officers who remained were to meet one-on-one with the commanding officer to learn their fate. I later learned that the other ranks were dealt with in a far less ceremonious fashion. They were gathered as a group and a series of candidate numbers were read aloud. If your number was called, you were in; if not, line up over there for a plane ticket home. It seemed like a fairly cold-blooded way to end someone's dream, but I guess it was like ripping off a bandaid: short and sharp.

When my turn came, I marched into the CO's office and the door was closed behind me. The CO was seated behind his large desk and I stood at attention and saluted him. After ordering me to stand at ease, he made a few throwaway remarks about how gaunt I looked before delivering the verdict.

'Congratulations, you've been selected for ongoing training with SASR.'

It was excellent news, but my elation was short-lived.

'Sit down,' the CO ordered. 'There're a few things I need to talk to you about.'

For the next twenty minutes he proceeded to rip into me, detailing everything I had fucked up during the course. It transpired that the decision to select me was not a unanimous one, and that some of the DS had viewed me as arrogant and felt that I was putting on a show, pretending to be a team player who cared about other candidates on the course, when I actually didn't give a fuck.

I was crushed to learn that this was how I was perceived, and while I had achieved my dream and passed the selection course, I felt completely deflated when I left the CO's office.

In the years that followed I would learn that one particular officer DS on the course had taken a profound dislike to me. He made it clear to the other DS that he didn't feel I was SAS material. That officer would go on to retrain as a doctor through the army, and over a decade later the tables were turned when he was a student in a trauma course I was instructing. While I joked with the other instructors that this was my long-awaited chance for revenge, I couldn't fault the guy – he was excellent.

That night a barbecue was held for the selected candidates. After the final cull there were five officers and 23 other ranks remaining. There were beers on offer but I didn't feel like drinking. I was physically and emotionally destroyed, so I left after eating and went back to my room to try to sleep. My right leg had worsened since the course ended, and by that point it was so swollen I couldn't bend the knee at all. The ulcer on the back of my heel had expanded to the size of a 50-cent coin and was constantly weeping pus. I was also starting to get fevers and chills, indicating to me that the infection was spreading throughout my body.

Over the course of the next few days, we were eased into a recovery PT regime and started to receive our administration and introduction briefs to the unit.

During a spare moment in the schedule I had presented to the RAP – the unit's regimental aid post – for medical review of my infected leg. The doctor there nearly hit the roof when he saw the sausage-like limb and berated me for letting it get so bad, though he settled down a little when he learned that I was a doctor and that I might very well one day be his boss.

The leg was in a bad state, and it was going to take some heavy-duty antibiotics to get the infection under control. The doctor inserted a drip into my arm and pumped me full of the maximum dose of the appropriate antibiotic, and I returned to the RAP at regular intervals over the next few days for further top-ups.

In the week following selection the SFTC representatives overseeing the course got in touch with 5 RAR and learned that the unit hadn't managed to find a replacement doctor for their deployment to Timor-Leste. I had to honour the deal I had made with my CO in Darwin and return to the battalion.

Although passing the SASR selection course was a significant milestone in my journey to becoming a beret-qualified doctor with the unit, to achieve my goal I still had to complete another year of specialist courses, known as the reinforcement cycle, or reo. Had I have known that I would never get back on reo, and therefore never achieve my ultimate goal of wearing the sandy beret, I may have dug my heels in and refused to return to 5 RAR. At the time, though, I was just happy that I was finally on the SOCOMD radar, and there were a bunch of positives in returning to Darwin, not least of which was being reunited with Kristy and making it home in time for little Henk's first birthday.

On my first day back at work at 5 RAR I was called up to see the CO. He informed me that my posting there was being cut short by a year and I would be posted to 4 RAR (CDO) the following year. Further to this, I would only deploy for the first four months of the eight-month Timor-Leste trip in order to potentially deploy again early the following year with special operations to Afghanistan.

I hadn't previously considered 4 RAR (CDO) – which would subsequently be renamed the 2nd Commando Regiment (2 CDO) – in my plan to serve in special operations simply because I was more familiar with the SASR through my brother. That said, 4 RAR (CDO) had well and truly established its credibility as a special operations unit, and a posting there represented the realisation of my special operations dream as well as being a significant step closer to my overarching goal of getting back to the SASR.

Things were falling into place career-wise, but on the physical side I was not doing as well. Most of the swelling in my right leg had resolved, but no matter how many antibiotics I pumped through my system, my right knee remained red, hot, swollen and painfully unstable. However I was reluctant to declare my ongoing infection for fear of being pulled off the Timor trip or, worse, having my posting to the commandos revoked.

By that time our mission rehearsal exercise for deployment was well underway, and a senior army doctor had been brought in to assess my professional suitability for deployment. On the second day of the exercise the assessing doctor noticed my limp and asked about my knee. I showed it to him and told him the associated story, upon which he hit the panic button and ordered a military ambulance to rush me to hospital for surgical review. The attending surgeon took one look at my knee and said: 'I'm taking you to the operating theatre this afternoon.'

It turned out the infection had set up shop in a small fat pad in front of my knee joint and was invading the surrounding tissues. The tendon joining my kneecap to my shinbone had also started turning to cheese, and about half of it had to be surgically removed. As a result I was laid up in hospital for eight days following the surgery.

It was a terrible time for me. I was physically broken and still mentally scrambled from the selection course, as well as the disappointment of missing my reinforcement cycle. It seemed my dreams were once more in jeopardy. Compounding this was the fact that things on the home front were strained to say the least. Kristy had been singlehandedly raising our infant son while I had been off selfishly pursuing my professional aspirations. She had been looking forward to me coming home and helping to care for little Henk; instead, I was now adding to her burden by being stuck in hospital. I needed her by my side and was longing to see my son, but her visits were short and her manner curt. She was hanging by a thread herself and had no emotional energy to spare for me.

As a doctor I naturally made a terrible patient, but despite my distaste for bed rest the early recovery went well. After eight days there was no physical need to keep me in hospital other than to feed me antibiotics through the drip. Henk's first birthday was fast approaching and I was desperate to get home for the occasion, and to start trying to rebuild bridges with my wife ahead of my impending deployment. The solution to my dilemma presented in the form of a large long-term drip, called a PICC line, that was threaded in through a deep vein of my upper arm and advanced almost all the way to my heart. A small bottle of antibiotics was attached which would slowly infuse over a 24-hour period, and a home nurse would visit to change the bottle daily.

Henk's first birthday was an excellent affair, although I look shocking in photos from the day. I was still gaunt from the weight loss of selection, and in most of the pictures you can make out the big drip hanging out of my arm with its attached antibiotic bottle in my pocket. When I look closely at Kristy's face, I see a look of weary resignation. She had known for years the professional life that I hoped to live, but that was only in theory. Now she was having her first taste of actually living it. The road ahead was becoming clearer, and it would be a rough one for both of us. Still, at least I was there. I would miss many subsequent family birthdays, but I'm proud to say that I beat the odds to get to Henk's first.

Post-surgery my knee continued to improve and was at long last starting to feel stable again. There was some back and forth about my medical suitability to deploy, but I eventually convinced the surgeon to sign me off. I was issued with my equipment for the trip and roughly six weeks after finishing selection I was on a plane bound for Timor-Leste.

To say that my trip to Timor was disappointing would be an epic understatement. Whatever threat had once existed in the troubled country had long since passed by late 2008, and on arrival my handover with the outgoing doctor was done over piles of banana pancakes doused in caramel sauce at one of the local waterfront cafes in Dili.

The medical mega-contractor Aspen had set up shop at the base where I was located and were providing every aspect of medical care to our battle group. Aspen had an all-singing, all-dancing capability, including aeromedical evacuation, 24-hour-a-day anaesthetic and surgical cover, and half-a-dozen general practitioners. There was literally no role at all for my ill-equipped medical element and, frustratingly, there was little chance of me ever treating any of my own soldiers. It was a demoralising situation to find myself in, with my self-pity further exacerbated by the fact that I was missing my SASR reinforcement training cycle to be jobless in a developing country.

After roughly a month of doing nothing to justify my deployment allowance, salvation came in the form of an opportunity to tag along on a sniper course being run out of a small town called Gleno in the hills to the south-west of Dili. The CO of 5 RAR, aware that I was kicking my heels in Dili, had arranged to upskill me prior to my move to special operations. I said it before, and I'll say it again: the CO of 5 RAR at the time was a good man. I didn't need to be asked twice, and quickly packed my things and took to the hills.

The following day I linked up with the sniper course and spent the next couple of weeks learning to accurately judge distances and stalk targets, while honing my navigation skills by day and night through the thick, humid jungle environment. It was excellent. Disappointingly, the course had covered most of its shooting phase prior to me joining them, so I missed that, but the rest of the competencies were valuable experience.

Around the same time the sniper course was wrapping up, a reconnaissance patrol commander course was starting in the same location. I got word through to the CO that I would like to stay on and join the recon course and was once again given the thumbs-up.

The recon guys were less standoffish than the snipers and, knowing that I had recently been successful on SASR selection, were happy to have me along. The purpose of the course was to assess recon soldiers for their suitability as patrol commanders. That was achieved through simulated mission profiles in which a five-man recon element would be inserted at a predetermined location in the hills, navigate some distance to a designated target, reconnoitre the target for a few days, and then stomp out and extract. A single DS would follow close behind the patrol to observe and assess. Every member of the recon patrol served a different function and I was inserted as the patrol medic. The experience was both challenging and fun, and it was during one of the patrols that I first had the sense that I just might enjoy combat.

On that particular patrol, our target was an infantry corporals course that was dug into the hills on the outskirts of Gleno and was going about its camp routine. They were made aware that we would be in the area and had been instructed to actively patrol for our element. Our job was to sneak in, and gain information on their numbers and disposition. Then, on the last night of our patrol, they would be given our location in order to assault us. At that point we would break contact and go into an escape and evasion scenario along a pre-planned route which would lead us to a helicopter extraction point.

Our insertion was by vehicle, which was meant to take us to a drop-off point approximately 5 kilometres from the 'enemy' camp, but due to a felled tree blocking the road we were forced to insert early and cover a little over 10 kilometres on foot. The jungle terrain was steep and going was tough. Being the middle of the wet season, it was hot, humid and airless in the thick foliage under the triple canopy above.

Our brief for the mission had been to avoid compromise by locals on insertion, which proved near impossible. No matter how stealthy we were, or how wide a berth we gave the villages, the Timorese seemed to be omnipresent in the jungle and would regularly pop out of nowhere and spot us. On more than a few occasions, we scared multiple shades of shit out of unfortunate locals who were dawdling through the jungle, minding their own business, only to stumble upon five camouflaged, armed men lying deathly still so as to avoid being seen.

We eventually made our way to a suitable position on an adjacent hill with a direct line of sight to the target camp. We set up a small camp of our own, making sure to minimise our footprint to avoid detection, and kept our kit ready to go in a hurry in case we were compromised.

Once established, we fell into the recon routine of information collection. Periodically we would send two-man patrols across to the enemy camp to conduct close target reconnaissance of their position. Cleanskin but for a rifle, spare magazines and water bottle, and often under the cover of the late afternoon tropical deluge, we would zip across to the enemy camp, crawling the last 100 or so metres, and observe them. It was like nothing I had done before and it got my heart racing. Admittedly the consequences of compromise were trivial, but I found it exciting all the same.

We managed to remain uncompromised for the three days of the activity, despite an enemy patrol passing within 10 metres of our position on one occasion. On the final night, the DS who had been observing us made his way off into the bush and, strongly suspecting that he was feeding the enemy our position, we prepped to bug out. Our suspicions proved correct; 30 minutes later a small group of the enemy approached our position, and after spraying them with blank gunfire we were off into the night.

The enemy patrol pursued us through the jungle for about an hour before handing over to another element with a tracking dog. Throughout the night we bolted along jungle tracks, making our way through several villages in the process.

Pausing intermittently to check our navigation, we could hear the tracking dog barking in the still night air, prompting us to keep moving. The experience took me right back to getting chased by the cops as a teenager; it was physically taxing but exhilarating.

We managed to evade the first dog, but just before dawn a new dog was set on our trail with a fresh set of handlers. By this time we were fatigued and our pace had slowed. The jungle had opened up into a small hilltop village, which was cloaked in mist that gleamed with the sun's early rays. The scene was silent but for the laboured breathing of our element and the dripping of heavy dew off nearby shanty rooftops.

Briefly halting at a crossroad in the centre of the small village, we performed a final navigation check before proceeding to our helicopter rendezvous. Engrossed in our maps, we were unaware that the tracking dog and its handler were within 100 metres of our position. A loud bark alerted us to their presence as they burst out of the jungle and onto the road in front of us. The dog stopped dead in its tracks and started going berserk. The handler froze. He was too far away for us to make out his facial expression, but his body language suggested surprise. For a split second we stood eying each other, before an explicit instruction came from our patrol commander.

'FIRE!'

I shouldered my Austeyr assault rifle, flicking off the safety, and the instant the dog handler's image occupied my scope I depressed the rifle's trigger completely, letting off a long burst of automatic fire that shattered the still morning. I felt calm and focused and completely in the moment. My field of vision had narrowed and was devoted to the target. The noise of my rifle, and those firing around me, appeared muffled. A warm surge of adrenaline, initiating in the middle of my back, crept up over my shoulders and head, cloaking me, and causing my scalp to tingle. I felt like a million bucks!

The enemy had been simulated, the scenario was contrived, and the ammunition was blank, but the adrenaline was definitely real. It was my first taste of the drug that is combat and I was left wanting more.

The bolt of my rifle locked back, indicating that my magazine was empty, and in coordination with the other patrol members I turned and ran, reloading on the fly. The rest of the dog team had caught up with their lead scout by now, and they were in hot pursuit. Managing to put a small amount of distance between ourselves and our pursuers, we split our element to confuse the dog and set an ambush in a series of ruined buildings. The ambush went like clockwork, and with the dog team notionally dead we proceeded up a nearby incline to the helicopter extraction point.

A perfect morning had dawned, and on cue our Black Hawk came booming in and picked us up, blowing the dodgy corrugated-iron roof of a nearby house with its rotor wash in the process.

The second we touched down at our base in Gleno, we were required to dump our packs and head back up to the extraction point by car to fix the roof before the afternoon rains. It was a shitty job, and we were all tired, but I didn't care – I was still riding the high of the morning's experience. My mind had broken through the taboo barrier that says you can't level a rifle at another human and pull the trigger, and it felt unnervingly good.

* * *

When the recon patrol commander's course finished I could no longer justify hiding away in the hills. I returned to Dili to endure the remainder of my tour, logging my first deployed Christmas and New Year's in the process. Then, early in January 2009, I returned home to Darwin, where Kristy and I packed up our house and moved our little family to Sydney for my posting to 4 RAR (CDO). After eight years spent pursuing my goal, I would finally be able to call myself a special operations soldier.

VI

FUN FOR THE FIRST
FIVE MINUTES

THE SENSATION OF FLYING WAS AS INTOXICATING AS IT WAS terrifying, and briefly I dared to lean my bodyweight back on the tube-tape harness that held my life. Glancing up, I caught a glimpse of the underbelly of the Black Hawk helicopter above. A glance down revealed the other half-dozen special operators attached by carabiners to the same flimsy caving ladder that I was. The ground rushed by hundreds of feet below and my senses were completely overwhelmed, but rather than panic, I felt a profound sense of calm, as if everything was as it should be.

Ten minutes later the helicopter returned us to the earth, and once unclipped I was signed off as competent in yet another capability required to be considered deployable as a special operator: suspended extraction.

It was one of many courses that filled my first months with

4 RAR (CDO), which also included training in a new suite of weapons and night fighting equipment. On completion of this induction I met the bare-minimum qualification for operational service and I was attached to the unit's tactical assault group (TAG) on high readiness for domestic counterterrorism response.

About one month later I was attached to my first TAG exercise. The scenario was a 'ship underway recovery', which, as the name suggests, involves assaulting and taking control of a moving ship that has been commandeered by an enemy force. The activity was being held in the vicinity of Jervis Bay, with my role being the real-time medical support. The trip down from Sydney to the exercise area was to be on board HMAS *Manoora*, one of the navy's Kanimbla-class landing platform amphibious ships.

On the morning of our departure I linked up with the TAG element out at the unit and we were bused to the Garden Island naval base in Sydney Harbour to board the *Manoora*. The reception from the TAG operators was frosty to say the least. As the new guy, and particularly one in a supporting role, I was treated with disregard at best. Undeterred, I went about my business as required, doing what I needed to do and offering my opinion only when it was asked for. It was clear to me that if I was going to gain acceptance into their world, I would need to prove myself with actions rather than words, and that would take time.

After a couple of days aboard the ship doing various training iterations, it was time for the full mission profile (FMP) of the activity. For the FMP, I considered the best position to locate myself was on a medium-sized dive boat supporting the activity. I packed my kit for the cross-load to the dive boat and dressed in a flight suit, personal flotation device, Pro-Tec

THE COMBAT DOCTOR

helmet, ballistic goggles and combat boots. Then I made my way down the ladder on the side of the ship and into a waiting zodiac to transfer me across.

On approach to the dive boat, I could see its crew members were dressed in board shorts, thongs and sunglasses, and as we drew closer I began to make out the smell of sausage rolls emanating from a pie-warmer lashed to the table on the back deck of the boat. *Yep, this is my kind of army exercise*, I thought as I jumped across onto the dive boat, quickly stripping out of my military attire in favour of a pair of boardies. It was a perfect afternoon out on the water, and I spent it eating sausage rolls and conferring with a medic attached to the commandos who had operational experience in Afghanistan. As well as discussing medical contingency plans for that night's activity, I listened intently as he spoke of his experiences treating combat casualties. After a few hours together, the medic presented me with a rectangular olive-green Velcro patch on which was an image of a voodoo doll stuck with pins. This marked the start of my induction into the Voodoo Medicine fraternity.

As thankful as I was for the gift, I couldn't have possibly appreciated at the time the full significance of that insignia, or the visceral sense of oneness I would come to feel with the tribe it represented. That very patch would adorn the front of my body armour during every mission I completed in my special operations career: facing the enemy in every gunfight I experienced, and facing the casualty every time I was called on to respond. Its tattered remnants would eventually be framed alongside a replica of my service M4 rifle, presented to me by my Voodoo Medic brethren on my departure from special operations. But this was all in the future; on that afternoon in Jervis Bay it was just a cool patch.

The phrase *fun for the first five minutes* is applied frequently to experiences in the SOCOMD environment, and I was about to get some solid, first-hand experience of the concept. As darkness fell, we made our way beyond the headland that protects Jervis Bay and into the open water. The wind and seas had begun to pick up and our boat started rocking and rolling. By the time the assault force was prosecuting the simulated target vessel, the conditions were approaching sea state five and I was vomiting uncontrollably off the back of the boat. My accompanying medic blasted me full of maximal doses of anti-nausea medications, but they did little to ease my symptoms. I spent the remainder of the night in a fetal position on the back deck of the boat praying that there wouldn't be a serious casualty, as I would have certainly struggled to treat them. Thankfully the exercise ended without any casualties and we made our way back to Sydney. It would be well over a year before I could face up to a sausage roll again.

I did a second exercise a few weeks later with an element from SASR who had flown across to use the same Jervis Bay training area. It was a more relaxed environment than the previous commando TAG activity, with many of the SAS guys involved having been DS on my selection course, making it easier for me to integrate. I had a good opportunity to practise some helicopter-winching scenarios from various watercraft, using different pieces of equipment and techniques. It proved to be an excellent start towards building my corporate knowledge of providing medical support to maritime special operations.

Back in Sydney following the SAS exercise, I learned that I would be deploying mid-year to Afghanistan for a six-month tour as the RMO for the Special Operations Task Group (SOTG). I promptly handed over my TAG responsibilities to the second RMO at the unit and was detached to the deploying commando company. I could hardly contain my excitement.

I was accepted well into my new company, helped in no small part by the officer in charge of the company. Known as the Hitman on account of his resemblance to the video game and movie character (minus the barcode tattoo on the back of the head), the Hitman was a fast-talking, high-energy individual who spoke his mind at all times. I liked him instantly. He was a friend of my brother and, appreciating the fact that I had done SAS selection, was keen to get me involved in all aspects of pre-deployment training with a view to employing me 'outside the wire' in Afghanistan – exactly the kind of scenario I'd been hoping for.

I threw myself into the training, learning everything I could about how to conduct myself on patrol and what to do when things went loud. As the doctor, there was no real role for me in a firefight other than staying out of the road of the operators and trying not to get shot. My experience in Timor had been a good starting point for my tactical training, but there was still a lot to learn about operating in an urban environment and patrolling under night vision. Even the simplest procedure – such as protocol for getting on and off helicopters, which was second nature to the commandos – was foreign to me. It was a steep learning curve.

The pre-deployment training culminated in a large mission rehearsal exercise (MRE) in a dusty region of South Australia. It was there that I had my first true special operations moment.

We had been allowed to grow our hair and beards for the three months prior to deployment, so by the time MRE rolled around I was well hairy. Coming from big army, where high-and-tight haircuts were the norm, the Sasquatch look held great novelty for me. In addition, I had been issued high-speed body armour, was allowed to wear non-issue boots, and had been allowed to paint my M4 rifle. Looking back now, I feel foolish at how important all this trivia was to me, but at the time it represented my arrival in special operations.

It was with my long hair, beard, armour and painted rifle that I loaded onto a Black Hawk to fly out for a night raid on a mock village. The back doors of the Black Hawk were open to facilitate a speedy egress when we touched down on target, and I was sitting on the edge of the bird with my feet dangling out the door. I felt as cool as cat shit, and with Jimmy Hendrix's 'Voodoo Chile' playing in my mind the chopper pulled on power and took off into the setting sun towards our simulated target. The training ground has a highway that passes immediately in front of it and a car had stopped on the side of the road to watch as our formation of helicopters took off. I gave the car's occupants a casual wave as we flew directly over them and gained altitude. I couldn't possibly have been happier at that moment.

In true SOCOMD *fun for the first five minutes* form, the coolness of the situation rapidly evaporated. We had flown through a rainstorm on the way to the target, and as I had been hanging out of the side of the chopper I got saturated. My role in the FMP was as an opportune aeromedical evacuation (AME) capability, and as such I stayed on the helicopter when the assault crew inserted. The Black Hawk then took off again and went into a holding pattern overhead to await simulated casualties. Night fell, and being soaking wet in the windswept back of the helicopter with the doors open I was starting to chill down. After about 30 minutes in loiter I was freezing cold and busting for a piss. I had huddled up into a ball and shuffled as far forward as I could in the passenger compartment to try to avoid the wind from the rotor wash, but it was no use. Pissing myself provided a solution to my full bladder and warmed me from the waist down for a blissful minute or two until my urine chilled down as well. It was miserable.

The assault team finally finished their clearance and called the helicopters back in for extraction. My bird landed and the guys piled back in, unknowingly spending the return trip to base sitting in my piss.

The remainder of the MRE was spent doing further FMPs, working out of both helicopters and Bushmaster Protected Mobility Vehicles. As part of my pre-deployment training I was qualified on the .50 calibre machine gun and the 40 mm automatic grenade launcher (AGL), being the two weapons mounted on the top of the Bushmasters, as well as the in-service shoulder-fired anti-armour rockets.

Immediately following the military MRE I bounced straight onto the medical-specific pre-deployment training for the medical elements of the deploying task group. Delivered over two weeks, these medical training exercises were designed to hone our skills in the application of medical interventions in a tactical situation. It had been recognised by the US special operations community after the Black Hawk Down incident in Mogadishu in 1993 that using civilian trauma response principles in a tactical situation was not appropriate. As a result, the concept of tactical combat casualty care (TCCC) was born, its aim being to provide appropriate medical trauma response during combat. It is down and dirty medicine, aimed at applying a minimum of life-saving interventions with brutal efficiency while giving primacy to neutralising the enemy threat and completing the mission at hand.

Our instructors were special operations medical elements, all of whom had recent operational experience in Afghanistan. Senior among them was a doctor named Marty, who would become my mentor. Marty was a thin, wiry, highly intelligent doctor with a deeply twisted sense of humour. He had blazed the trail for special operations doctors going outside the wire in Afghanistan and had been the first SOTG doctor to be decorated for his actions in that theatre of war, being awarded a Commendation for Distinguished Service for his involvement in a mass-casualty situation resulting from a suicide bomber detonating in a local marketplace. Under Marty's lead we were pumped through two intensive weeks of TCCC training by day and night, starting with simple, single-casualty scenarios and culminating in a night mass-casualty scenario. During the final scenario I was required to take the lead on triage and management of the situation. It was highly realistic training and I found it fantastic. I felt as though I had finally found my true calling. I fucking *loved* tactical medicine.

After the TCCC package, we rolled straight into another block of high-fidelity trauma training, this time under the tutelage of a surgeon named Jim. Jim, a confident, outspoken bloke of Greek descent, was one of a kind. Despite never deploying with SOCOMD, Jim has contributed more to Voodoo Medicine than most of the rest of us combined. He is one of a very short list of overachievers who have completed specialty training in both cardiothoracic *and* vascular surgery, and he is a professor at a prominent teaching hospital.

My initial interactions with Jim were a little icy. We were in a preliminary theory lesson and Jim was showing us a series of chest X-rays displaying different pathology. As we studied a film illustrating a condition known as tension pneumothorax, Jim pointed at me for a description. At medical school, we had been taught to follow a set sequence when examining X-rays, so I started on my spiel accordingly.

'This is an anterior-posterior chest X-ray of a Mr John Smith, taken on 5 December 2004, which appears well exposed, but slightly rotated. The trachea appears –'

'Blah, blah, blah,' Jim interjected. 'What are you, a medical student?'

'I used to be,' I replied, taken aback by the interruption.

'Just tell me the pathology and how you'd fix it,' Jim ordered.

I answered the question to his satisfaction and we moved on with the lesson.

Later, during a practical session, Jim approached me.

'So, you said that you used to be a medical student,' he said. 'What are you now?'

'A doctor.' My tone was a little cool after our recent interaction.

'Oh shit, are you the doc going over?' Jim's expression brightened. 'I was just fucking with you before. Come with me – I want to show you a few things.'

And with that, Jim proceeded to impart knowledge that would prove life-saving in the years to come. The two of us have since become great friends, and I remain in awe of his selfless contribution to Voodoo Medicine.

My anticipation was rising; I couldn't wait to get to Afghanistan. I wanted to experience combat and I was itching to treat some war wounds, the worse the better. I had the naivety and bravado that came with being a young man about to go to war for the first time. I understood in theory that guys I knew might be injured or killed, but I had no concept of the reality. It seemed like something that happened only to others – people we saw on the news. We were special operations, and in my mind we were pretty much bulletproof.

I returned from the medical courses and spent my predeployment leave on an *in case I die in the 'Ghan* holiday with Kristy. My parents came to Sydney to look after Henk while Kristy and I spent a week cruising around the Hunter Valley in my newly purchased vintage Lamborghini, tasting wines and eating at expensive restaurants. It was a brilliant experience, but I wasn't fully present. Part of me had already deployed to Afghanistan and I had begun to subconsciously distance myself from my family.

Before I left, I sat down and composed a letter for Kristy in case I was killed on deployment. It was a tough thing to do, and it was only through writing the letter that the full consequences of my death occurred to me. Kristy would be widowed and Henk would grow up without his dad, or with another dad. It was a horrible realisation and I was hit by the selfishness of what I was about to do. I pushed the thought out of my mind and sealed the envelope, writing *Dead Dan* on the front of it.

Our deployment date rolled around and Kristy and Henk once again dropped me at the airport. Naturally Kristy was teary, but I found myself more excited than sad. I had already emotionally detached from home life and was mentally set for the adventure that lay ahead. I handed Kristy the *Dead Dan* envelope, kissed her and Henk goodbye, and joined the large group of heavily bearded soldiers attempting to look inconspicuous in the civilian airport. I was at long last deploying on special operations.

VII

AFGHANISTAN

THE FIRST THING THAT HIT ME ABOUT THE MIDDLE EAST WAS the heat. Stepping off the plane at our staging base in Kuwait was like stepping into a fan-forced oven.

The American base in Kuwait was a real eye-opener, particularly mealtimes in the massive mess facility, with American stereotypes and cliques in abundance. It made for excellent people watching, and sweetened by the all-day access to Krispy Kreme doughnuts and Baskin-Robbins ice cream, it quickly became my favourite place on base. A close second was the postal exchange, a large store that sold all manner of items at heavily discounted prices to service personnel. They had things we couldn't get in Australia, including double-edged knives, and I took the opportunity to purchase a small Gerber boot knife to attach to my chest rig. (A couple of years later that Gerber would save a life

121

and land me in a bunch of trouble at the same time, but I'll get to that in time.)

After a couple of days in Kuwait our deploying special operations element boarded a C-130 Hercules in full combat order and a few hours later touched down on the dirt airstrip at the base in Tarin Kowt, the capital of Afghanistan's Oruzgan Province, that would become our home for the next five months.

My initial impression of TK was the stark contrast between the beauty of the mountains surrounding the base and the stench of shit-filled dust and burning rubbish that hung in the air. We made our way across the dusty airstrip to a series of waiting cars and proceeded to the heavily fortified front gates of the Australian special operations base. The gates were flanked by 3-metre-high reinforced walls topped with razor wire. Mounted on the wall to the left of the entrance was a faded sign with an image of a red kangaroo wielding an assault rifle and the words AUSTRALIA. CAMP RUSSELL printed on it. Named after SASR Sergeant Andrew Russell, who had been killed by an IED blast in Afghanistan in 2002, Camp Russell housed the Australian SOTG and was a self-sufficient base complete with accommodation, mess hall, vehicle stables and workshops, Q-store and regimental aid post, all linked by a dusty ring road.

I made my way to the RAP, dropped my kit, and immediately began the handover process with my outgoing counterpart. The medical support to the SOTG was divided into three groups: the integral medics in the SASR squadron and those embedded with the commandos (both of which shared accommodations with their respective elements), and the primary health care team. This team consisted of a doctor, a nurse and two medics, who lived and worked out of the RAP. Their role was to provide round-the-clock health care and medical administration to the task group, as well as to supplement the outside-the-wire medical capability of the fighting elements when required.

Owing to the slightly different operational application of the commando and SAS elements, it was the commandos who more often came looking for additional medical support. To use a crude analogy, the SAS were akin to a scalpel, performing surgical strike operations in small teams, where the commandos were more like a sledgehammer, deploying into the field in larger numbers and more likely to start a big fight. Even when posted to SASR, during my time in Afghanistan I would do the majority of my missions with the commandos.

During the week-long handover with the outgoing RMO, I was introduced to the key players at the two surgical facilities, as well as the American aero medical evacuation crew on the TK base. During downtime from operations, the SOTG medical elements would supplement the American flight medics on forward helicopter AME missions, as well as getting valuable hands-on experience at the surgical facilities, where we would help manage all manner of war wounds, from resuscitation in the emergency department through to initial wound surgery. The SOTG was most closely aligned with the surgical element on Camp Ripley. Inhabited at the time by a US special forces group, the forward surgical team on Camp Ripley comprised some of the most experienced war surgeons in Afghanistan. A constant stream of trauma came through the door and the staff there were incredibly accommodating in letting us get our hands dirty.

By the end of the handover week I felt well and truly ready to get down to business. The outgoing medical team departed and we took the reins. As I had integrated well with the commando element during pre-deployment training, by the time operations started it was assumed that I would be along for the ride. I relished the opportunity to do the medical support planning for missions and would link in with the operational planning guys to provide advice on the positioning of medical elements on the ground to optimise support. I took a keen interest in where the company medics would be placed, where I would be, how long it would be before we could get an AME bird overhead, and where the closest surgical facility was located. I was acutely aware that this was it: after eight years, I was doing the job I'd set my sights on.

To further reinforce my arrival in special operations, I was walking down the main corridor of our headquarters demountable one day when I noticed a familiar-looking soldier coming towards me. Somewhat embarrassingly, it kicked off a bit of a fanboy response in me. Trying desperately not to appear like a teenage girl in the presence of Justin Bieber, as the soldier got closer I was preparing to give him a friendly nod and pass without speaking when he stopped, extended his hand for shaking, and greeted me with a friendly, 'G'day, Pronky,' before introducing himself as Mark Donaldson, as if there was a chance I wouldn't know who the fuck he was. Like the rest of Australia, I knew damn well who he was following his highly publicised award of the Victoria Cross for Australia just a few months prior. Donno and I had a quick chat before parting ways, leaving me with a profound respect for the guy that continued to grow from that day forth.

Within a week of handover, the commando element had planned its first job to clear Taliban fighters from a regional village and I was out the door on a real-time special operation.

Ours means of transport to the target village was Bush-masters, being ten-tonne military monster trucks, easily capable of carrying and sustaining half-a-dozen soldiers for days at a time, and with armour that would resist enemy machine-gun fire and IED blasts, and armament that could give as good as we got in any gunfight. I was, perhaps inappropriately, designated as the rear machine gunner in one of the vehicles, manning a MAG 58 machine gun from the back hatch of the vehicle.

Driving through the night for a dawn raid on the target, I got my first look at the vast expanses of *dasht*, the desert landscape of Afghanistan, which appeared as a desolate moonscape under night vision.

Shortly after midnight our vehicles pulled up in a pre-determined defensive formation in what was to be our vehicle drop-off point. Having stopped about 10 kilometres from the target village, the plan was for us to walk from that point to retain an element of surprise that would be lost if the enemy heard our cars approaching. A skeleton crew was left to guard the vehicles and the rest of us shouldered our packs and patrolled off into the night. My heart was thumping with excitement as I forced myself to consciously recall the appropriate pro-cedures for patrolling at night. It would soon come naturally to me, but on that first job it still took a conscious effort.

Just before dawn we silently approached the target village and formed up amid a craggy outcrop of rocks on a feature overlooking the village.

As we were about to step off into the village, real-time intel-ligence feedback indicated that we had been compromised, and the enemy were eagerly preparing themselves for our arrival. I would come to learn that most of the time Taliban smack talk really was just that; it would seldom result in the large-scale attacks they promised. On that first job, however, I was convinced that every last insurgent threat was going to come to pass, and I was pumped.

The time came to move. I tapped the magazine of my M4 to ensure that it was properly engaged and then slapped the bolt assist to guarantee I had a round properly chambered and ready to go. With nervous energy surging through my system, I followed my teammates into the village.

The clearance of the village commenced without incident, and the huge fight promised by the Talibs failed to eventuate. We found half-a-dozen AK-47s and our lead elements had a few fleeting exchanges of gunfire with the enemy but otherwise things were quiet.

During one of the brief firefights, my group was positioned to move up and flank the fleeing enemy. The guy in command of our eight-man team was initially keen on the move, then suddenly became hesitant, deciding against the flanking manoeuvre. He couldn't come out and say it directly over the radio – I suspect because I was within earshot – but it was obvious to me that he didn't want to move the element because of my presence. Whether he was (quite rightly) concerned that I would be a tactical liability, or just feared the repercussions of getting the task group doctor shot, I'm not sure. Either way, I was furious: first, because I didn't want to be the sole reason our element wouldn't attempt to cut off the fleeing enemy, and second, because I was desperate to be involved in the fight. In the end, another team chased the enemy for over an hour before calling in an Apache helicopter gunship to resolve the situation with a Hellfire missile.

Regrouping in the village, we destroyed the captured weapons with explosives before hiking back to our vehicles. No longer requiring stealth, our Bushmasters had driven towards the village to meet us, significantly shortening our exfiltration walk. It was a welcome relief to see the cars, as it was nearing midday by that time and the temperature had climbed above 40 degrees Celsius. I reached my car, dumped my pack inside and climbed up into the hatch to man the gun for the dusty trip back to base. As we drove, I reflected on the job. It had all gone to plan and I hadn't fucked anything up, but I was still dirty at myself for holding back my group. I hoped that in time I would get the chance to prove myself and would no longer be considered a liability.

Within a few days of our first mission, we were back out the door on a similar job. Once again, we drove through the night before parking up, debussing and walking onto target.

We had left our cars parked at the top of a large feature and our walk to the target compounds was down a near-vertical cliff crisscrossed by goat tracks.

Walking while using night vision goggles can be challenging at the best of times due to the lack of depth perception and the limited field of view making it hard to see what is immediately in front of your feet. Between my inexperience on NVG and a 50-kilogram combat load, I spent about as much time on my arse as I did on my feet during the descent into the valley.

Reaching low ground, we had to stomp hard to get in position before dawn. I was allocated to an overwatch command group, which was to be located on high ground overlooking the assault elements. As we neared the objective, our group peeled off from the main body and began the climb into position.

On cue the assault teams swept through the target compounds unopposed, detaining several suspicious persons as they did so. With the compounds secured, and dawn breaking, our overwatch element broke cover and regrouped with the assault force to help process the detainees and determine if any should be taken back to base for further interrogation.

As the tactical questioning was going on, intelligence reports indicated that a group of Talibs was massing on the reverse slope of a nearby feature with the intent of attacking us.

The ground force commander drew everyone inside the mudbrick compound and set about securing all the points of entry and establishing defensive positions with guns pointed out of every window and door.

From what I could gather, things were about to go loud and, although my role in the situation was limited to trying not to get shot, I was excited. There was, however, one small issue. Perhaps coincidentally, or maybe due to the adrenaline dump from the impending circumstances, my bowel chose that moment to let me know that it was in urgent need of evacuation. Over the preceding week we had been eating a lot of ration pack food and I had become a little constipated, leaving me with a backlog to clear. Unable to go outside due to the impending threat, my only option was to find the one room in the compound that was vacant. Propping myself in the corner of the dirt-floored room, I backed out a herculean turd. Then, with my eyes still watering, I made my way back into the main area of the compound.

It transpired that we were able to get a couple of Apaches overhead, which quickly dispersed the would-be attackers using their 30 mm cannons. By that stage it was approaching midday and the tactical questioners had determined that we should take a few of the detainees back to base with us. One of them had some fairly incriminating video footage on his mobile phone that was duly bagged up and attached to his flexi-cuffed wrists to serve as evidence in the case against him.

The walk off target was emotional due to the effects of the extreme heat in our un-acclimated state. The temperature was in the high 40s by the time we hit the base of the steep climb back up to our vehicles, and a few guys were already starting to buckle.

Midway up the climb I came across one of our explosive detection dogs lying in a small sliver of shade cast by a low rocky outcrop, panting feverishly and looking close to death. Its handler didn't look much better, but figuring that the dog would be the lighter of the two, I slung my rifle and carried the dog over my shoulders. Reaching the top absolutely exhausted, I shoved the near-dead dog into the back of one of the Bushmasters and doused it with water to cool it down. Taking a minute to catch my own breath, I then assembled a few IV drip sets in one of the cars for some of the worse-off guys as they arrived. As anticipated, a few of our team dropped at the top of the climb, but they recovered quickly after a bag of fluids in the back of an air-conditioned car.

While the other medics and I were looking after the heat casualties, our intelligence continued to monitor the enemy. The remaining Taliban from the group that had been dispersed by the Apaches had made their way into the compound we had occupied and were having a look around. Through intelligence means I cannot describe in this book, our group was informed (with some degree of delight) that the Talibs had found a huge pile of faeces in one of the rooms.

'*That's my shit,*' I yelled excitedly.

'The Talibs decided that the Americans must have had a large animal with them, because they have found animal shit,' was the end of the verbal report.

I was ecstatic. Naturally I had been personally satisfied with a good crap after a few days of constipation, but to draw such praise from the enemy was a particularly proud moment. The only downside was that the Talibs had mistaken us for Americans and were unaware that it was an Australian offering. (For a couple of days afterwards I attempted to persuade people to refer to me as 'The Animal' on account of the Taliban description, but like all good nicknames that you actually *want* to stick, it didn't.)

For the next few months the task group fell into the routine cycle of planning and conducting missions. Most of the jobs were vehicle-mounted, lasting between one and ten days, and utilising a combination of Bushmasters and long-range patrol vehicles (LRPVs) in the form of an open-topped six-wheel Land Rover. The jobs all blurred into one, with enemy contacts frequent but fleeting, and several close calls for our guys but no serious injuries. Despite getting out on almost every job with the commandos, my rifle remained unfired.

My only memorable moment from that series of operations came as we were returning to base after several days patrolling in the north of Kandahar Province, to the south of Tarin Kowt. We were required to cross a medium-sized, fast-flowing river, and as we did so one of the LRPVs became stuck in the middle of the waterway. In the time it took to recover the car with a Bushmaster, a crowd had gathered from the local village, with one family bringing out an infant for medical attention.

I was called across to review the baby, and on first glance thought the young girl was already dead. Her flyblown, sunken eyes were closed and her tiny body was limp and lifeless. Her ribcage protruded through her emaciated torso. On closer inspection, however, I realised she was still alive, though only just.

Through the terp we learned that the girl had been suffering from diarrhoea and vomiting for the past four days and hadn't been able to feed. I inspected the girl's arms for potential veins to insert a drip but found nothing. Her dehydrated body had shut down all blood flow to her peripheries to maximise perfusion to her vital organs. She was dying. With no other way to access her bloodstream, I took out a small drill known as an intraosseous device and drilled a metal cannula into the top of the infant's shinbone, accessing the bone marrow directly. She didn't so much as flinch.

Estimating her body weight to be no more than 5 kilograms, I drew up the appropriate volume of intravenous fluid and injected it slowly through the cannula. At this, the young girl squirmed with pain and cried out. It was terrible to witness but a good sign overall; she was still with us. Within minutes of the life-saving fluid bolus, she opened her eyes and became quite animated, screaming and flailing her limbs about. Blood began to flow back to her arms and legs and her previously collapsed veins reappeared. Within ten minutes she had a vein in her arm large enough to insert a drip. I pushed a dose of intravenous antibiotics through the vein in hope of killing off whatever infection had caused the child's gastroenteritis.

Just as the antibiotics were through, I got word that the LRPV had been recovered from the river and it was time to move. I removed the needle from the child's shin but left the arm drip in place. Through the interpreter I gave a brief set of instructions to the child's father on the dosing of intravenous fluids and antibiotics until they could get her to hospital, and left a supply of both behind for the girl's parents to continue her treatment, but whether they would manage to do either successfully was far from certain.

While I was packing up to go, the ground force commander approached me and we briefly discussed the possibility of taking the girl and her father with us to TK. It would be a breach of protocol, and I had no idea if we would be allowed back on base with local nationals in our vehicle, nor whether the child and father would be safe in town alone. All my training leading up to deployment had been focused on looking after my teammates in combat; I hadn't considered the broader objective of also providing medical care to the locals. The importance of that would become clearer to me in future deployments, however at that stage it was – regrettably – all too easy to pack up my kit and depart.

We passed through that village again a few weeks later and learned that the child had died the day after I had treated her. I had held her tiny life in my hands, and I had failed her. For years following that event she would visit me in my dreams, and when she did I would try to talk to her. Most of the time I couldn't get any words out, but when I could, I would apologise.

During the first few months of deployment I spent about as much time outside the wire as I did back at base. When on base I would attend to the administration of running the medical element, including attendance at regular CO's orders, as well as mandatory reporting to my medical technical chain of command at rear-echelon bases and back home in Australia. My clinical workload was a spectrum of routine GP presentations from members of the task group through to gunshot wound and blast casualties at the forward surgical team and on the AME helicopter. When in camp I'd work out at the gym daily, and every few days I'd phone home to touch base with Kristy and little Henk or my parents. I found myself not missing home at all, and apart from when I phoned them I rarely thought of my family. As callous as that sounds, there was no place in my mind for thoughts of my family while at war; my cerebral bandwidth needed to be completely devoted to the life-and-death task at hand.

Around halfway through the tour a job came up that was guaranteed to result in an epic firefight. The mission was into a known insurgent safe haven in Helmand Province and required a large special operations element to infiltrate the village and recover some sensitive items that had fallen into Taliban hands after a British helicopter crashed nearby.

As I listened intently to the initial mission briefings, it became clear that there would be a high chance of casualties and a very realistic possibility of fatalities.

The medical support on the ground for the job would consist of the two commando company medics embedded with their platoons, plus a further medic and myself attached to the tactical headquarters element. I pushed hard for, and was given, a six-wheeled all-terrain vehicle (ATV) to kit out with extra medical supplies. This would allow us to carry a cooler box filled with blood and blood products for immediate transfusion into serious casualties on the ground. We also loaded up two body bags for the worst-case scenario.

The mission would employ the task group in its near entirety, with an SAS element inserting early and occupying strategic locations in the mountains surrounding the village. From there they would provide battlefield reconnaissance and commentary to the commando element that would be providing the infiltration force. On insertion, commando snipers would also make their way to the high ground surrounding the village to provide support as required.

To preserve an element of surprise, the plan was for us to insert by helicopter 15 kilometres off target and walk through the night to hit the village just before dawn. A small convoy of ATVs, mostly transporting the snipers, with our medical bike trailing, would crawl along quietly beside the procession of ground soldiers during infiltration.

After days of meticulous planning, briefing and organisation of all the assets required to conduct such a large-scale mission, it was finally go time.

I felt excited by the prospect of using my tactical medical skills for the first time in the field and possibly getting some rounds off in combat. By that time, operating on night vision had become second nature and I felt comfortable moving tactically in the field. As I evolved as a soldier, I had begun to crave involvement in combat as well as treating the wounded incurred. Firing my weapon in anger seemed to me to be a rite of passage I must undergo if I were to truly assimilate with my new tribe.

At 2200 hours on the night of the job, we made our way down to the airstrip where our three insertion CH-47 Chinooks were already turning and burning, rear ramps down and ready for us to load on. After a short shake-out and communications check, we climbed aboard the birds and took our seats for the flight. The ATVs were loaded on last, reversing into the helicopters so as to be facing forward for a speedy egress on insertion. I was amped. Most of our jobs to that point had been vehicle-mounted, so helicopters still held significant novelty appeal. Heightening my excitement was the fact that we were bound for Helmand Province, where it was rumoured the Taliban would stand their ground and fight, as opposed to the shoot-and-scoot tactics we had been seeing up until that point on the tour.

In the noisy, dark confines of the back of the Chinook I tried to calm myself by breathing deeply, but it was pointless; I was jumping out of my skin with excitement. To focus my mind, I forced myself to run over a mental checklist of my equipment. That process would later become my almost subconscious ritual on insertion helicopters. I ran my hands over the kit on my chest rig, confirming the location of my tourniquet, my specialist QuikClot bandage, my radio push-to-talk and my spare magazines. I completed the check by ensuring the readiness of my rifle.

As was protocol on helicopter insertions, we received warnings when we were ten, five and one minute out from our insertion point, screamed by the door gunners over the deafening whine of the helicopter engines.

By the time of the one-minute warning, the inside of our helicopter was a hive of activity. The door gunners were swinging the barrels of their machine guns left and right, scanning for targets, and the 40-odd tooled-up commandos on board were poised and focused on the rear ramp of the aircraft, ready to run off into the night.

The bird flared, tilting its rotor systems to wash off forward speed by forcing the aircraft into what felt like a near vertical posture, and then levelled out into a low hover followed by a gradual descent. The instant the wheels of the massive helicopter touched down, the ATVs were off, closely followed by the lead commandos, fanning out in a perimeter around the back of the bird and taking a knee to scan their surroundings.

I followed, dashing down the ramp of the chopper and into the sandstorm created by the rotor wash. Finding a gap between two other soldiers, I kneeled and surveyed the dark desert through my NVG, bracing myself against the hurricane force generated by the departing Chinook. Within seconds the birds were gone, the dust had settled, and the night was deathly quiet.

Our element remained in position for a few minutes further, silently studying our environment to ensure we were in fact alone, before commencing our insertion. Then the order to move came over the radio and the night silence was broken by a familiar sound which seemed slightly out of place in that context: the hiss of Red Bull cans being opened as the commandos loaded up on sugar and caffeine for the long mission ahead. Drinks downed, we rose one by one and moved off in single file towards the target village. By the time it came for me to move, the procession stretched further into the distance than I could see through my NVG. It was hard for me to imagine such a large element sneaking into the target village undetected, but that was exactly what we planned to do.

The march in was flat and the terrain was favourable for moving quickly. By that stage my pack fitness had improved significantly and the 50-kilogram load on my back felt far more comfortable than it had on earlier missions. We stomped on, and at around 0300 hours I began to make out the features of the target village in the distance. Our final approach to the village offered us little in the way of cover, so we increased our pace for the last couple of kilometres to reduce our exposure before dropping into the relative safety of a creek bordering the village. We waited there for our entire element to arrive, and then postured for our planned synchronised infiltration.

I was sitting with a group that contained the executive officer of the commando company, and as one of the commando platoon commanders filed past the XO got his attention.

'Hey, Jacko,' the XO whispered.

'Yeah, what?' the platoon commander snapped; his mind was clearly focused on the job ahead and he didn't appear to appreciate the distraction.

'You suck,' the XO whispered, a grin creeping across his face.

'Fuck you,' Jacko fired back.

'Don't get killed.'

'Fuck you,' Jacko repeated, before leading his team off towards his specified compound.

The XO seemed pleased with the reaction he had provoked, and I certainly appreciated the humour. While it may appear juvenile and grossly inappropriate to the outsider, that sort of black humour is perfect for diffusing the tension, and it is often employed among those who operate in complex, high-consequence environments.

After all the individual elements had moved off towards their respective positions in the village, the time came for our headquarters element to move. I picked up and followed my group into the village. It was a strange sensation, moving stealthily at a slow walking pace, literally through people's backyards, as they slept on unknowingly.

The compound that our headquarters element was to occupy was a vacant, roofless mudbrick structure in a slightly elevated position overlooking a marketplace running down the centre of the village. As we neared the compound the dull green night sky, as viewed through my NVG, was instantly illuminated, and a second later an almighty explosion rocked the village. Our element froze where we stood. The Hitman, who was immediately to my front, turned and looked at me wordlessly. Seconds passed with radio silence. We had been briefed that the IED risk in the village was high, and I suspected that the unannounced explosion was one of our teams hitting a device. My mind raced with triage procedures and treatment protocols and my heart beat hard against the Kevlar plate of my body armour with anticipation. It was time to put my training to the test.

Thankfully, but somewhat disappointingly at the same time, a radio transmission came across the net shortly after the blast informing us that it had been an explosive entry into a compound and everyone was all right.

With our presence now made abundantly clear to the enemy, our element made best pace to the security of our designated compound and set ourselves up for the day ahead. The blast had woken the village, and intelligence soon suggested that groups of insurgents were coordinating the retrieval of weapons from caches in preparation for a gunfight. Having heard it all before, I thought, *I'll believe it when I see it.* I would learn subsequently that, when in Helmand, the intelligence picture of enemy intent was accurate and should probably be taken seriously.

Just on first light women and children began streaming from the village in large groups, which served as a strong indicator that word had got out and combat was imminent; the Taliban needed the support of the local villagers, and having non-combatants killed was as bad for them as it was for us. Intelligence updates pointed to the insurgents launching an attack the instant the sun rose over the mountains towering over the village. And so it proved: the very second the sun peeked over the mountains the village erupted with enemy small-arms fire and a volley of well-aimed rocket-propelled grenades. It was well and truly on.

By design, our headquarters compound was situated out of the town centre where the bulk of commandos were located, and we were therefore removed from most of the fighting. Early in the day a handful of rounds intended for other people had snapped over our compound, but our position appeared to remain unidentified by the enemy.

I had become quite complacent in what I figured was the perfect safety of our position and was wandering freely around the compound, taking a good look out of the large gaps in the mudbrick walls facing slightly uphill to one side and down towards the village centre to the other. The signaller from our element, who had positioned himself on the uphill side of our compound, had detected movement in another dwelling about 100 metres from ours and I joined him to have a look for myself. Scanning through our scopes, we quickly ascertained that the movement was a group of small kids playing.

With that mystery solved I was walking back to my original position to resume watching the marketplace, where most of the action was unfolding, when an enemy bullet snapped past inches above my head and smashed into the compound wall immediately to my left, showering me in dust and sending me diving face first into the dry dirt below.

I had always wondered how I would respond in such a situation, and wasn't entirely surprised to find myself giggling like a schoolgirl at how close I had come to being ended. With hindsight, I don't think I comprehended the magnitude of the situation, and I certainly didn't take it personally. A Talib had seen me, had a clear shot, and took it. It was as simple as that. I lay there in the dirt for about twenty minutes, until I was certain no more rounds were coming my way, then got up and made a mad dash back to the downhill edge of the compound.

As the day progressed, the fighting moved closer and closer to our position, with rounds regularly zinging overhead and coming through the gaps in the walls of our compound, smashing chunks out of its inner perimeter walls.

There was a small pit located in the open some 15 metres towards the village centre from our compound, and at one stage two members of our element had taken an 84 mm rocket launcher and bolted out to try to get a bead on the enemy in the marketplace. Being in the middle of my first proper gunfight and having very nearly had my head taken off by an enemy bullet, I felt the time was right to get involved. Seeing the opportunity, I raced out and joined the others in the pit, hitting the deck to their left and immediately taking up a sight picture through my rifle scope. Sensing that I was being watched, I glanced across at the soldier lying next to me. He was the senior soldier in the commando company, the company sergeant major, and he was eyeing me with a look of disbelief on his face. While technically I outranked him, on the ground he held the authority.

'Doc, what the fuck are you doing?' His voice was more disappointed than angry. He pointed back at the compound I had come from, gesturing for me to return like a parent might admonish a misbehaving toddler. I picked up my rifle and skulked back to the safety of the compound.

Less than a minute after my departure, the two soldiers in the pit came under intense and accurate enemy fire, with one round striking the rocket launcher. After being pinned in position for several minutes by the weight of fire, they were eventually able to retreat to the compound under the concealment of a smoke grenade.

Having then pinpointed our position with the smoke, the enemy proceeded to unleash a barrage of fire, with one well-aimed RPG slamming immediately into the other side of the thick mudbrick wall I was leaning against, demanding my attention with the percussion it caused. My first decent gunfight was exactly as I had hoped, and I continued to giggle away as the bullets and rockets flew around us. A pair of Apache gunships joined the fight and added to the ambience by periodically engaging with Hellfire missiles and bursts of 30 mm cannon. Eventually losing interest in shooting up our position, the enemy turned their attention back to the commando elements that were systematically clearing the marketplace, and our compound stopped receiving effective fire.

The hot afternoon dragged on and the fighting continued intermittently throughout the village. Chasing some shade, I had set myself up in a sheltered corner of the compound, on the other side of the gap in the downhill side wall to the rest of the element. Sitting there alone, and with nothing specific to do, the fatigue of the previous night started to catch up with me, and I was drifting off to sleep when the excited voice of the Hitman snapped me back into the moment.

The Hitman had seen an Afghan dart past the uphill side of our compound and disappear towards the same compound in which the signaller and I had seen the kids playing that morning. The Hitman was convinced he had seen an ICOM radio in the Afghan's hand which, in the context of the fighting going on, made him a legitimate target.

Due to our disposition on the ground at the time, I happened to be the only one with a view up the hill to the compound that the Afghan had entered. I took a position on my guts and, supporting my rifle on a large rock, stared intently through my rifle scope, watching the compound for signs of life. Before long, an Afghan male wearing aqua-coloured robes made his way out of the compound and stood behind the chest-high mudbrick wall in its courtyard. He was looking directly down through the gaps in the walls of our compound and into the marketplace and was seemingly oblivious to my presence. I froze, desperate not to move and declare myself. From that distance, his head and torso were visible above the wall and almost completely filled the reticle of my rifle scope. I have never been a great shot, but he was unmissable. At a loud whisper, I double-checked with the Hitman that the guy he had seen was dressed in aqua. It was confirmed. My heart raced and my breathing quickened, causing the Afghan man's image to dance around a little in my reticle.

'Do I shoot him?' I asked.

'Can you see the ICOM?' the Hitman responded.

'Nah, his hands are behind the wall.'

'Wait until you see the ICOM.'

My entire attention was focused down the scope of my rifle. I steadied my breathing as best as I could, and flicked the safety switch of my M4 to semi-auto. *It's time to kill,* I told myself, the concept causing conflicting emotions and an unexpected degree of hesitation. *Show me the ICOM, show me the ICOM.* My mind raced as beads of sweat formed on my forehead and began dripping down into my eyes. The effort of remaining completely still was exhausting, and every fibre of my body tensed with the anticipation of taking another man's life. As I watched, movement flickered in the bottom left corner of my scope. I turned my attention momentarily to its cause to find the same kids that had been playing before popping out past the corner of the wall, right next to where I judged the Afghan man's feet to be. Turning my attention again to the man, he appeared to be chastising the kids and sending them back into the compound. I watched as he briefly turned and looked back into the compound behind him before turning once more in my direction.

A second later the mudbrick wall to the immediate front of the Afghan man exploded in a cloud of dust, and a fraction of a further second after that the man's chest erupted in a spray of pink and he dropped behind what remained of the wall, like a puppet whose strings had suddenly been cut. I had not pulled my trigger and it took me a moment to register what the fuck had happened. We had snipers positioned on a hill to the rear of our position and one of them had taken the Afghan out with his second shot from a .50 calibre sniper rifle, the first round hitting the wall. Talking with the sniper later, he explained that from his vantage point he could positively identify the ICOM in the Afghan's hand.

I had acted in accordance with the rules of engagement, but when I learned that the man had been a legitimate target I found myself jealous of the sniper who'd pulled the trigger. The same unnerving but empowering sensation I'd felt during the simulated ambush in Timor the year before had returned in me, this time intensified by the fact that the bullets were real. Further psychological boundaries were crumbling in my mind as I realised that not only was I capable of killing under the right circumstances, there was a shadowy component of my psyche that actually wanted to. I had begun the process of desensitisation that combat operations brings, and the normalisation of very abnormal experiences.

The remainder of the afternoon passed without incident, and the sensitive items from the British helicopter that we had been sent to find were duly recovered.

With dusk approaching the fighting intensified as the insurgents made one final attempt to claim an infidel life before dark, when our night-fighting overmatch would reduce their chances significantly.

Night fell and the fighting ceased. Our individual elements regrouped and postured for exfiltration. At around 2100 hours we exited the village as silently as we had entered some eighteen hours prior. The only indication that the insurgents knew we were leaving came in the form of a message left for us and translated by our interpreter.

'We have very much enjoyed fighting with you today – you are welcome back anytime,' the insurgent leader told us, despite the fact that estimates from subsequent intelligence suggested that enemy dead numbered between 25 and 30.

The rotation drew towards its end, the previous months blurring together into a mass of miles covered in Bushmasters peppered with village clearances, combat and the occasional close call for our guys. No-one had been seriously injured, and my M4 remained unfired in anger. I felt that I had integrated into special operations and to some degree earned the respect of the soldiers around me. I was no longer treated as a liability, and my presence didn't hinder any further offensive action. If anything, I began to sense that my presence lent confidence in combat; the men appreciated knowing that a doctor was nearby to help make sure any casualties had the best chance of survival. To some degree I had validated my tactical medical training, and I had begun my on-the-job training in gunfighting. Under the circumstances, the apparent paradox between those two contrasting skillsets never struck me as anything but normal.

Our final job for the trip was yet another valley clearance for which I was in an overwatch position, at a remove from any action that might occur on the ground. The clearance force on the day was met with significant resistance and a decent gunfight erupted in the valley, which I watched through binoculars from the safety of our position on a feature hundreds of feet above.

During the firefight an Afghan boy was caught in the enemy crossfire and shot through the leg. I listened to the radio transmissions enviously as Brad, one of the commando medics on the ground, treated the kid.

Brad was not much more than a kid himself, his career trajectory having streamlined him into special operations at an age younger than would be expected. Fortunately, his thick crop of black hair allowed him to grow a passable beard, and his competence as a medic had won the respect of his commando platoon. I had trained closely with Brad leading up to deployment and trusted his medical judgement. Brad's assessment of the wounded child suggested that the bullet had damaged an artery in his leg and that he could lose the limb without urgent surgery. An AME bird was called in and I watched it swoop down into the hostile valley and recover the young child before turning its tail towards Tarin Kowt, and the bright lights and sharp steel of the operating theatres at the American military hospital.

The clearance force fought its way to the end of the valley, and once the mission was complete we began regrouping for the final time to proceed back to base and the end of our tour.

Our car had consolidated with the rest of the Bushmasters, as well as the snipers, who were mounted on ATVs. As we waited for the last of the clearance force to make their way out of the valley, our sniper element was initiated on by AK-47 fire from a small group of insurgents in a fighting position 300 metres away. Being incredibly brave, or extraordinarily stupid, the enemy had chosen to engage despite the fact that six heavily armed Bushmasters were in plain sight. With the snipers dodging bullets and ducking for cover behind their bikes, the Bushmasters quickly orientated their main armaments towards the insurgent fighting position and unleashed their full fury.

The main weapon on our car was a 40 mm automatic grenade launcher, manned by the XO, and with the car aligned for it to pummel the insurgent position I found myself behind my machine gun, pointing in the exact opposite direction. Craning my neck to see what was going on, I watched the XO deliver devastating bursts of high-explosive grenades into the insurgent position. As my frustration at not being able to get involved in the fight escalated, an opportunity suddenly presented. The 40 mm grenade fire from our car had abruptly stopped, and this along with the XO's calls for another box of ammunition alerted me to the fact that he was reloading. Knowing that process would take a minute or so, I ducked my head into the car and yelled at the driver to turn the car around so I could have a blast. He accommodated and the Bushmaster did a rapid three-point turn, bringing the insurgent fighting position directly into my arc of fire. It was my time. I pressed my shoulder hard into the butt of the mounted MAG 58 machine gun and clicked the safety button to the fire position with the base of my index finger, its tip taking up the first pressure of the trigger. Within a split second the red dot of the gun's scope swung onto the insurgent position, and I depressed the trigger with the intent of unleashing a sustained burst of machine gun fire onto the enemy, but instead let off a single round before the gun jammed. I yanked desperately

146

at the cocking handle of the gun to clear the stoppage, but it didn't budge. *You're fucking kidding me!* I thought. *I've waited six fucking months to shoot at some fucker, and I get a fucking first-round stoppage!* I eventually reefed the cocking handle back and was in the throes of clearing the link that had jammed the gun when the Bushmaster performed another violent three-point turn and the XO re-engaged the target with his grenade launcher, leaving me once again pointed in the opposite direction to the action.

Shortly thereafter the shooting ceased, as it was assumed that the several thousand rounds that had been sent in the enemy's direction had probably done the trick.

The six-month rotation ended, and we handed over to the incoming task group. I boarded the plane home wanting more. I had tasted the drug but I hadn't had a decent fix. I would have to wait fifteen more months before I could score again.

VIII

PLAYING FOR KEEPS

BACK IN AUSTRALIA EVERYTHING HAD CHANGED. LIFE AROUND me was the same as when I had left for Afghanistan, but the way I viewed it was different. Although my trip had been largely un-traumatic, I struggled to fit back into normal society and found myself agitated and highly anxious, especially in crowded, noisy areas such as shopping centres and pubs. In those surrounds my heart would race, my palms would sweat, and my eyes would dart from person to person, assessing them for threat.

The catalyst for me to avoid shopping centres for a while came in the form of an altercation with a middle-aged man in the Christmas crowd at a local mall. We had both gone to step onto an escalator at the same time, and in doing so had knocked shoulders with one another. I had been involved in a situation in Afghanistan late in my trip where a local had tried to grab the knife out of the front of my body armour in a crowded marketplace, and for a split second I was right back there. I responded to the man in the same way I had to the Afghan, with an abrupt, open-palmed shove to the chest that knocked him back a few steps and left him gasping to catch his breath. The crowd around us in the shopping centre froze, all eyes on me. The man I had struck stood completely still, staring at me with a mixture of terror and disbelief on his face. I offered a mumbled apology and then bolted to my car and drove off before security could get their hands on me.

Throughout the 2009 Christmas break I remained unsettled. While it was fantastic to reconnect with my family and have some time away from work, there was a nagging sensation in the back of my mind. I was slowly processing my experiences from Afghanistan and had reached the conclusion that I *had* to get back there, the sooner the better. Unknowingly, I had commenced a metamorphosis from which there would be no return to my former self. I had started my transition from ordinary doctor to Voodoo Medic. I found normal life boring and felt guilty that I wasn't satisfied by having a beautiful wife and child and a career that most would consider successful. I found it increasingly difficult to interact with people outside of the military and dreaded the predictable questions about Afghanistan and platitudes about how terrible it must have been. I found it impossible to convey to people how exciting Afghanistan had been and why, given the opportunity, I would jump on the next plane back over. I did what most would do in the same situation and internalised my feelings, while adopting a facade that allowed me to interact with society the way I knew I was supposed to.

It was a welcome relief to return to work and not have to keep up the pretence any longer. As penance for my year of fun on TAG and deployment the previous year, in 2010 I inherited the senior doctor's position at 2 CDO and the administrative frustration that came with it. The job entailed assisting in the running of a medical centre servicing approximately 1000 troops, as well as being the military point of contact with the civilian services that provided rehabilitation to our wounded soldiers.

The latter role came to the forefront in June that year when an American Black Hawk carrying ten Australian commandos crashed in Afghanistan, killing three of them and severely wounding the remaining seven. An American crewmember also lost his life in the incident. The crashed helicopter had been one of a formation of insertion birds on the mission, and fortunately the remaining aircraft were able to land immediately and extract the casualties from the crash site. The actions of the commandos who responded to the scene, and the rapid evacuation of the wounded, unquestionably reduced the death toll from the incident.

I had turned up to work as usual early on the morning of 21 June 2010 and was immediately ordered up to headquarters. Once there, I was ushered into a bustling briefing room. Phones were ringing incessantly and soldiers were tapping away diligently on computer keyboards. The walls of the briefing room were covered with the photos of the commandos involved in the crash, and underneath each photo were regularly updated documents outlining their injuries and current status. Three of the photos had the letters KIA printed underneath them in bold, indicating that the soldiers had been Killed In Action. Of the remainder, most were categorised VSI, signalling a very serious injury, which meant they were still at risk of losing their lives or limbs.

I moved from photo to photo, reading the accompanying documents, as the profound magnitude of the situation slowly registered. The atmosphere in the room was solemn but purposeful, with the primary agendas being the timely notification of the next of kin of the soldiers involved, as well as gaining regular and accurate updates on the status of the injured. My role was to decipher all the medical jargon coming back from the treating hospital in Kandahar, to ensure that the notification teams could explain to the next of kin what was going on in terms they would understand.

Despite vaguely knowing some of the guys involved in the crash, and understanding perfectly the seriousness of their medical conditions, my emotional response to the situation was muted. The crash had happened half a world away, and I was experiencing an attenuated version of events with no visceral cues to attach to it.

The injured commandos were stabilised in Kandahar and then rapidly evacuated to the Landstuhl Regional Medical Center in Germany. Once there they received further surgeries as required and were prepared for their return flight to Australia.

Two weeks later I found myself standing next to Lieutenant General Ken Gillespie, then Chief of the Australian Army, in the bitter pre-dawn cold on an airstrip at RAAF Base Richmond, about 50 kilometres north-west of Sydney, awaiting the arrival of the wounded commandos. The herculean C-17 Globemaster aircraft touched down and taxied to our location, its huge tail ramp opening to reveal the impressive medical configuration that had been fitted in its cargo bay to sustain the casualties during the flight.

Two of the commandos were still in comatose states and had made the journey on full life-support machinery. As the wounded were wheeled out past us, the human toll of the incident finally began to register with me. Two weeks earlier, these men had been highly functioning special operations soldiers in the prime of their careers; now, in a split second of misfortune, they had been reduced to shattered shells of their former selves.

The casualties were loaded onto waiting ambulances and transported to a nearby hospital, where half of the intensive care unit had been cordoned off for their arrival. Their families were waiting at the hospital, and witnessing their response gave me some insight into the devastating second-order effects that can result from events overseas.

When an Australian soldier dies or is severely wounded on operations, all the general public sees is a brief summary of the incident that is quickly superseded by the next news item. What they don't see, and couldn't possibly appreciate, are the years of grief and mourning that ensue for the loved ones of the dead, and how the lives of those close to the severely wounded are put on indefinite hold as they support the casualty's recovery. I saw this first-hand in the period following the injured commandos' return to Australia.

Assigned as the medical liaison between the treating hospital and 2 CDO, I spent long hours in the hospital engaging with the casualties, their families and the treating doctors. The medical response was second to none, with the commandos undergoing dozens of scans, X-rays and surgeries daily, but it was the response of the families of the injured – many of whom had dropped everything and travelled interstate to be there – that I found most impressive. Most were appreciative of the efforts being made to help the patients, but frustrations would boil over periodically at the perceived lack of progress being made or the occasional need to assign blame for what had happened.

The behaviour of the injured commandos was similarly impressive as they began to come to terms with the deaths of their close friends and teammates as well as their own career-threatening injuries. One of the guys, despite having broken his neck in the crash, refused to stay in bed, and at every opportunity he would get up and walk down to the hospital lobby to get a coffee, causing significant friction with his treating surgeon.

Another two of the guys who had been severely head injured in the accident remained in comas for weeks following their return to Australia, and their wives and families spent every permitted hour of visiting time by their bedsides.

Meanwhile, kids needed to get to school, bills needed to be paid and pets needed feeding. It was truly awe-inspiring to see the families rally to the occasion, supported by the Defence Force's services for dealing with such situations.

After a week of being stuck in their hospital beds, the less seriously injured commandos were pulling their hair out and pushing the limits of their rehabilitation. All of them were demanding to know when they would be released from hospital and, more importantly, when they could return to soldiering. Such was the nature of the guys that, despite having suffered severe injuries in a crash that had claimed the lives of their friends, all they wanted was to get back to the job they loved, and once again fulfil the commitment they had made to their mates and the army. Their collective attitude was an excellent prognostic indicator for their long-term rehabilitation, but at the time their impatience was a significant challenge for the treating medical team, who had to constantly remind them that no matter how motivated they were, their broken bodies needed time to heal.

Further stress was added to the situation by the steady stream of high-ranking officials, from the defence minister down, who filed through the hospital to wish the soldiers the best in their recoveries. All in all, it was a pressure cooker of a scenario, and I was thankful when the casualties were all finally established in their rehabilitation routines and I could return to my day job at 2 CDO.

By the time I returned to work on base, the other 2 CDO doctor had deployed to Afghanistan, leaving me as the sole RMO for the unit and therefore denying me the opportunity to get back across to Perth to commence my SAS reinforcement training. As disappointing as it was to miss reo for a third year running, the period of stability in Sydney afforded me the perfect opportunity to knuckle down and complete my general practice specialist training. This required me to complete two days a week in a civilian clinic – the other three being at the unit – and then sit a series of written and practical exams. During the back half of 2010 I spent three days a week getting special operations soldiers ready for war, as well as periodically blowing things up and hanging out of helicopters, and two days a week dealing with Uncle Derek's erectile dysfunction and high blood pressure, and Aunty Betty's urinary incontinence and diabetes. The dichotomy of my existence was epitomised by a situation that occurred towards the end of that year.

Through a contact at 2 CDO I had been approached by an agency that required a security-cleared doctor. I was briefed in detail, and the task was set for a day coinciding with a mandatory paediatric dermatology seminar run by the GP training consortium, conveniently located within walking distance of the agency gig.

I spent the morning sitting through lectures and workshops on all manner of skin conditions in kids. Shortly after lunch, it came time for me to disappear to my other commitment. Slipping out of the lecture theatre, I hurried on foot to the designated meeting point, conducted the sensitive task, debriefed with a representative of the agency over coffee, and then raced back to the GP training session. Upon arrival back at the lecture theatre, a presentation was underway on differential diagnosis of skin rashes in infants. I crept into the darkened theatre and resumed my seat towards the rear of the room. The guy I had been sitting next to for the day looked up and gave me a knowing nod, as if he had a clue as to what the fuck I had snuck out for. I thought for a brief second about telling him the truth, but of course dismissed the idea. He wouldn't have believed me anyway.

At the time, I struggled to engage with GP training and couldn't see the relevance of most of it to my military role. My primary motivations for completing the training were threefold: first, the job at SASR theoretically required me to be GP qualified; second, the qualification brought with it a hefty pay rise; and third, becoming a GP specialist would carry with it a promotion to major. And so I persevered, sitting and passing my exams towards the end of 2010.

My GP fellowship was awarded at around the same time as both my promotion to major and my posting order for 2011, confirming that I would be headed for SASR. Furthermore, I had been pencilled in for the first SOTG rotation of 2011, which was due to leave in early March the following year. The plan was for me to touch base in Perth, march into SASR and then pack my bags again for Afghanistan. After the best part of a decade, I would finally fulfil my aspiration of being the RMO at SASR (albeit not yet beret-qualified) and, sweetening the deal, I would get another trip overseas.

Kristy, heavily pregnant with our second son at the time, didn't share my enthusiasm, but I was largely oblivious to her needs. The SOCOMD bug had bitten me and to my mind little else was as important.

I made a whirlwind trip to Fort Bragg, North Carolina, in December 2010 to liaise with the medical elements of some of America's premier special operations units, and then attended a special operations medical conference in Florida. I returned home briefly for Christmas and was present for the death of our cat and the birth of our second son, Gilbert. We spent a couple of nights in hospital after Gil's birth, and were then discharged to an oceanfront Sydney hotel, which the hospital used to accommodate new mothers. With uninterrupted sea views, room service meals and a midwife in a room down the hall providing assistance as required, I spent a brief but magical period with Kristy and Gil while my parents cared for little Henk. Then, after ten days bonding with my second little man, I once more packed my bags and left for pre-deployment training.

Kristy, meanwhile, packed up our Sydney home for a move back to her home town of Adelaide to be closer to a support network of family and friends in my absence. In my mind, Kristy moving back to Adelaide provided the solution to her stress of looking after our three-year-old and newborn sons alone, and absolved me of guilt. Such was the stoicism of the woman I married that she never even ventured her opinion on the unfairness of the situation; she simply clicked into single mum mode and got on with it. To my shame, even if she had voiced her objections, I suspect they would have fallen on deaf ears. The impending deployment was going to be my chance to tick all the boxes that I hadn't ticked on my first trip. I was smarter, fitter, better prepared and keener than I had ever been. It was going to be brilliant.

Years later, when I asked Kristy what she had done in Adelaide during the period I was deployed, she replied, 'I cried.'

IX

THE GERBER INCIDENT

MARCH 2011 FOUND ME BACK IN TARIN KOWT, AFGHANISTAN, and back in the job I loved: RMO SOTG. Overall, things in Camp Russell were largely the same, with a few significant exceptions. A big one was Operation Voodoo.

From the early years of Australian special operations involvement in Afghanistan there had existed an informal relationship between Australian medical personnel and the American aero medical evacuation (AME) helicopter crews, call sign Dustoff, who supported our missions. By 2011 this relationship had been formalised under the title of Operation Voodoo.

Voodoo, as we called it, involved 24-hour shifts in which an Australian SOTG medic, nurse or doctor would live with the Dustoff crew manning the primary response aircraft (the 'first-up' bird) and launch with them on any AME missions during that period. For Category A missions (immediately life-threatening injuries), the slowest acceptable time to be airborne was fifteen minutes, meaning that the first-up crew had to stay close to the aircraft and carry individual handheld radios with them at all times. Casualty notification would come in the form of a 9-liner, which was a standardised sequence of relaying pertinent information about casualties from the field, and contained details including the number, severity and location of the casualties, as well as whether there were any enemy in the area. On occasion we would get advance warning that there was a casualty in our area of jurisdiction and we could make our way to the bird in a more leisurely fashion to await the formal notification of the casualty. More often than not, however, the first indication that there was a CAT-A casualty was the call 'MEDIVAC, MEDIVAC, MEDIVAC' coming over the radio. To expedite our response, we would leave all of our equipment inside the guarded helicopter and sleep in our uniforms and boots. Even simple acts such as going to the toilet were a gamble, and I was caught out on several occasions in that frantic scramble.

Operation Voodoo proved to be a highly successful enduring operation for the SOTG, with hundreds of missions flown between 2009 and the end of 2013 in support of coalition and partner force operations, as well as civilian medical evacuations. It was a good news story for the task group and our successes would periodically circulate in the Australian and even international press. I had the privilege of flying around 30 Voodoo missions during my cumulative time in Afghanistan, and worked with some amazing helicopter pilots and crews. These aviators were some of the very best. They took great pride in their work and, in my experience, would regularly choose to risk their own lives, and that of their crews, rather than leaving one of our severely wounded in the field – often flying by night, landing under heavy enemy fire, or precariously balancing one wheel on the pinnacle of a mountain to extract casualties.

I always got a buzz when launching with Dustoff, but there was one mission that stood out. It would come to be known as 'the Gerber incident', and it incited multiple storms in teacups.

The shift started like any other, with the 1530 hours hand-over procedure between the outgoing and oncoming first-up crews. The meeting was held in a cramped, bombproof oper-ations room on Camp Ripley, which the Dustoff crew was sharing with a US Navy SEAL team at the time. Being the middle of summer in Afghanistan it was hot and dry, with daytime temperatures consistently in the mid-40s Celsius. I was running late for the shift and belted down to Camp Ripley on an ATV, riding directly to the handover meeting as opposed to dropping off my equipment first at the Dustoff bird. As a result, I still had my body armour on with my M4 slung to my front when I burst into the briefing room a few minutes into handover. Everyone in the room stopped and glared at the interruption. I apologised, and the meeting continued.

It was as hot as Hades in that stuffy briefing room and sweat began to stream down my back and into the crack of my arse. I was desperate to take off my body armour but dared not, as doing so would require the rip of several tabs of Velcro and a bit of a wrestle getting the 15-kilo rig off over my head, which would further disrupt the meeting. Instead, I stood and suffered through the remaining updates on weather conditions, moon illumination and enemy surface-to-air missile threat. An uncomfortable hour later, I joined the first-up crew for the day. We made our way back to their accommodation to hurry up and wait for someone to get hurt.

The Dustoff crew at the time were from Alaska and called themselves 'Artic Dustoff'. For reasons that I never completely understood they had a pink flamingo as their emblem, which they wore with pride on patches starkly contrasting against their MultiCam flight uniforms. From living in each other's pockets for 24-hour blocks on Voodoo shifts, I had got to know most of the pilots and aircrew quite well. I made myself a cup of dreadful coffee from the best machine on offer and sat down on some dodgy, homemade outdoor furniture to catch up with Nick, one of the pilots for the first-up bird. Nick was a highly experienced Black Hawk pilot and was the second most senior pilot with the Dustoff element based at TK. He had a healthy disrespect for military authority, and both he and another of the pilots, Josh, had grown horrible moustaches with the primary intent of pissing off their bosses. The pair of them together were like a comedy duo, full of pranks and puerile jokes, mostly at the expense of other crewmembers. On first meeting Nick and Josh, you wouldn't trust either of them to be responsible for their own farts, let alone a multi-million-dollar Black Hawk helicopter and the lives of its crew; however, the moment they put on their flight helmets a trans-formation would occur, and the juvenile pranksters became consummate professionals, commanding and piloting their aircraft with pinpoint precision and instilling absolute confi-dence in all on board.

On the afternoon of the Gerber incident, I had been engrossed in one of Josh's bow-hunting for caribou in knee-deep snow in the wilds of Alaska stories when we had our first indication that we might be required to launch. A message came over our radios that an Afghan National Army element had sustained a casualty who was taken to a nearby coalition base for AME. Pre-empting the 9-liner, and our official authority to launch, we proceeded to the helicopter at a jog. As I began putting on my helmet and armour, the Dustoff crew started their pre-mission checks and fire-up procedure for the bird.

As weapons were not allowed to be mounted on a dedicated AME bird displaying the Red Cross, it was protocol for a second helicopter, a chase bird, to launch with Dustoff. Usually an armed Black Hawk or an Apache, the chase bird would stay in the air and provide overwatch and security to the Dustoff helicopter as it landed to pick up the casualty. On the Gerber mission the designated chase bird was a Black Hawk, and a second aircrew had paralleled us out to their aircraft and was going through their own start-up procedure. Having donned my body armour, Peltor noise-cancelling headset and helmet, and with my rifle slung across my front and my medical kit carabinered to the floor, I climbed into a seat in the back of our bird and plugged into its communications system. Then, while the American flight medic with the first-up crew took a seat and strapped into a four-point harness for the flight out, I connected myself to the airframe of the helicopter using a reinforced cord known as a strop. Attached to my combat belt at a reinforced point, the strop loosely restrained me within the aircraft while still giving me the freedom to move around a casualty on the floor in the back of the helicopter. Although not offering anywhere near the same level of safety as the seats and harness systems in a Black Hawk, the mobility afforded by the strop was essential to provide the best care to a casualty in flight.

Through the aircraft's internal communications system I could hear the voices of the pilots and crew going through their usual pre-flight checks, confirming with one another as they went. I watched one of the loadmasters move purposefully up and down the left side of the airframe, checking it over and taking care not to tangle up the communications lead that tethered him to the helicopter.

The pungent smell of jet fuel filled the hot cabin as the engines groaned to life, the whine intensifying as the main rotor system stirred into motion. The rotor gained momentum and within seconds appeared as a blur, the rotor wash ridding the cabin of the fuel smell.

Through the open side door next to me I glanced across to see the chase-bird crew racing around their aircraft and frantic-ally ripping off its engine covers. One of the loadmasters from the disabled bird came bolting towards us, his flight helmet still on. At a yell he informed our pilots that the chase bird had an engine malfunction and wouldn't be able to fly the mission. As he walked away, the 9-liner for the mission came over the radio. With both hands I pressed my headset tightly against my ears to better hear the transmission over the roar of the helicopter. I noted the time and the casualty's injury details and vital signs, documenting them with a permanent maker on a piece of strapping tape stuck to my right thigh specifically for that purpose. It looked grim. The casualty had been shot twice at close range with an AK-47, one bullet ripping through his upper-left chest and the second passing through the left side of his neck. The subsequent transmission of the casualty's vital signs was broken and the only part that I caught was the blood pressure, which was 80/50, indicating that the soldier had lost a significant amount of blood and his cardiovascular system was struggling to compensate. Without rapid surgical intervention to stem the bleeding, death was imminent, and yet there we sat, in a turning and burning helicopter with no chase bird to accompany us to the casualty.

Seconds later, word came over the radio that an Apache

crew had been scrambled but would take fifteen minutes to get their machine into the air. The casualty was located approximately ten minutes' flight time away from us, meaning that we could get there, load the casualty and start heading back before the Apache was even ready to launch.

Nick came up on the internal communications of our bird, questioning the significance of the casualty's blood pressure.

'Is eighty over fifty bad?'

'It's not good,' replied the flight medic.

'Has he got fifteen minutes to live?'

'Doubt it.'

'Fuck it, we're launching.' And with that Nick made a decision that could save a stranger's life and end his own career at the same time.

Just prior to take-off, he radioed in the mandatory calls to the air traffic control tower. As I was only wired into the bird's internal radio, I could only hear Nick's half of the conversation, but that was more than enough to deduce that the tower was not in any way authorising the launch.

Our helicopter's engines changed pitch and it lifted directly up before turning into the setting sun, dipping its nose and gaining forward momentum towards the location of the casualty. The chase-bird crew, still working on their aircraft, turned their backs and shielded their faces against the cloud of brown dust stirred up by our departure. I watched them grow smaller as we gained altitude. The sun setting over the ring of mountains that forms the 'TK Bowl' around the town lit the sky in hues of orange and pink. Afghanistan certainly could be picturesque from the air, and under a different set of circumstances would be a beautiful place to spend some time.

As we flew I ran over the details in my mind. *Gunshot wounds to the chest and neck, BP eighty over fifty. The low pressure means he's definitely bleeding into that chest. Lung's probably popped, possible build-up of trapped air in his chest that could be dropping his blood pressure further.*

Even if his lung was leaking only a small amount of air and he was fine on the ground, taking him to altitude in the helicopter would cause any trapped gas to expand, generating pressure inside his chest and potentially creating a condition known as tension pneumothorax that could lead to both lungs collapsing, his heart stopping and, ultimately, death.

I ran through the treatment for the condition in my mind, opening one of the front pouches of my body armour to confirm I had a good supply of appropriate needles for releasing any pressurised air in his chest. I then got on the aircraft's communications and voiced my thoughts to the flight medic. 'He'll probably tension when we get him to altitude,' I said, getting a knowing nod in return.

We approached the forward operating base where the casualty was located and went into a low, left-banking circuit to allow the pilot to visualise the landing zone. In the failing dusk light I scanned the ground through the window of the aircraft, observing a hive of activity, with multiple tray-backed cars parked on the outskirts of the landing zone, one of which contained the casualty.

We touched down and the moment I flung open the door of the Black Hawk we were greeted by the stretcher party, who hurled the wounded soldier into our aircraft. The casualty's chest and neck wounds were covered with dressings and his eyes were open but wandered without focus. I attempted to make eye contact and gave him a thumbs-up, but there was no response. I attached a pulse oximeter to one of the casualty's fingers to get a reading of his pulse rate and oxygen levels. The screen of the device flashed to life, indicating a pulse rate of 135 beats per minute and oxygen saturation of 92 per cent. Not great, but not terrible under the circumstances.

The flight medic had taken a few steps out of the bird and was getting a handover from the treating medic on the ground, which I was unable to hear over the noise of the aircraft.

Having launched single-ship we had no guardian angel hovering above us to provide protection and I noticed Nick casting a nervous glance back towards us as the bird sat on the ground, vulnerable. A few moments later the flight medic bumped knuckles with the treating medic before climbing back into the aircraft and reefing the sliding side door shut behind him.

I had unhooked my strop to help load the casualty and was untethered, and unprepared, for the ferocity of our launch back into the sky. Keen to get the fuck off the ground, Nick cranked the aircraft to eleven and we hurtled into the air like a ride at the Easter Show. The force of our launch caused me to lose my balance and fall across the back seat of the helicopter before bouncing off it and landing on top of the casualty on the floor. Regaining composure, I reattached my strop and kneeled at the casualty's right side to assess him. The flight medic had also been thrown around by the ballistic take-off and was getting himself reorganised on the opposite side of the casualty, readying an oxygen mask.

My pulse oximeter was attached to a lanyard on my belt and had been yanked off the casualty's finger by my violent movement as we launched. I reattached it, and as I waited for a reading to appear I glanced up at the casualty's face. It was dark in the cabin by that time and the pilots and aircrew were flying on NVG. So as not to interfere with the goggles, the back of the aircraft was dimly lit with blue light. I could see that the casualty's eyes were now closed and his breathing was rapid and shallow. Fearing that in his unconscious state his tongue might flop back and occlude his airway, I retrieved a flexible rubber airway tube from a pouch on my chest rig and, after lubricating it with saliva from the casualty's mouth, inserted it into his right nostril. It passed without resistance and, once in, the flight medic strapped the oxygen mask to the casualty's face to bolster his dangerously low levels.

Despite the oxygen, review of the pulse oximeter showed that the casualty's pulse rate had continued to climb and his oxygen saturations had plunged. As anticipated, it appeared that trapped gas inside his chest was expanding and collapsing his lungs. I turned the LCD screen of the small device towards the flight medic, who reached the same conclusion as I and began to reach for a needle from his medical kit to release the pressure. I was quicker on the draw, and I ripped the packaging off a large gauge needle, inserting it into the upper-left side of the casualty's chest, a little down from his collarbone. The casualty didn't flinch to indicate he had felt the needle being inserted, and owing to the noise of the aircraft it was impossible to hear any telltale hiss that would indicate the release of pressurised air from the chest. The best we could do was monitor his conscious state and watch the numbers on the pulse oximeter as indicators of improvement. Within seconds, his pulse rate started to drop and his oxygen saturations began to climb, confirming our diagnosis and the effectiveness of the intervention.

But the success of the decompression was short-lived, and within a minute of inserting the needle it started bubbling with blood and blocked off. The flight medic retrieved his needle and reached for his communications switch. Depressing the switch, he came over the bird's comms.

'I'm going to try one in his left axilla,' he said, indicating his intention to try an alternative site to relieve the pressure in the side of the casualty's chest. With that he tore the packaging away from his large-gauge cannula and plunged it in between two ribs high in the soldier's armpit. Leaning over the casualty to observe the procedure, I watched blood immediately start dripping out of the needle.

I looked back down at the pulse oximeter to see the casualty's pulse rate now higher than ever and his oxygen saturations plummeting. He was dying on us.

Convinced that we were losing the soldier due to both blood loss and an ongoing build-up of trapped air in his chest, I decided that we needed to make a bigger hole in the side of his chest wall to vent the pressure. I reached into my medical kit for a vacuum-sealed bag containing all the equipment – or so I thought – required to create the surgical hole. I ripped open my kit and drew up the vial of local anaesthetic contained within. Identifying the exact point I intended to create the hole, I inserted the needle and began to infiltrate the anaes-thetic, slowly advancing into the casualty's chest wall until I felt the give of the needle entering the air space around his lung. Withdrawing the needle, I turned back to my kit to grab a scalpel to make the initial cut. Ferreting through the kit under the weak blue light I couldn't find it. Convinced that it must have fallen out due to the vibration and movement of the heli-copter I began searching the floor of the aircraft for the scalpel. Nothing. It was nowhere to be found and the frustrating reality dawned on me that I had fucked up and failed to put one in my kit in the first place. Over the comms system I hit up the flight medic.

'Have you got a scalpel handy?'

He shook his head in response.

'What's going on back there?' Nick asked from the cockpit, but I ignored him.

Scouring the floor of the helicopter in a futile attempt to find a scalpel that was never there, infuriated with myself for failing to pack my kit correctly, a thought struck me. *I could use my Gerber*. I reached down to the front of my body armour and drew my Gerber boot knife from its sheath and held it up for the flight medic to see, seeking his approval to use the knife for the procedure. He responded by drawing one of his hands back and forth across his throat, the universal body language for *don't even fucking think about it*. I re-sheathed the Gerber on my rig, rage at myself building. As I did so, the flight medic came up on comms.

'We're only three minutes out.' The procedure could wait until we got back to the hospital, he was saying.

Turning my attention back to the casualty, I reviewed him once more. I rubbed my knuckles vigorously on his chest, attempting to get some sort of response. Nothing. I peeled open his left eyelid to reveal a lifeless eyeball rolled high into the back of its socket. My pulse oximeter had once again been yanked off the casualty's finger and was dangling at the end of its lanyard. I reattached the device and fixed my attention on its LCD screen, willing the numbers to appear. They didn't. What did appear, however, was a flashing red light that indicated every pulse beat that the device detected. It flashed rapidly and in an irregular fashion, suggesting to me that the soldier's heart had gone out of rhythm and was in its dying throes. We were losing the guy.

At that moment, in my mind there was only one option – however inconceivable – to save the soldier's life.

I drew my Gerber boot knife from the front of my body armour and drove the tip of its blade into the anaesthetised area between two ribs in the upper-left side of the soldier's ribcage. With the initial cut made, I re-sheathed the knife and continued to burrow deep into the casualty's chest wall with a set of surgical forceps until I felt the satisfying pop that confirmed the instrument had entered the desired space around his left lung. As it did so, a pressurised torrent of bright red blood sprayed out of the soldier's chest, spilling over my knees and flooding the floor of the helicopter.

Seconds later the bird slammed down on the TK landing ramp closest to the American surgical hospital. A waiting ambulance crew flung the side door of the chopper open and began dragging the casualty out, blood from the helicopter floor flowing out onto the airstrip and pooling on the concrete below. Looking out, I could see the back of the waiting Humvee ambulance, doors open and ready for the casualty to be loaded. I released my grip on the forceps, leaving the instrument in place to keep the cavity open, before clambering out of the helicopter on my knees. Stepping out of the aircraft, I was pulled back by something tugging at my belt. Looking down, I saw the lanyard attached to my pulse oximeter, which had once again fallen off the casualty's finger and was caught inside one of the door panels of the aircraft. I drew my trauma shears and cut the lanyard, making no attempt to recover the trapped device.

By that time the casualty had already been loaded into the back of the Humvee ambulance and the flight medic had jumped in with him, positioning himself at the casualty's head end. In his hand the flight medic had a bag-valve-mask (BVM) device, a self-inflating rubber bag used to breathe for patients incapable of doing so adequately for themselves. I leaped into the ambulance behind the flight medic, reaching across him and banging on the back of the driver's window to indicate we were loaded and ready to move. Someone slammed the doors shut behind me.

The pod on the back of the Humvee ambulance was modular and independent of the driver's compartment, and as we moved off the lights in the pod were off. With the doors closed too, it was almost pitch-black in there, making assessment of the patient impossible. The flight medic screamed at the driver to turn the lights on in the back, and as they flickered to life the medic and I stared at the casualty and registered that he had stopped breathing. I immediately leaned over his lifeless form and initiated chest compressions, pumping vigorously directly over his heart. Blood spurted from the hole in the left side of the casualty's chest, painting the inside wall of the ambulance and running down onto the floor. The flight medic had simultaneously commenced breathing for the patient in concert with the chest compressions.

The drive to the hospital took less than one minute, and when the back doors were reefed open at the reception area for the emergency room the casualty had begun to breathe for himself once more, albeit fast and shallowly. He was hauled out of the ambulance and onto a waiting trolley. I picked up the artery forceps that had fallen out of his chest during compressions and reinserted them in a wiggling fashion to re-establish the tract leading into his chest cavity. Once done, I forced the forceps open again, initiating a further flow of bright red blood that left a thick trail on the concrete and then linoleum floor of the emergency room as we raced him to a resuscitation bay.

The room was warmed to combat the hypothermia that accompanies blood loss in trauma, and the heat hit me as we entered. A waiting team of anaesthetists and surgeons stood ready to receive the patient, and I relinquished my grip on the artery forceps in the casualty's side and stepped away. My job was done.

The medical team enveloped the casualty, industriously attaching monitoring devices and establishing intravenous cannulas. A tube was immediately inserted into the hole I had made in the casualty's chest and commenced draining fresh blood, indicating ongoing internal bleeding. The intravenous access was connected immediately to warmed bags of blood for a life-saving massive transfusion.

I made my way back to the entrance of the resuscitation bay, where the flight medic was standing, and shook hands with him.

'We just saved that dude's life, man!' I was jacked up on adrenaline and couldn't stand still. My eyes like dinner plates, I must have looked quite a sight – hair to my shoulders, thick beard, still wearing my armour and helmet, with my camouflaged M4 slung at my front and the casualty's blood sprayed all over me. I moved back over to watch the resuscitation take place and noticed that there were no antibiotics being administered. I got the attention of one of the treating doctors and pointed out the apparent oversight.

'Hey, I know you know this, but that guy is going to need antibiotics; his wounds are pretty dirty.' Then I added foolishly, 'Plus I had to use a non-sterile instrument to open his chest.'

'Oh yeah? What did you use?'

And with that I did something that I regret to this day: I drew my bloodstained Gerber and showed it to the treating doctor. In my defence, I wasn't thinking straight due to my adrenaline high, but – unquestionably and embarrassingly – there was some ego involved, too. I secretly considered that opening a chest with a boot knife in the back of a helicopter at night was the coolest fucking thing that I had ever done and I wanted the whole world to know.

173

The treating doctor looked me up and down with utter disdain, and without responding turned back to continue working on the casualty. It was years before it hit me that I hadn't even tried to explain the lack of a more appropriate instrument for the procedure. Rather than understanding that my Gerber was a tool of last resort, the surgeon must have thought it was my instrument of choice. I probably looked to him like some special operations cowboy lipping off about how cool he thought he was. Regrettably, that's exactly what I was at that moment, and my simple, stupid admission undermined everything else the Dustoff pilots, crew, flight medic and I had done to save the casualty.

Once stabilised in the resuscitation bay, the casualty was wheeled next door into the operating theatre to have his chest surgically opened and his neck wound explored to find and fix the sources of bleeding.

The flight medic and I grabbed our kit and made our way back outside to the casualty reception area, where the ambulance crew were busy washing out the back of the Humvee. I glanced into the pod of the ambulance at what appeared to be a murder scene, the casualty's blood sprayed everywhere, and apologised for the mess. The ambulance crew was used to it, though, and laughed it off. The flight medic and I then headed back towards the flight line, where our helicopter had shut down and was waiting for us. As we walked, the flight medic had gone quiet, clearly contemplating something serious.

'You all good, man?' I asked.

'We're going to be in the shit for this one. Our boss hasn't signed off on opening chests in the bird.'

It was my first indication that a storm was brewing. While I was qualified to perform the procedure myself, and despite it being included in the overarching document that outlined what could and couldn't be done on an AME helicopter, the senior AME doctor at the time had not signed off on it. Due to her own lack of expertise in the procedure, she had not felt confident to authorise her medics to open chests. Under the memorandum of understanding that underpinned Operation Voodoo, Australian elements were technically subordinate to the flight medic and we were not meant to exceed their protocols. I had inadvertently opened a huge can of worms. But I reassured the flight medic that we could sort it all out. *Thank fuck the guy lived*, I thought as we neared the waiting helicopter.

The blood that had spilled from the patient's chest had congealed and started to dry on the aircraft floor like black-crusted jelly. The aircraft rules were *you make the mess, you clean it*, and so the flight medic retrieved a cleaning kit from one of the storage compartments in the back of the helicopter and we set to work sanitising the floor of the bird with bleach. It was tedious work, owing to all the nooks and crannies in the floor of a Black Hawk. As we scrubbed, we debriefed the pilots and crew on what had gone on in the back during the flight back to base and up at the hospital. They, like me, thought that opening a guy up with a Gerber was outrageous, as well as being a practical solution to the problem of not having the appropriate instrument available.

Once all the blood had been cleaned from the bird – I had retrieved my pulse oximeter in the process – we piled back aboard the aircraft, the pilots kicked it over and, after stopping for a refuel on the way, flew back to the Dustoff flight lines and shut the machine down.

With the time approaching 2300 hours, and still on shift, I made my way back to our accommodation to try to get some sleep in case we had to launch again during the night. But it

175

was useless; I was still wired from the experience and my mind was playing repeats of the event on loop, processing what had gone well and what hadn't. I kicked myself for not having a scalpel in my kit and then for being stupid enough to tell the doctor at the hospital about using the Gerber. That was just plain dumb; the patient would have been given antibiotics anyway on account of his wounds, and analysing the situation further I concluded that I had simply been showing off to the surgeon. That was uncharacteristic of me and I was appropriately furious with myself. Furthermore, a new concern was building in my mind about overstepping the medical protocols allowed on the bird. I tossed and turned for hours before finally coming down off my adrenaline high and drifting off to sleep just before dawn.

I was woken with a start a few hours later by some chatter on my radio. In my groggy state I didn't catch what had been transmitted, so I leaped out of bed and bowled out of my room, only to find the Dustoff crew leisurely drinking coffee. The radio call had been for a routine transfer of the previous night's casualty down to a higher medical facility in Kandahar, about 45 minutes' flight south of our location.

The Kandahar hospital had a higher medical imaging and specialist surgical capability than what was on offer in TK, as well as a greater holding capacity for casualties. Due to the small size of both the hospitals on the TK base, the emphasis at those facilities was to perform initial surgery to stop bleeding and stabilise the wounded and then dispose of them to Kandahar for definitive surgical procedures and longer-term hospital care. The surgeons at the treating hospital from the night before were happy with the clinical state of the gunshot wound casualty and we had been given the task of transferring him down to Kandahar.

After we finished our brews, we walked out to the helicopter and went through the spin-up procedure. There was no urgency to the mission; the patient was in an induced coma, with a tube securing his airway and a machine breathing for him. We took off from Camp Ripley and landed briefly on the same ramp where we had unloaded the wounded soldier hours earlier. A Humvee ambulance with the casualty on board was waiting at the ramp and we loaded him, and all the equipment hanging off him, onto the helicopter. A flight nurse from the hospital was coming along for the mission and she had primary responsibility for looking after the patient. There was not much for me to do other than sit back and enjoy the flight.

On arrival at Kandahar another ambulance was waiting to meet us on the airstrip, and we loaded the casualty onto it. The flight nurse, flight medic and I then jumped in with him for the short drive.

We were in the process of unloading the casualty at the hospital when the front doors of the emergency room burst open and about twenty medical staff and assorted randoms ran out of the facility towards us. Among them was a film crew carrying video cameras and sound booms, cords trailing behind them as they tried to keep up with the stampede. Having no idea what on earth was happening, and not really required for any of the handover procedure, I stepped back from the scene as the crowd engulfed the stretchered patient and ferried him into the facility. I would later learn that a documentary was being filmed at the facility, which accounted for the commotion.

Long-haired and bearded, armed to the teeth and with my uniform still covered in dried blood from the night before, I felt a little out of place in the sea of clean-cut, high-and-tight haircuts. I drew a few curious looks, but no-one spoke to me until I heard a female voice from behind me.

'Voodoo? What's that?'

I hadn't noticed the gorgeous Canadian nurse sitting nearby. She was pointing to the Voodoo Medicine patch on the right shoulder of my uniform.

'It's the logo of Australian special operations medical elements,' I replied, trying to sound composed, and attempting to appear nonchalant despite her beauty.

Her reply was encouraging. 'Special operations – that's so cool.'

Though happily married, I sensed an opportunity to dust off my mojo and take it for a harmless test drive. I casually tore the Velcro patch off my shoulder and handed it to the nurse.

'No. Really?' She hesitated briefly before accepting my gift.

I looked over my shoulder, pretending to check how the casualty handover was going, but really just trying to appear aloof and desirable. She thanked me and I nodded.

Seconds passed in silence, then a minute. Two minutes. *Say something cool, say something cool*, I urged myself, but it was useless. What little mojo I once possessed had clearly atrophied from disuse. Without another word I walked away, no doubt leaving the nurse confused as to why such an arrogant prick had bothered to give her a patch.

With the casualty handover complete, I rejoined the flight nurse and medic and we climbed back into the ambulance for the return trip down to the flight line. A message had come through that our Dustoff bird had been required to pick up some mission essential equipment from a different landing ramp on the base and we had to wait a short while for it to pick us up for the flight home. As we shut the doors and strapped in I smelled something strange in the cabin. It was not a bad smell but was certainly out of place for that environment. Also odd was the fact that the back of the bird was completely empty, when we'd been told it had been diverted to pick up equipment. The two thoughts came together to make perfect sense when I spotted the huge pile of pizza boxes stacked between the two loadmasters. While we were at the hospital, the cheeky buggers had nicked off to a pizza joint on base at Kandahar and grabbed a stack of pizzas for the crew back in TK. Mission essential equipment indeed!

The Gerber incident shift ended, but the fallout from it had just begun. On arrival back at Camp Russell, I tracked down the executive officer of the SOTG.

'There *may* have been an incident on Voodoo last night,' I opened with.

The XO was sitting with several other officers who appeared to find my wording amusing.

'There *may* have been, or there *was?*' the XO asked.

'There was.'

And with that the XO sent me straight to the task group legal officer for some guidance and to write an incident report while the detail was still fresh in my mind.

The commanding officer of the SOTG was away from TK at the time, and later that afternoon I received a message to phone him about the incident. I was shitting myself, and with my heart in my throat I called the number and braced myself for a reaming from the boss. As the phone rang I started to feel hopeful. *Maybe he won't answer and I can just leave a message*, I thought.

'Hello?' The boss's voice crushed my hopes.

'Ah, yeah, boss, it's Dan Pronk here – I got a message to call you.' I braced for the tirade.

'Yeah, Dan, I'm glad you called. I heard about the incident and just wanted you to know that I fully support your actions. If you need me to call anyone to help smooth things over just let me know. Well done, mate.'

Fucking hell, I hadn't been expecting that! I thanked him for his support and hung up the phone feeling a whole heap better than I had minutes earlier. The boss was a great man and it was awesome to have his support at a time like that.

Several investigations ensued, with the surgeons from the TK hospital fixated on the use of the Gerber on the patient, and the American AME senior doctor asking questions as to why I was opening chests on their helicopter. Operation Voodoo was suspended indefinitely until the issues were resolved.

Eventually the investigations concluded that I had acted pseudo-appropriately given the circumstances. The fact that the casualty survived went a long way towards saving my skin, I suspect.

I met several times with the US senior AME doctor and brokered a new set of protocols for use by Australian medical staff on Operation Voodoo. A few weeks later the grown-ups from the AME task group eventually let us back on the birds and, on our best behaviour, we recommenced Op Voodoo.

I never had the chance to talk to Nick about his punishment for launching on the mission without an armed escort. However I did notice that he was spending an unusual amount of time down in Kandahar, where all his superior officers were located, and when I saw him next he had shaved his cheesy moustache.

As for the offending Gerber, I would lose it several months later while clambering out of a crashed helicopter.

* * *

Voodoo missions, as well as my time spent with the forward surgical team, were starting to provide some great experience in treating war wounds and an insight into the potential consequences of our task group's operations. And yet even while it was playing out right in front of me, it all still seemed so distant. Most of the casualties were Afghan local nationals or coalition soldiers; I was yet to treat a seriously wounded Australian soldier, and certainly not one that I knew. I continued to hold the naive illusion of our invulnerability – an illusion that would be shattered by three incidents in the following months.

X

INTO THE
HORNET'S NEST

'FIVE MINUTES!'

I looked up and scanned the dark confines of the helicopter, eyes moving from one bombed-up special operations soldier to the next. All were clad in MultiCam uniforms, combat boots, body armour and Kevlar helmets with NVG attached, and were bristling with weapons ranging from M4 assault rifles through sniper rifles to shoulder-fired anti-tank weapons. On their backs were packs crammed with extra ammunition, explosives, specialist equipment, and food and water to sustain themselves for 48 hard hours of fighting. It was exactly where I wanted to be at that moment.

'THREE MINUTES!'

I instinctively tapped hard on the bottom of my magazine to ensure it was firmly slotted into my rifle and followed that by slapping the bolt assist of the M4 with the palm of my right hand, as was my ritual.

'ONE MINUTE!'

The atmosphere inside the bird was electric. I angled my body towards the back of the helicopter and looked out the open ramp at the night sky. Silhouetted against the bright green glow stood the Chinook's tail-ramp gunner, scanning left and right with his 7.62 mm machine gun.

I leaned my weight forward over my knees, ready to stand and run off the ramp the instant the helicopter touched down. We would be landing out in the open, well within machine gun and RPG range of the enemy village, and as a result the emphasis on insertion was to disembark the helicopters at pace.

'THIRTY SECONDS!'

I fixed my gaze on the guy who was to be immediately in front of me in the order of march, and braced for the impact of the bird touching down.

The Night Stalkers of the US 160th Special Operations Aviation Regiment flew their helicopters at the limit, with the objective of getting troops in quickly and then getting the hell out of there. The result was routinely safe but harsh landings.

The bird hit the deck and into a cyclone of dust and rotor wash we evacuated the Chinook, filing left and right of the tail gunner and jumping off the back ramp. I kept my eyes glued to the guy in front of me; I couldn't afford to lose sight of him and become dislocated from my element on the ground.

Often when inserting via helicopter we would take a knee close to the aircraft and wait for it to take off prior to getting up and moving off. Not that night. We raced into the darkness towards the target village, our backs sand-blasted by the savage rotor wash of the departing Chinooks. Within one minute of insertion, and with the helicopters still well within audible range, machine-gun fire belched from the village and poured into our insertion point. Thankfully, we were safely away from the area by that time. Lacking any sophisticated night-fighting capability, the insurgents had likely been aiming at the point where they heard the birds land, hoping we would still be there. I turned and watched the tracer rounds from the enemy gun light up an arc between the village and our insertion site. We were clearly not welcome there.

The date was 22 May 2011, and I was two months into my second tour of Afghanistan. Our mission was to infiltrate the Taliban-held village and then degrade their ammunition supplies and manpower to soften them up for a planned sweep-through by US forces. In essence, we were there with the singular focus of fighting. Hard.

We had landed about 400 metres from the edge of the village and we covered that ground quickly, bunching up as we reached the nearest compounds. I rested behind a large dirt berm, observing the village for any signs of life. All was quiet apart from the barking of dogs. The machine-gun fire into our insertion point had ceased, the gun no doubt being set up elsewhere to greet us again. There had been no attempt to surprise the enemy; our priority on insertion had been speed.

Our leading teams moved forward, making their way between the compounds on the village's perimeter and into a series of crop fields. The moon was high and full and the sky cloudless, making for excellent NVG visibility but also meaning the enemy had a better chance of seeing us. As I watched the green image of the soldiers proceed into the crops a radio transmission came through to inform us that the first of our elements was approaching their target area, a bazaar in the centre of the village. That was my group's cue to move. I turned towards the ground force commander for the mission,

Sean, who acknowledged the transmission over the radio and then picked up and began moving.

I kept my distance from the guy in front, making a conscious effort to step exactly where he had and not venture off the path left by the special operations engineers. The field was wet underfoot, making it easy to identify the footprints of the soldier I was following. I was gazing down, watching my step, when my attention was abruptly diverted high and left by a blaze of light in the corner of my goggles. The flash was quickly followed by the unmistakable *whoosh* of a rocket-propelled grenade. I stood still, hypnotised by the sight of the rocket zipping across the night sky and then airbursting precisely above our forward element, causing them to scramble for cover. Thankfully the rocket was aimed too high to inflict any damage on our guys, and the only casualties from the incident were no doubt a pair or two of underpants.

The village once again fell quiet but for the ubiquitous barking of dogs, and after a short pause we picked up and moved on.

Rifle-mounted infrared torches and aiming lasers, invisible to the naked eye but bright as day through NVG, lit up every dark alleyway, doorway and window as we patrolled. Covering one another as we crossed potential fire lanes, we moved through the dirt alleyways before dropping down into a creek line towards the centre of town. After patrolling through the murky, warm knee-deep water for a distance, we reached a steep embankment immediately to the rear of our designated target compound. The creek bank had turned to mud from the guys before me exiting the water, and with 60 kilograms of equipment on my back I struggled to climb it. Eventually resorting to crawling on all fours, I made my way ungracefully up and out of the creek.

A small clearance party had moved forward into our target building and the remainder of us sat and waited for the compound to be cleared before entering. I had my back to a two-storey mudbrick wall, the creek I had just climbed out of running to my immediate right. In front of me was a field of waist-high crops bordered by small mud berms approximately 30 centimetres high and designed to keep irrigation water in the field. While not as protected as my position, the mud berms were the perfect height for sitting on, and two members of our group perched on them while we waited. We were talking quietly among ourselves when we were rudely interrupted. *Crackcrackcrackcrackcrack!* A burst of machine-gun fire erupted, passing within metres of my right side and shredding the foliage on the small trees lining the creek. I was perfectly safe, out of sight of the shooter and with the wall behind me shielding me from the hail of bullets. The burst was clearly intended for the two guys sitting on the berm and it sent them ricocheting backwards into the crops. Unhurt but suitably invigorated, one of them immediately got up and scurried towards the safety of the compound wall. The other soldier, heavily burdened by a massive combat load, had launched backwards into the crops and was stuck like a turtle on its back, arms and legs flailing as he tried to right himself. Before I had a chance to get up and help, he managed to roll over and clamber through the crops to join us, chuckling nervously.

Minutes later the clearance party gave us the green light, and we made our way into the abandoned structure. The time was approaching 0300 hours, and after establishing a machine-gun position on the roof and a rotating piquet roster, which would make sure at least one member of our group was awake at any given point during the night, we took it in turns to get some sleep. The sniper element with our assault force had occupied the compound adjacent to ours and had established a similar gun position on their roof.

I had been allocated first piquet and spent the hour roaming around on the roof, scanning the dark village for any signs of enemy activity and periodically catching sight of the sniper next door doing the same. All was quiet, and when my hour was up, I woke the next guy for piquet and then retired to one of the dirt-floored rooms of the compound. Scrounging a few ragged blankets from a corner, I laid them out and took off my body armour to use as a pillow. We had all been awake for around twenty hours by that time and I was exhausted. With my boots still on, I placed my M4 within arm's reach next to me and lay down on top of the blankets, immediately falling deeply asleep.

The snapping sound of supersonic bullets passing over our compound roused me out of my slumber just on first light. My mind scrambled for a few seconds, confused as to where exactly I was, before registering that I was safely within a compound. Reluctant to wake fully after only a couple hours of sleep, I dozed for a few minutes before becoming aware of a scratching sound in the room with me. Forcing my tired eyelids open, I rolled over to be greeted by a large chicken scratching around in the dry dirt and pecking at the occasional grain it found.

It was light enough by that time for me to better appreciate my surrounds. The compound was typical for rural Afghanistan and appeared well maintained, obviously owned by middle-class Afghan villagers. The room I was in appeared to be a dining room of sorts, with shelves dug into the mudbrick walls which were lined with jars of herbs, spices, pots and pans, and cooking oil. The centre of the dirt floor was covered with a large hand-woven rug which back in Australia might fetch hundreds, if not thousands, of dollars at some chic interior design shop. Here it was simply a practical floor covering for the family to sit on at mealtimes. In one corner of the room, I found several large pieces of naan bread wrapped in a thin cloth tea towel. I picked one up and inspected it for freshness, wondering how recently the occupants of the compound had left. The bread was slightly stale but felt no more than a day old, leading me to conclude that the family who owned the compound had probably left just prior to us arriving, no doubt prompted by the sound of helicopters and gunfire. The locals in these areas would have seen it all before and they knew the drill.

I put my body armour back on, grabbed my rifle and walked out of the dining room into the protected central area of the compound. A survey of the courtyard in the morning light revealed the charred dirt of a dug-out cooking pit up against an inner wall, a second large room – a bedroom, perhaps – adjacent to the dining room, and several smaller storage rooms full of hay on the opposite side of the courtyard. The walkway to the main entrance of the compound led to an area where animals were kept. A set of mudbrick stairs in another corner of the courtyard led onto the roof, with the outer perimeter walls of the compound extending some 1.5 metres above the roof level. A second set of stairs near the main entrance of the compound led to the separate roof area where we had set up our machine gun the night before, and one of our guys was up there now on the final piquet of the night.

One by one the members of our group emerged from their sleeping locations. Ours was the company headquarters (CHQ) element, the nucleus of the fighting force on the ground. Our element consisted of Sean, the ground force

189

commander; Mick, the commando company's senior soldier; a signaller; a joint terminal attack controller (JTAC) responsible for controlling and deconflicting all the aircraft flying in support of us and for orchestrating the dropping of warheads on foreheads; two guys responsible for more secretive communications functions; and myself as the medical authority for the mission. As the CHQ element, our role in the first instance was not to do any of the fighting but to provide higher tactical command as well as higher communications back to base. My primary purpose was to support the platoon medics as required.

We all congregated in the courtyard to receive an update on overnight events. Situation reports came in from all elements in the village reporting probing enemy activity throughout the night but no sustained engagements. The reports confirmed that there was no evidence of any women or children left in the village, suggesting word had got out that a shit fight was about to ensue. We had kicked the hornet's nest and it was time to wait and see what happened.

As I sat and listened, I cracked open a US ration pack known as an MRE, or 'meal ready to eat', and sorted through it to find something for breakfast, settling on the pound cake. Mick had rustled up an old open-fire kettle from the compound and, after filling it with bottled water, had started a small fire to get a brew going. Occasionally rounds would snap overhead, causing Mick to flinch every time, making the rest of us laugh.

As I ate my pound cake I broke off small crumbs and threw them to the chicken, which had followed me out of the dining room and was wandering purposefully about the courtyard scratching for food.

The sun started to rise, and as the day heated up so did the fighting. Having worked out our rough disposition on the ground, the insurgents set about attacking us, moving between pre-established fighting positions throughout the village. The enemy fire was mostly small arms, consisting predominantly of AK-47 and machine gun with the occasional RPG thrown in for good measure.

By mid-morning our snipers in the adjacent compound began to receive accurate fire from a series of compounds approximately 150 metres to our front and were retaliating with precision single shots from their sniper rifles, as well as bursts from the machine gun in their position. I sat in the safety of our compound listening to the firefight escalate around me and chatting with one of our secretive communications guys, Hollywood.

I had got to know Hollywood on my previous special operations tour when he had crashed a motorbike and badly injured his ankle, forcing him to return to Australia prematurely. A solid, good-looking bloke, Hollywood had a colourful sleeve tattoo covering one of his shaved arms and was fairly particular about his personal grooming and diet. In preparation for deployment, Hollywood had purchased a food dehydrator and made all manner of dried meats and fruits that were then vacuum sealed and sent over periodically by his girlfriend. Despite his role not requiring him to be a qualified special operations soldier, Hollywood had chosen to complete the arduous commando selection course and subsequent reinforcement training to earn the right to wear the coveted Sherwood green beret of Australia's Commando Regiments. He was passionate about his work and his enthusiasm was contagious.

As we sat talking, the volume of enemy fire directed at the snipers next door picked up. Hollywood and I decided we'd head up onto the roof to see if we could get a look at where it was coming from and try to get involved in the fight ourselves. We made our way up onto the roof, walking in a crouched position to keep our heads below the perimeter walls of the compound. There were no appropriate gaps to look or shoot through, and the perimeter wall was slightly too high to comfortably shoot over without standing on something and exposing ourselves to the enemy. If we wanted to get into the fight, we were going to have to dig a keyhole through the mudbrick wall.

Heading back downstairs, we searched the compound for digging tools and then returned to the roof with a sickle and a large screwdriver to begin hacking away at the wall. It was hard going in the midday sun, with the mudbrick wall being about 50 centimetres thick and built to last. After about an hour we broke through to the other side, expanding the diameter of our keyhole to give us a decent field of view of the Taliban compounds, while leaving the hole small enough that it would be difficult for the enemy to hit us through.

We took turns sticking the barrels of our rifles through the keyhole and, through our magnified scopes, observed the likely gun positions in the enemy compounds. It didn't take long to identify where the insurgents were firing at us from. They were quick, popping up at any given firing position, letting off a burst of machine-gun fire at the snipers next door, then disappearing again. The key was to watch a firing position intently through our scopes then engage the second we saw movement behind it. Hollywood had a 40 mm grenade launcher attached to his M4 and we established a system whereby I would identify the enemy and engage with my rifle through the keyhole while he launched high explosive grenades over the compound wall at the position. Predictably, as soon as we started shooting our own position drew fire, and the enemy spent the afternoon alternating their attention between our position and the sniper position next door.

While we were having our stand-off with the Taliban in the compounds to our front, we could hear the other friendly elements in the village being more decisively engaged from multiple directions. The enemy forces appeared to be growing in size, doubtless reinforcing throughout the day through a series of underground tunnels the Taliban used for concealed movement and caching of weapons. Originally designed to carry water over great distances without loss through evaporation, these centuries-old 'Karez' systems afforded the Taliban a means of clandestine movement, undetectable by coalition intelligence, surveillance and reconnaissance platforms, our eyes in the sky.

By late afternoon the entire village was engulfed in battle. Completely surrounded, our individual elements fought outward in all directions, fending off the insurgent attacks. Enemy bullets snapped overhead constantly, and periodically our keyhole would be subject to an accurate hail of bullets, spraying dust and debris back into our position and sending Hollywood and me diving for cover. The crack and thump of friendly shoulder-fired high-explosive rockets came frequently from our platoon headquarters element located in a nearby compound, as well as from the element in the bazaar in the centre of the village. A pair of Apache helicopter gunships had been called on station and cut slow menacing laps above the battlespace. Under the control of the JTACs on the ground, they would swoop in low overhead and bring their full fury to bear on enemy positions with devastating bursts of 30 mm cannon and Hellfire rockets. By sundown several enemy compounds had been razed to rubble and several more were consumed by fire, sending black plumes of smoke billowing into the twilight sky.

As the sun set the fighting stopped and the village once again fell silent. That was typical of the Taliban; knowing they couldn't match our night-fighting capability, they would unleash all hell on dusk and then retreat to safe positions during darkness to regroup for a first-light attack.

We drew back into the courtyard and once again began to prepare for our night routine, fixing NVG to helmets and drawing up a piquet list.

The heat and activity of the day had left us low on water and reports coming in from our other positions confirmed that they were in the same predicament. The intensity of the day's fighting had also left us critically low on ammunition. With the Taliban reinforcing and anticipating fighting of similar intensity the next day, Sean set about organising a resupply drop. He also requested that a vehicle-mounted platoon of commandos, on a separate mission in the vicinity of our village, drive through the night to reinforce us the following day. The platoon was mounted in Bushmasters and would bring some handy firepower to the fight in the form of .50 calibre machine guns and 40 mm automatic grenade launchers, not to mention 30-odd more commandos.

I hadn't felt much like eating during the day due to fatigue and the heat, but I knew I should force myself to choke back a main meal from the MRE I had opened at breakfast. I retrieved an 'imitation pork riblet' meal and began to warm it in the chemical heating satchel provided. As I did, my chicken friend made her way over to see if there was anything in it for her. Suddenly becoming quite hungry, I eyed the chicken and cast my mind back to the herbs, spices and cooking oil I had seen in the dining room that morning. In between radio transmissions I got Sean's attention and hit him up.

'Hey, Sean, can we eat that chicken?'

Dad, beer in hand, and Mum, heavily pregnant with me. Townsville, Queensland, early 1977.

Fat baby Dan, late 1977. It would take about fifteen years to finally burn off all that baby blubber and become lean!

Me (standing), Ben (right) and one of his mates playing army when we lived in Holsworthy, New South Wales, in 1985. Ben seemed destined to join the army from an early age and was seldom seen without his trusty plastic M16 rifle.

Back in the good old days of army aviation when it was considered appropriate to take your kids for helicopter rides. I can't recall this exact flight, but I reckon I would have been about ten at the time.

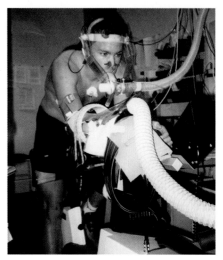

At age fifteen I discovered triathlon and never looked back. While I didn't become the triathlete that I had dreamed of being, the discipline of training and the foundation of fitness served me well when training for SAS selection.

Maximal exercise (VO₂ max) testing in the lab at Griffith University, Gold Coast, 1998, where I was studying Exercise Science. The mouthpiece is capturing my expired gases, while my right arm is in a heating device to facilitate easier blood-taking for analysis during testing. Out of picture is the core temperature probe inserted 30 cm into my rectum for the sessions!

Long haired and with earring in place at one of Ben's parades at ADFA during his officer training in 1995. I could have never imagined at the time that just a few years later I'd find myself clean cut and formed up on the same parade grounds.

Ben and I, jacked up on adrenaline after a rock-climbing fall in the Glass House Mountains during the early hours of Christmas Day, 2000. I would later learn that I had broken three ribs, bones in both of my ankles, and my left arm!

Weekends during medical school were spent at the range, gaining experience in rifle and handgun shooting. Perhaps not your average medical student . . .

Exhausted after stomping 82 kilometres in 27 hours straight on Tasmania's Overland Track in the middle of winter, 2004. Pack-marching was the cornerstone of my training for SAS selection; on this trip my pack weighed around 40 kilos.

Kristy and I on our wedding day, November 2006. Who could blame me for falling head over heels for such a beauty!

Our meal, consisting of tongues, eyeballs, and testicles, set in cold, blue gelatin, during the last phase of selection. After three days of no food or sleep, anything tasted good. Well – almost anything!

The body language says it all: heads down, dejected. Carrying the impossibly heavy box on the second last day of SAS selection. I'm Candidate 18, to the right of the photo, taking a break from carrying.

Physically and emotionally broken at the end of the three-week selection course. I started the course weighing 73 kilograms and finished it a mere 58 kilograms.

Tagging along with a recon patrol commander's course in the hills of Timor, gaining experience that would prove useful on operations in Afghanistan in the years to come.

Awaiting Black Hawk extraction on a hill in Timor after an all-night escape and evasion exercise. I've removed my rifle's blank firing attachment to try and look cooler in the photo, but I'm not sure anything could compensate for that moustache!

On the 'ship underway recovery' training exercise with the 4 RAR (CDO) tactical assault group in Jervis Bay, New South Wales, early 2009. I was new to Special Operations Command and loving every second of it.

Finally in Afghanistan on my first tour in 2009. I'm manning the machine gun on the back of one of our Bushmaster armoured vehicles during a mission. The vast expanses of desert, or *dascht*, that cover much of Afghanistan can be seen in the background.

In overwatch, waiting for our clearance force to complete its mission on the 'American animal' job in 2009.

Watching a battle rage in the valley below from the frustrating safety of an overwatch position. The final job of my first rotation of Afghanistan, November 2009.

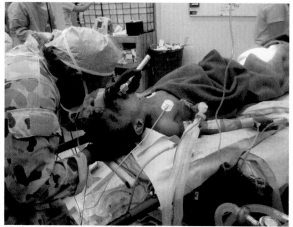

While I didn't see as much action as I would have liked on my first tour, I gained valuable medical experience working with injured Afghan local nationals with the American Forward Surgical Team, Tarin Kowt. Here I am intubating a local Afghan child for surgery.

Providing intravenous fluids and antibiotics to an infant Afghan girl who was close to death following days of gastroenteritis. I would later learn that, despite our efforts, she died the following day.

Stitching up a local who had been badly stabbed by the Taliban. Luckily, the cuts were relatively superficial, and his left lung was intact.

Treating Mick's shrapnel wound in the Platoon Headquarters compound during my second tour, just hours prior to Brett Wood's death on 23 May 2011.

With the Viking,
a fellow medic, on a
mission into Helmand
Province in 2011.

23 May 2011. Hollywood fires
a 40 mm grenade as I engage
the Taliban in the compound
150 metres away through a
keyhole in the rooftop wall of
our compound.

Burning one-kilo bags of pure
Afghan heroin, and hundreds of
thousands of dollars of
Afghan and Pakistani drug money.
The solid brick structure and the
barred windows of the heroin
packaging facility can be seen in the
background, clearly out of place
amongst the surrounding structures.

Immediately prior to extraction
from Target One, 6 June 2011. A fuel
depot ignited during the firefight can
be seen burning in the background.
Within hours of this photo being
taken, Rowan Robinson would be
shot and killed.

Sporting a mohawk on the last job of my second tour of Afghanistan, July 2011. By this time, my work as a combat doctor was starting to take its toll.

It was a difficult transition at the time, but I was happy to be back with my family in late 2011. Henk is on my shoulders. I'd left Gilbert when he was just a couple of weeks old and returned to the little chunker you see in Kristy's arms!

At the range at Tarin Kowt at the start of my fourth and final tour, December 2012. Kristy was pregnant with our third child, but I was still excited to get back to Afghanistan.

When we weren't out on missions we were training for missions. Tactical combat casualty care is down-and-dirty medicine specifically designed for high-threat environments. It's not pretty, but it saves lives.

With a fellow Voodoo Medic after a mission in early 2013 on which two of our guys were shot, one through the leg and the other in his fingers. Thankfully, they both made good recoveries.

Tooled up for a job in the common room of the regimental aid post, the Blue Voodoo Lounge near the end of my last tour, in May 2013. The voodoo doll logo on my uniform patch is on full, colourful display here.

With fellow Voodoo Medic Brad in front of the Forward Surgical Team compound, 2013. This logo was freshly painted on my first tour of Afghanistan in 2009 but, like my passion for the role as a combat doctor, had been degraded over the years by the harsh environment.

With Kristy (above) and baby Toby (below left) after my investiture ceremony where I received the Commendation for Distinguished Service, in December 2013. My self-esteem was high at the time but I had failed to realise that it was all contingent on wearing that uniform. Within months of these images I would lose my identity and purpose, and the downward spiral would begin.

With Mark Donaldson VC at the investiture ceremony, December 2013. It was my last week with SASR and a humbling way to finish my time at the unit.

Rebuilding my self-esteem and forging a new identity proved challenging post-army discharge. I credit this man, Gog, with helping me to do both. Pictured in the emergency department of the regional Queensland hospital that I helped him run 2015–17, and where some of the trauma skills we honed in Afghanistan came in very handy.

At the unveiling of a 2016 display at the Australian Army School of Health commemorating medical corps members who were decorated for gallantry and distinguished service in Afghanistan. It was the greatest honour to be among those medical corps personnel recognised.

An unexpected turn in my post-army career saw me on set as the doctor for the hit TV show *SAS Australia*, 2021 and 2022. Above with British special forces veterans DS Jason 'Foxy' Fox, Ant Middleton, Ollie Ollerton and Mark 'Billy' Billingham; below with one of my partners in crime, TacMed Australia paramedic Matty. With looks like Matty's, he should have been the one in front of the camera!

Proudly displaying *The Resilience Shield*, the bestselling book I co-authored with my brother Ben and fellow SAS veteran Tim Curtis. All the lessons I've learned in facing, overcoming and adapting to the challenges of military and civilian life are in here.

Making up for lost time with my little team, Kristy, Henk, Gil and Toby. Above at a family member's wedding in the Adelaide Hills in 2014, and below on holidays in London, 2019. It's hard to believe how quickly the kids grow – Henk now towers over me!

'Eat the chicken?'

'Yeah, I'll kill it, gut it, pluck it, and then we could roast it on a fire with the oil and spices from in there.' I gestured to the dining room.

'Good idea, man,' Hollywood weighed in, his vacuum pack bag of dehydrated whatevers suddenly losing appeal.

'Nah, the fire would give our position away,' Sean replied.

I pondered that for a second. What he said made good tactical sense, however having fought from our compound for the last twelve hours straight, I suspected that the enemy would have a pretty decent idea where we were.

'I reckon they know we're here,' I said.

'Doc, we're not eating the chicken and that's that,' Sean fired back. It was clear he didn't appreciate my persistence.

With that, I begrudgingly went back to eating my luke-warm, imitation pork product.

The sun had fully set by the time I finished my meal and the moon was yet to rise. We began our night routine, sleeping in shifts with at least one of us on a roving rooftop piquet and monitoring the radio. Shortly after midnight we all stood-to for our ammunition and water resupply, which was to be delivered by a low-flying C-130 Hercules.

The Hercules crew claimed to have perfected a supply drop technique which involved them flying extremely low and slowing to the verge of stalling to allow pallets of supplies to be dropped out of the back ramp of the aircraft without requiring any form of parachute. They boasted of their ability to achieve pinpoint accuracy, with little to no damage to the supplies. Anecdotally, the technique had been trialled with a caged goat strapped to a pallet, and it had apparently landed unharmed.

Slightly sceptical, Sean requested that the aircraft do two passes, the first to drop the pallet of water and confirm the drop point, before delivering the more crucial ammunition pallet on the second pass. (The ramifications of dropping a pallet of bullets and high-explosive munitions in a Taliban village where we couldn't retrieve them were pretty obvious.)

The location chosen for the supply drop was a walled-off field immediately in front of our compound. As the Hercules pilots would be flying on NVG, with the aircraft completely blacked out to reduce its signature, the drop point was marked with an infrared strobe in the centre of the field.

I climbed up onto the roof of our compound and, figuring that the risk of being seen and shot in the pitch-black was minimal, sat up on top of the perimeter wall to observe the supply drop through my night vision. As I watched the IR strobe flash away in the field, I started to make out the distant rumble of the C-130. The noise got louder as the intimidating black shadow of the massive aircraft lumbered across the night sky, seeming to be flying impossibly slowly and with little clearance over the village rooftops. I eyeballed the rear ramp of the aircraft for the resupply pallets, waiting to witness the drop into the designated field, but nothing emerged from the plane. It passed directly in front of me with a deafening roar and then began to disappear into the distance. Just before pulling into a steep climb several hundred metres past the designated drop point, the supply pallets were turfed out. They slammed into the ground with a crash that was audible over the noise of the Hercules' engines. *Glad there were no goats on that one*, I thought to myself.

Communications with the aircraft confirmed that the drop had consisted of both the water *and* the ammunition pallets, the request for a split drop being denied. Radio transmissions from the platoon headquarters position to our east reported that the resupply drop had hit hard and the pallets had disintegrated on impact, spreading the water and ammunition across an open field between the platoon headquarters position and the Taliban compounds. Making matters worse, the supplies were located less than 100 metres from an enemy machine-gun position that had been engaging the PHQ element and our guys in the bazaar all day. Recovering the supplies was going to be interesting.

Under the cover of darkness, Hollywood, the JTAC and I made our way across to help recover the supplies and retrieve our element's allocation of water and ammunition. We arrived at the PHQ position to find the supply recovery already well underway, orchestrated by a sergeant by the name of Brett Wood, a mate of mine. We weren't best buddies, but I had known him for two and a half years and we would stop and chat if we passed each other in the hallway at work.

Brett was a no-bullshit warrior who was legendary in special operations circles as being one of the first commandos to receive the Medal for Gallantry. I never heard the full story, but I gathered Brett had been part of a combined US and Australian clearance in a Taliban-held area in southern Afghanistan. During the mission their elements had been ambushed, sustaining heavy casualties and with one US soldier killed in action. Brett, despite being injured himself although not admitting it, led his team of commandos to aggressively clear a series of nearby enemy compounds, allowing the coalition casualties to be extracted. He then continued to lead his team on a further assault, neutralising all remaining enemy threats. It was only then that he admitted to his injury from the initial ambush and was medically evacuated.

We touched base with him for instruction and then fell in with the work party. The next couple of hours was spent moving out into the open ground to retrieve the supplies before returning to the PHQ area and laying out the water and ammunition in organised piles. I tried hard not to dwell on the prospect of the enemy machine gun bursting to life, as with dozens of us out in the open like that we would have been cut to shreds. There was no other option but to proceed, though, as we couldn't leave a pallet load of ordnance out there and we needed the water.

The supply recovery went without incident, the enemy machine gunner likely fast asleep following his big day of infidel hunting. Hollywood, the JTAC and I claimed the CHQ allocation of the ammunition and water resupply and I let Brett know that we were departing his location. In the still and quiet of the warm Afghan night, a near-full moon was beginning to rise. None of us could have possibly predicted that it would be the last moon Brett would ever see.

XI

BRETT WOOD

Scanning the horizon from the rooftop I could see the Bushmasters in the distance. As the sun broke the horizon at dawn of day two of our mission we found ourselves surrounded on all sides by Taliban, who had overnight found themselves flanked on one side by our armoured vehicles. The scene was set for a good showdown.

Hollywood and I resumed observing the firing positions in the enemy compound series through our keyhole. Mick had decided to go and join the fight from the PHQ position and we watched him from the roof as he dashed through the village between the compounds, crossed a bridge over a small creek, and then disappeared into a maze of alleyways lined with mudbrick walls.

Throughout the morning there was little activity to our front, with only sporadic engagements from the snipers next door and the occasional burst from me and Hollywood when a shadow appeared in one of the enemy firing positions. Most of the fighting was occurring on the opposite side of the village, indicated by regular rifle and machine-gun fire, cracks and thumps from friendly shoulder-fired rockets, and the occasional gun run by the Apaches, which were once again buzzing overhead. Somewhere around mid-morning a Hellfire missile materialised seemingly out of nowhere from above and came tearing from the sky to demolish an enemy machine-gun position with a devastating thump. Having not been privy to the radio communications with the Predator drone lurking somewhere above, the first I had known of the missile strike it delivered was the same warning that the enemy had. Very little.

Shortly before midday, a transmission came over the radio that the PHQ position had sustained a casualty and they were sending an escort to come and get me. I watched from the roof as a shooter purposefully made his way to us along the same route that Mick had taken earlier. As he drew closer, I could see that it was Brett Wood.

I climbed down from the roof and met up with Brett in the courtyard area, where he briefed me on the casualty as I grabbed my medical kit. It turned out that the casualty was Mick. In an exchange of rocket fire with the enemy, some high-velocity shrapnel had struck him in the left lower leg, taking a large chunk of flesh out of his shin in the process. I heaved my medical kit onto my back and followed Brett back to the PHQ compound to review Mick. The route was safe from enemy fire and took us along a convolution of dry dirt tracks surrounded by mudbrick walls of varying heights, punctuated by doorways and windows that opened into compounds. These compounds had been cleared on our initial infiltration to the village, and Brett and I made small talk as we walked with no concern for tactical movement. After 36 hours holed up in the CHQ compound it felt good to get out and explore more of the village by day.

The PHQ compound was similar to the one I was based in, although smaller. It was a single, large, square construction surrounded by mudbrick walls extending two storeys high. Single-storey rooms lined the inside perimeter, with roof access allowing our guys to be in elevated positions with clear line of sight in all directions. The compound walls extended approximately 1.5 metres above the height of the roof and were the perfect height to shoot over from a standing position while only exposing a small profile of the shoulders and above to enemy fire. I greeted a few of the guys on the way in and was ushered to the room where Mick was located.

As I walked through the courtyard of the compound one of the soldiers on the roof yelled, 'EIGHTY-FOUR FIRING!' He was warning us that he was about to unleash an 84 mm shoulder-fired rocket, meaning we should cover our ears and get out of the back-blast area of the weapon. I put my hands over my ears and ducked into the room where Mick was waiting, immediately under where the rocket was being fired. I braced for the boom, which came a few seconds later and was accompanied by dust and debris raining down on us from the ceiling above. Once clear, I set about reviewing Mick. The platoon medic, Chris, had arrived in the compound shortly before me and had already dressed the wound. I briefly discussed my management plan. I knew the wound was going to be contaminated with dirt containing a high faecal content, and there would likely be a delay in evacuating him, so my highest priority was to get some antibiotics into him. Other than that, the immediate plan was to get his pain under good control and clean the wound as best as we could.

I took the dressing down and inspected the wound. There was no ongoing bleeding, but the chunk taken out of Mick's shin was significant. Chris established a drip in Mick's arm through which we gave him some morphine for the pain and then commenced an infusion of intravenous antibiotics. I then drew up a vial of local anaesthetic and was injecting it directly into the wound – to numb the site before we cleaned it and save Mick a bit of agony – when one of the shooters on the roof above said something that made my ears prick up.

'Fuck, I've just been shot.' The voice sounded very casual given the content of the statement.

I dropped what I was doing and stuck my head out of the door, craning my neck to look up to the roof. The guy who had spoken was holding a lead projectile from an enemy rifle. The projectile was complete and un-deformed and had struck him in the chest with minimal force, lodging in his body armour without significant impact. It was a lucky escape; the well-aimed bullet must have been at the very end of its trajectory when it struck our guy. He laughed it off, but I did notice him exchanging his baseball cap for a Kevlar helmet before resuming his fighting position.

I went back to Mick and commenced cleaning the wound with a bag of sterile intravenous fluid. The hole in his shin was around the size of a 50-cent coin and it had left the bone exposed. Running a gloved finger along it confirmed that the bone too was damaged, with a considerable chip taken out of the front of it, but there was no obvious evidence of a fracture extending through it.

I was finishing up – packing the wound with gauze and applying a new dressing – when Brett entered the room to get an opinion on the injury. We weren't due to extract until the early hours of the following morning, and although Mick's wounds weren't life- or limb-threatening we decided that the best plan would be to get an AME bird in to take him off target during daylight hours. That way, Mick could receive surgical care in a timely fashion and it would save us having to stretcher-carry him out to our planned extraction point.

No sooner had we decided to call a bird in for Mick than a transmission came over the radio informing us of two more casualties who were inbound to our location.

The two turned up on foot, which was a good sign. They had been part of a patrol conducting a clearance of an enemy compound from which their element was receiving intermittent fire. Hugging the outer wall of the roofless compound as they tactically approached the main door to make entry, they were stopped in their tracks by the crackle of a Taliban radio immediately on the other side of the wall. One of the commandos had instantly grabbed a grenade from his chest rig and, after pulling the pin from it, let it cook for a couple of seconds before lobbing it over the wall at the enemy. Just one metre away, though shielded from sight by the wall, the enemy fighter had heard the approach of our guys and was doing the exact same thing. The grenades hit the dirt on both sides of the wall simultaneously. After a split-second pause to recognise the threat, the friendly element had starburst in all directions away from the enemy grenade as it detonated. Small pieces of frag from the grenade had caught two of our guys but fortunately hadn't inflicted critical injuries.

The pair joined us in the room where we were finishing up Mick's treatment, and Chris and I reviewed their wounds. The first commando had got away lightly, with a single piece of frag entering his inner right arm at the level of the elbow. Initially concerned about a potential arterial injury, I checked the shooter's wrist pulses, confirming that they were both present.

I tasked Chris with putting a drip into that casualty to administer intravenous antibiotics, and I set about assessing the second grenade casualty. He had copped a few more fragmentation wounds located in slightly more concerning places. Fortunately, his body armour had taken the brunt of the blast and frag, but a few small pieces had found their way around his Kevlar and lodged in the left side of his chest wall and his back. He seemed fine, but there was no way of knowing with certainty whether the frag had penetrated his lung or other vital organs. I had a good listen to his heart and lungs with my stethoscope, reassured that it all sounded normal, but I was still concerned that there might be a blood vessel or a lung slowly leaking in his chest that would declare itself later.

I spoke again with Brett and we concluded that we should AME both grenade casualties on the same bird we were calling in for Mick. Better to get them to a medical facility, where they could be X-rayed and have their wounds assessed properly, than keep them in the field and risk having them deteriorate during a firefight, or at night, when AME extraction would be far more complicated and dangerous. Brett composed a 9-liner and transmitted it through to request non-urgent AME for our three guys.

Due to the complexity of the urban terrain in the village, the only place for the AME bird to land was the field we had walked through on our insertion two nights earlier, where the Taliban had airburst the RPG above our lead element; a field overlooked by the very compound the two grenade casualties had been attempting to clear when they were injured.

We formed a stretcher team for Mick, and a security party for the move, then, using the only stretcher we had with us on the mission, loaded Mick up and made our way to the edge of the field.

During the walk to the landing zone I discussed with Brett the pros and cons of trying to reclaim our stretcher after we had loaded Mick onto the aircraft. My primary concern was the amount of time the bird would have to spend on the ground while trying to get Mick off the stretcher in the cramped confines of the back of a Black Hawk. My feeling was that we should race out, chuck Mick onto the aircraft, and cut our losses with the stretcher to allow the bird to get away faster. Brett was adamant that we didn't want to lose our only stretcher. What if we had another casualty that afternoon? he argued. I eventually conceded that keeping the stretcher was a good idea, and we agreed to unload Mick onto the bird and then reclaim it.

Immediately upon arrival to a safe compound at the edge of the field we were greeted with a burst of machine-gun fire, which kicked up dirt about 20 metres away from us and confirmed that the casualty extraction was not going to go unchallenged.

'Still want to fuck around keeping our stretcher?' I asked Brett.

He ignored me.

A pair of Apaches had been dispatched with the AME Black Hawk, and the three-bird package became audible over a nearby mountain range. Safely concealed in the foyer of our compound, the JTAC, who had moved forward with our element, called the Apaches onto the enemy machine-gun position. One of the shooters with our group loaded up a red smoke grenade in the 40 mm under-slung grenade launcher of his M4 and fired it at the enemy compound. Using the red smoke as a target indicator, the two Apaches came in low and slow over the field and hosed the enemy compound with 30 mm cannon fire. To their credit, as the second bird came in for its run, the insurgents lit up the gunship with a PKM machine gun, causing the aircraft to up the ante and deliver a Hellfire in response. The missile annihilated the front wall of the enemy compound – and, I suspect, any occupants – with the thunderous explosion from the strike rocking the compound we were in. Seconds after delivering the Hellfire, the Apache gained altitude and banked away as the AME Black Hawk swooped in on its final approach to collect our casualties.

Brett dashed out into the field and threw a green smoke grenade to designate the landing zone. The Black Hawk approached from diagonally opposite our position on the edge of the field, and flew low and fast directly towards the recently destroyed enemy compound. Not registering immediately what was going on, we all stood bemused, watching the bird heading in the wrong direction and on a trajectory directly towards the enemy, before it clicked.

'GREEN SMOKE, GREEN SMOKE, GREEN SMOKE!' the JTAC yelled into his microphone. The AME pilot had mistakenly taken the red smoke used to mark the enemy position for the Apache as the landing indictor for the medical evacuation.

I have no idea whether a Black Hawk has the aerial equivalent of a handbrake, but to the uninitiated that is what it appeared the pilot used to turn his bird around. The machine stood almost vertically on its tail and pivoted harshly, proceeding at speed towards us before flaring forcefully and thumping down in the field, sending a vortex of green smoke and debris into the air. Our party of casualties, stretcher-bearers and myself ran towards the rotor wash of the chopper, and I searched through the dust for the flight medic to hand over to.

The casualty handover process varied between medics and was dependent also on the tactical situation; on that occasion it became abundantly clear that the flight medic had no intention of disembarking the bird to hear what I had to say. The pilots and crew knew that the landing zone was hot, and their sole function was to land, load the casualties and go – quickly. I leaned into the helicopter and identified the flight medic, grabbing him by the collar of his flight suit and pulling him in close.

'THREE CASUALTIES, ALL PENETRATING TRAUMA, ALL STABLE,' I shouted, holding my right thumb up to indicate that all was good with the guys.

He nodded, seeming happy enough with my limited handover.

I gave him the casualty cards for the guys, which contained written detail on their injuries and management, and backed out of the helicopter.

One of the aircrew had thrown out a replacement stretcher that I stumbled backwards onto as I moved away from the aircraft. Unfortunately, it was a rigid, fixed, full-length stretcher, and was of little use to us in our situation due to it not being easily man-packable. I picked it up and slid it back onto the floor of the helicopter. As I shoved the stretcher back in, I looked across at the guys who had loaded Mick onto the bird and saw them struggling to get our small stretcher out from under him. The helicopter seemed to have been on the ground for an eternity, and over the noise of its engines and rotors it was impossible to tell if we were being shot at or not. I looked around to the compound where the remainder of our element was to try to gauge whether they were in contact with the enemy, but they didn't appear to be. I then looked back past the tail rotor of the AME bird and studied the recently destroyed enemy compound for signs of life, but I didn't see anything of concern. As I did so, one of the Apaches passed low over the compound to assess the destruction caused by their missile strike and dissuade any further enemy activity. Reassured that no-one was shooting at us, I glanced back into the passenger compartment of the AME bird in time to see a businesslike Brett draw his Spyderco rescue knife and cut the final straps that were snagging our stretcher on the aircraft, reefing it out from under Mick. The moment it came free we all turned and ran from the bird so it could power up and depart. Escorted by the Apaches, it disappeared back over the mountain range.

We rejoined the guys in the compound foyer on the edge of the field and I retrieved my medical kit, which I had left there when I went out to do the handover with the flight medic.

One of the shooters in the group had brought with him a six-pack of local orange-flavoured soft drink that he had liberated from a shop in the bazaar. Seeing it made me realise I hadn't had anything to drink since my coffee that morning, and I couldn't remember the last time I had taken a piss. It was after midday by that stage and the temperature had climbed into the mid-40s Celsius. My mouth was as dry as a chip, so I cracked one of the soft drinks and threw it back. It was disgusting, the warm fluid tasting like Fanta mixed with a teaspoon of dirt. It left me feeling worse than I had before, but at least it delivered some much-needed fluid and sugar to my system.

On return to the CHQ compound I debriefed Sean on the casualties and dropped my kit in the shade to get some rest before the next session kicked off.

As the afternoon progressed, the enemy was rousing from their midday intermission. Continuing the trend of the previous 36 hours, their activity recommenced with intermittent fire, building momentum as the sun began its march towards the horizon and the air cooled. Hollywood and I took our position on the roof and once again exchanged periodic fire with the enemy in the compounds to our front.

At around 1600 hours we heard a firefight break out close to our position.

A small team of commandos, led by Brett Wood, had been advancing through an aqueduct towards the enemy compounds to clear the machine-gun positions when two Taliban fighters compromised them. Immediately engaging the enemy, Brett's element hit one of the Talibs before they both fled, leaving a blood trail in the dirt for the commandos to follow.

My understanding of what happened next comes from talking with the guys involved and helmet camera footage of the clearance. Like a pack of the very wolves that feature on the commando company's logo, Brett's team mercilessly pursued the enemy through a convoluted series of compounds and alleyways. Knowing that all civilians had long left the village by that time, they threw grenades over compound walls and shot locks off doors before kicking them in and rapidly clearing the mudbrick buildings. Moving at pace through the enemy compounds, Brett's team found the machine-gun positions the enemy had been using, but no enemy. Probing deeper into Taliban territory, the team burst out of one compound midway along a dirt alley, bordered on both sides by high walls. Moving tactically, the team was split, two down one side and two down the other, staggered from each other and hugging the walls. They slowed as they approached a T-intersection at the end of the alley. The front-left shooter in the team, Matty, peered cautiously around the left-hand bend of the intersection, his M4 on instant and finger poised on the trigger ready to engage. The way ahead was clear and, with Matty covering him, Brett, who had been following close behind, moved past Matty's right shoulder to lead the team deeper into the enemy's lair.

From my position I could hear the sporadic gunfire and grenade blasts as the clearance force blew locks and cleared compounds. I was squinting through our rooftop keyhole to gauge where the clearance force was when, 150 metres to the front of our position, I caught sight of a telltale plume of dust and smoke that was instantly followed by the ear-splitting blast wave from a massive explosion.

For a few moments the village fell deathly quiet. My heart sank. The blast had come from the exact area where Brett's team had been pursuing the two insurgents they had engaged minutes earlier.

I raced down from my rooftop position and grabbed my medical pack in anticipation of casualties. After hastily donning my pack, the JTAC and myself made our way to the front entrance of our compound, where we anxiously awaited a radio transmission to clarify the situation. My heart thumped steadily in my chest. Clearly, I wasn't the only one craving information; as I listened through my earpiece, the back half of a broken transmission came through the radio from Sean requesting information on the blast.

'Yeah, all good,' responded one of the snipers who had been providing overwatch to the clearance force. Relieved, I started making my way back into our compound, but it turned out the sniper had mistakenly interpreted the broken transmission as a communications check and was confirming that he had heard it.

The next voice in my earpiece was that of a shooter with Brett's clearance force, and in a voice that was pressured without being panicked, he delivered a message that would change things forever.

'We need a fucking medivac right now – we've got a triple amputee.'

The JTAC and I turned and ran towards the PHQ position. We bolted through the same maze of dirt alleyways that I had traversed with Brett that morning, screaming the friendly force identification code as we approached the entrance to the PHQ compound. On arrival, a quick reaction force (QRF) had been assembled and were kitting up to respond to the situation under the leadership of a commando named Todd Langley.

Todd was a consummate professional: a highly passionate and experienced special operations soldier who had been decorated with the Commendation for Distinguished Service for leadership in combat not once but twice. He was not the model of fitness one might expect of a special forces soldier, and was seldom seen without a cigarette hanging out of the corner of his mouth (I once heard another shooter suggest that Todd treated his body more like an amusement park than a temple), but when the chips were down, Todd was the guy you wanted leading the charge – and the chips were definitely down.

I touched base with Todd and suggested that the casualty would likely require a blood transfusion, and that at least one member of the QRF should have O-type blood in case I needed to harvest blood from them to transfuse into the casualty. In a hospital situation, a complex series of blood checks and a process known as a cross-match is undertaken prior to blood transfusion, but this was in extremis.

Todd put out the call for anyone with O-type blood, with a positive response coming from a shooter who was already part of the QRF. Scott was a tall, solid, bear-like individual who spoke infrequently. He was a man's man, who I had only ever seen present medically on one occasion, after sustaining a significant injury in a training accident. I had assumed he was presenting to get a medical certificate and was somewhat surprised when he just wanted some basic analgesia to knock the edge off the pain and allow him to get on with his soldiering.

The remainder of the QRF comprised Chris (the medic who had helped me treat the casualties from that morning), the JTAC and a few more shooters. Within minutes of us arriving at the PHQ position, our element was ready to respond.

Led by Todd, we set off single file at a running pace across the open ground where the resupply drop had gone awry the night before and reached the boundary of the enemy compound series. Clinging to the mudbrick walls for cover, we continued running to the start of the dirt alleyway leading to the compound Brett's team had fallen back to. Todd paused and scanned the alley briefly before turning to the rest of us and issuing an instruction that I believe to this day may have saved my life.

'It looks a bit dodgy down here – stick to the hard-packed dirt.'

And with that Todd disappeared around the corner into the alleyway, heading towards the incident site.

Todd had noticed areas of loose dirt on the ground that could easily be concealing IED-initiating pressure plates. Having just sustained a casualty from a blast, Todd was expecting that there would be further bombs littered around the place to maim or kill more of us. With that thought in the forefront of his mind, and clearly understanding the risk to himself, he warned us of the danger and then proceeded into the fray without hesitation to help an injured mate. That was the calibre of the man.

I bolted down the alleyway with my eyes glued to the ground, playing a lethal game of hopscotch over the loose areas of dirt and attempting to step precisely where the soldier in front of me had. Up ahead, the lead QRF elements were peeling left through a doorway. As I approached the entrance to the compound I saw thick, blood-soaked drag marks; this was my first indication of the severity of the injury suffered by the casualty within.

I turned into the compound, ducking my head to pass through the low doorway, and as I entered my eyes fixed on a large chunk of burned debris for a brief second before moving a few metres past it to the wounded man. Lying on his back, ashen grey from shock, in a pool of black, bloodstained dirt, was one of our own, horrendously damaged, and flanked by two shooters industriously cutting away his clothing and assessing his wounds. A second casualty stood stunned, several metres behind the first, his pants and shirt cut up the sides of their legs and arms respectively, and hanging loosely off him like rags. His helmet and glasses were still intact, and he was caked in dirt.

I directed Chris to the second casualty and I made my way towards the first, approaching from the end where his legs had once been. Passing down his left side, I noticed the glistening white of exposed bones providing a dramatic contrast with the dirt below. Moving towards his head, I could see wounds on the left side of the casualty's torso, raising concerns that, while the blast had initiated from below, he may have chest injuries. I cast off my medical kit and kneeled in the dirt with the casualty's head between my knees to begin my management. I was assaulted by the coppery smell of blood mixed with burned flesh and cordite as I leaned forward to assess his airway and breathing, while surveying his body for any evidence of ongoing bleeding.

The initial medical treatment of the casualty had been outstanding, with arterial tourniquets in place on his amputated limbs stemming the loss of further blood. One of the first responders had inserted a plastic airway in the casualty's mouth, which was moving air effectively. Breathing was fast and shallow, and owing to the injuries on his torso, I feared that pressure was building inside his chest from a punctured lung. I instinctively drew a needle from the front pocket of my body armour and swiftly inserted it through the casualty's left upper chest wall. Expecting to hear a rush of air and to see an immediate improvement in his breathing, I was instead met with silence, and the casualty's breathing remained unchanged.

His eyes were open and wandered around the compound, a peaceful look on his face; he was clearly unaware and in a deep state of shock.

Up until this point, I hadn't thought to wonder who I was treating. I'd seen him as a casualty rather than a person, a medical puzzle to be solved rather than a dying teammate; I had started my drills with no emotional involvement. But now, as his wandering eyes briefly met mine, I registered who it was.

'Fuck, is this Woodrow?' I asked of one of the assisting shooters.

The shooter confirmed that it was indeed Brett Wood, and the dreadful reality of the situation hit me like a wrecking ball.

Over the years, both as a junior doctor and during my previous stint in Afghanistan, I had seen dozens of people die horrible deaths. But the patient was always a stranger, and I was generally subordinate to a senior doctor running the resuscitation. This time was different. This time it was a friend of mine dying in the dirt in front of me, and it was my job to save him.

Having excluded ongoing external blood loss and a tension pneumothorax in the left side of Brett's chest, his shocked state was most likely the result of the blood already lost prior to the application of tourniquets. Brett's body was lethally low on blood and was shutting down flow to the peripheries to preserve his vital organs. I assessed the carotid pulse in his neck. It was barely palpable.

I called for Scott, the shooter with O-type blood, to come over. Taking a purpose-specific transfusion bag out of my medical kit, I slid the large needle attached to the bag into one of his correspondingly large arm veins. The flow of dark red, venous blood was instantaneous, tracking down the tubing and collecting in the bag. I turned back to Brett to see that his eyes were now closed, and his laboured breathing had become even more rapid.

While I had been cannulating the blood donor, one of the other shooters had been unsuccessfully attempting to insert an intravenous drip into Brett. With no alternative, and an urgent need to bolster Brett's failing blood pressure, I retrieved the intraosseous drill from my pack and established access into the bone marrow of the top of his left upper arm bone. Having confirmed the cannula's placement, I attached a bag of fluids, instructing another bystander to squeeze the bag tightly to force the fluids into Brett's system. It wouldn't be as lifesaving as blood, but it might buy us vital time.

Glancing back at the blood collection bag, I assessed it to be half full and resisted the temptation to unplug it at that point to commence the transfusion. The collection bag contained a series of chemicals to stop the blood from clotting, and if these were not diluted with the appropriate volume of blood, they might do more harm than good. Brett was hanging by a thread, and it was a risk we couldn't take. As impossible as it seemed in the moment, we had to be patient.

I yelled out to Chris to give me an update on the second casualty. He responded that the patient – it was Matty – was badly fragged through his arms but had no life-threatening injuries.

Turning my attention back to Brett, I saw he was now unconscious. His breathing had become increasingly shallow and the movement of his chest with his breaths was almost imperceptible. I turned back to Scott and reassessed the blood collection bag, which was finally full. Removing the needle from Scott's arm, I hastily started to attach the transfusion-giving set.

Behind me, one of the shooters at Brett's side said, 'I think he's stopped breathing. Should I start CPR?'

I spun around to confirm that breathing had indeed ceased and told the shooter to commence chest compressions. Handing the blood to another shooter to hook up to the intraosseous cannula, I drew up a shot of adrenaline and injected it in a last-ditch attempt to jolt Brett's heart back into activity. I hoped against hope that if we could just get some adrenaline into him to stimulate his heart and top him up with fresh, warm blood, we could keep him going long enough to get an AME bird in.

Compressions continued as the blood moved steadily through the giving set and into Brett's system. More adrenaline followed. After a further minute of chest compressions, Brett let out a long sigh, which I now believe was the exact moment at which we lost him. It was a noise I had heard before during failed resuscitations. I imagine it has something to do with the diaphragm relaxing for the last time, forcing all the air out of the lungs, but I associate it with the sound of the soul leaving the body.

At that moment, a shooter with the QRF who had positioned himself on the roof of the compound let off a few rounds, causing me to start. I had been completely absorbed in Brett's medical management and was oblivious to the tactical situation developing around me. It was getting dark and the Taliban, sensing that we were bogged down with a casualty, were probing our position.

Scott approached me and quietly suggested that time was running out. AME birds had been called in and were in a holding pattern waiting to extract our casualties. They could only stay on station a further 30 minutes before they went bingo on fuel. We needed to move.

I ordered chest compressions to stop and assessed Brett for any signs of life. There were none.

Standing, I turned to find everyone in the room watching me in silence. I offered them two words: 'Brett's gone.'

One shooter reacted with a brief emotional outburst, kicking a nearby door before immediately regaining composure.

I wrote the time of death – 1750 hours – on the back of my hand with a permanent marker then looked back at the men.

All eyes were still on me, waiting to see what came next.

Fortunately, prior to deployment I'd had an in-depth discussion with a fellow special operations medic who had lost a soldier in the field under similar circumstances, and I had a mental framework in place to deal with this situation. The medic had advised me to cover the remains of the casualty to avoid anyone seeing their face or injuries unnecessarily and forming memories that would likely come back to haunt them. With that in mind, I put out an open request to the other members of the QRF to find some blankets in the compound to cover Brett, and requested the stretcher that we had used to carry Mick to the AME bird that morning. The very stretcher that Brett had been so intent on retaining would be the stretcher on which we carried him off target. It was as if, on some level, Brett knew the fate awaiting him, and his determination to retrieve the stretcher was his final selfless act; he would not inconvenience his brothers by forcing them to carry him without a stretcher.

A shooter recovered some blankets from another room in the compound, and I gently wrapped Brett's remains in them. Another two shooters unrolled the stretcher and began loading Brett onto it.

The light was starting to fail as I repacked my medical kit and prepared to leave the compound to affect the AME for the other casualties from the blast. As well as Matty, who was badly fragged through his arms, there were two shooters who had been on the opposite side of the alley when the device initiated. They had copped the full force of the blast wave of the bomb, which knocked them to the ground. Even though they seemed more or less unscathed, I would need to keep a close eye on them for developing signs of internal injuries not visible at first glance.

I fell in with the other members of the QRF, filing out of the compound and heading back down the alley on our way to the AME location. I had been looking down at my chest, attaching my M4 back to the sling on my body armour, when a commando in front of me yelled, 'STOP!'

I froze dead in my tracks, and looked up. With terror etched on his face, the shooter was holding up one open hand, as if to somehow arrest my movement. Once he had my attention, he pointed to the ground in front of me. My right foot was resting inside the perimeter of a pink circle spray-painted on the dirt.

While we had been working on Brett inside the compound, the brave men of the Special Operations Engineer Regiment had searched the alley and, finding two additional IEDs in the soft dirt, marked them with pink paint. Todd had been right when he assessed the alleyway as dodgy; I had come within inches of detonating a device. I thanked the shooter profusely, gingerly removed my right foot from within the pink circle and continued down the alleyway, making sure to give the other pink circle a wide berth.

Our move to the AME landing zone was slowed by sporadic enemy fire, and we arrived at the field just on dusk. The 9-liner we'd sent indicated that we had two CAT-A casualties, and so there were two Black Hawk AME birds on station to extract our guys, with a pair of Apaches once again providing gunship support.

On arrival at the same compound foyer from which we had staged that morning's evacuation, one of the shooters who had been on the opposite side of the alleyway with Brett's clearance force approached to inform me that something felt unusual in his left ear. Moving his jaw in circles, he was clearly trying to pop, or equalise, his ear as he spoke to me. Inspecting the ear canal with a scope, I saw that his eardrum had been ruptured by the massive pressure of the blast, leading me to suspect he may have sustained further injuries from the explosion. Fearing blast lung, a condition in which the lungs becomes damaged as a high-explosive blast wave imparts energy into the tissues as it passes through the body, I assessed the shooter's oxygen levels with my pulse oximeter. The low reading suggested that he had indeed suffered a degree of blast lung, and I recommended we get him out of there with the AME for fear of him deteriorating over the next few hours in the field. He reluctantly agreed to go on the first AME bird with Matty. Suspecting that the fourth member of the clearance force may have similar injuries, I examined him to find that he too had a burst eardrum and evidence of blast lung, although not as severe. He begrudgingly agreed to be evacuated on the second AME bird and escort Brett's remains back to base. Remarkably, despite their injuries, these two shooters had been the ones to drag both Matty and Brett to safety and initiate their medical management. It was only at this point, long after the blast and after ensuring that everyone had safely retreated from the enemy compound series, that they had admitted to their injuries.

The Taliban had seen our AME that morning and knew what was coming next. Anticipating the opportunity to target the AME bird, they began to fire a few ranging bursts from a machine-gun position in the compound directly adjacent to the one the Apache had destroyed that morning. Racing against time before the Black Hawks ran out of fuel and complete darkness set in, the Apaches did a low suppressing gun run on the enemy machine gun, and the first of the AME birds screamed in and smacked down in front of us, again vectored in by a smoke grenade. We ran out with our first two casualties – Matty and the shooter with the worst blast wave injuries – and helped them on board. The AME medic had no interest whatsoever in a handover, waving me off as I leaned into the helicopter to engage him. That was perfectly fine with me, and in a matter of seconds the casualties were loaded and the bird was airborne.

As we ran back to the compound, a sustained burst of enemy machine-gun fire cracked high over our heads, aimed at the AME chopper and prompting a second strafing run from the Apaches. Several shooters from our element were engaging the enemy position with their M4s and 40 mm high explosive grenades.

In the foyer, the JTAC was on the radio with the second AME Black Hawk, and it was clear from his side of the conversation that they were reconfirming the absolutely necessity of them coming in, given the guarantee of taking enemy fire. The JTAC and I had a quick exchange and concluded that the risk to the second bird was not warranted. We had one guy with a blown eardrum, and Brett's body, which we could carry off target with us. It wasn't worth risking a helicopter, and the lives of the crew, by attempting to bring them in to land. The JTAC dismissed the second AME bird as darkness fell, and we set about preparing for night operations by mounting NVG on our helmets, and switching on and testing our aiming lasers.

I radioed Sean at the CHQ position to give him an update on the situation, and was advised to stay in my current location; the CHQ would need to come through my current location to extract and could pick me up on their way. The plan was for our entire element to consolidate on the edge of the village then walk the 8 kilometres out into the desert where Chinooks would come in and pick us up.

I sat with Brett's wrapped remains, and under subdued red light from a head torch wrote notes on his medical management while the detail was fresh in my mind. I also completed his confirmation of death certificate, a supply of which I had carried in my pack for just such an occasion, though I'd hoped I would never need them. As I documented the events, it occurred to me that I hadn't eaten all day, so I retrieved some dry biscuits from my MRE and forced them down, despite my lack of hunger.

With the onset of darkness the enemy fire had died down and a strong wind was picking up. When the time came to begin our exfiltration, a dust storm was raging, with gale-force winds ripping through the village. The long procession of special operators started snaking its way off target and into the dust and darkness. I was the very last man in the order of march, and I stood looking back down the windswept centre of the village through my NVG, waiting for every other member of our element to leave, before picking up my kit and moving off.

I stopped and turned back towards the village occasion-ally, to ensure we weren't being followed by the enemy. It was an eerie sight. Several of the compounds in the village were ablaze from the fighting, and they glowed bright green in my goggles amid the otherwise dim scene. Doors to abandoned compounds were being slammed open and shut with the wind, and the moving shadows of trees danced across the ground, drawing my attention and the beam from the aiming laser on my M4. I stood for more than a minute surveying the scene, and feeling a sickening sensation in my core, as if I was in the presence of pure evil and looking back at the very gates of hell.

When I turned again into the dust storm, the soldier in front of me had stopped and was looking back at me, his body language saying, *What the fuck are you doing?* I gestured to him that everything was fine, and he turned and continued marching.

The going was slow, across fields of crops and then a series of low hills before we cleared the outskirts of the village and entered the moonscape of the desert.

The platoon of commandos mounted in the Bushmasters had made their way down to secure our exfiltration route and provide support to us in case we were pursued out of town by the enemy. They had heard the news about Brett and were out of their cars to greet us in the darkness, and to hear first-hand what had happened. Some of Brett's closest friends were among the platoon, and his body was briefly placed in one of the Bushmasters to allow his mates to pay their last respects to him.

As I filed through the Bushmaster position, I stopped to talk to one of the commandos who was a good mate of mine. From the small fridge in his vehicle he had been handing out bottles of ice-cold Gatorade to our element as we came past.

After 48 hours of drinking warm water and disgusting soft drink, the chilled Gatorade was heavenly.

We left the Bushmaster position shortly after and continued to our designated helicopter extraction zone for a 0200 hours pick-up. Precisely on time as always, the Night Stalkers emerged out of the dark sky and began their final approach to our position, zeroing in on a flashing infrared strobe, and touching down just long enough for us to board before taking to the skies again. I dropped my pack on the floor of the bird and fell exhausted into my seat, switching off my NVG and cramming in a set of earplugs to dull the noise of the helicopter. I closed my eyes and rested my head back against the airframe, my tired mind racing with the activities of the past 48 hours, and tried to organise my thoughts for the mortuary affairs procedures I would need to follow when we landed.

Forty minutes later we touched down on the same airstrip we had departed from a little more than two days prior. An ambulance was waiting to take Brett's body to the hospital, along with the blast casualty we hadn't been able to AME off target. I handed over the relevant paperwork to the ambulance crew, and trudged back to my room on base to drop off my kit. Then I made my way down to the hospital, where Brett's body was being medically processed for handover to the relevant authorities.

Although it was past 0300 hours by now, a large crowd of devastated special operations soldiers had massed outside the resuscitation room where Brett had been taken, hoping for a chance to pay their final respects to their fallen brother. I made my way past them and into the room to find Brett's body covered up to the chest by a clean white sheet while hospital staff washed his torso and face. The look on my face must have indicated a desire to be alone, and they respectfully left without a word.

I could hardly bring myself to look at Brett. I felt broken and racked with guilt for not being able to save him. I gently rested my hand on his head and apologised to him for not being able to do better. His face was undamaged and appeared peaceful; if not for its lack of colour, you might have thought he was sleeping.

By the time I had repacked my kit with everything required it was after 0500, and I was due on a helicopter at 0645 for a job with another element. I showered and lay on my bed for the first of countless sleepless nights I would spend running through Brett's failed resuscitation in my mind.

The alarm came as a welcome distraction from my thoughts. The deep fatigue I felt was irrelevant; this was what my selection and training had prepared me for. Jacked up on caffeine and stress hormones, an hour later I found myself sitting on a US State Department Mil Mi-17 'Hip' helicopter, once more on my way deep into Taliban territory.

We would have an IED initiate on us that day as well, followed by a good burst of AK-47 fire to complete the ambush. Fortunately, the IED was initiated by the enemy a little early, when we were still about 30 metres from it. The ground erupted in front of us, spraying a plume of dirt and debris in all directions but leaving us unharmed. A pair of Taliban in the vicinity then opened up with a long automatic burst from an AK-47 that shredded the knee-high grass between members of our element. I remember watching, as if in slow motion, as the grass to my immediate right was raked with fire and swayed as though a strong breeze was blowing through it.

The enemy's intent was clearly to follow up the small-arms fire with an RPG, however the Talib wielding the rocket was shot before he could unleash it, dropping the rocket launcher before managing to run away with his AK-47-toting friend. We followed his blood trail for several hundred metres before losing it.

The rest of the day passed without incident and we extracted that afternoon unopposed.

We paid our final respects to Brett several days later with a memorial service, followed by a slow-marching funeral procession behind an SOTG fighting vehicle that contained his coffin draped in an Australian flag. The procession made its way down to the main airstrip on base, where Brett was loaded onto a waiting C-130 Hercules to commence his journey home.

The complete SOTG stood on the hot airstrip as the Hercules closed its back ramp and taxied to the start of the runway. We stood at attention and saluted our fallen brother as the large aircraft gained speed down the airstrip and lumbered into the sky, banking left over the mountains surrounding Tarin Kowt then disappearing over the horizon.

The war went on much the same, but everything had changed. The confronting reality of our vulnerability finally struck me. If a soldier of Brett's calibre could be killed, none of us was safe.

XII

JOHN'S SECOND ARSEHOLE

B<small>RETT'S</small> <small>DEATH SERVED AS A FULCRUM, A TIPPING POINT AT</small> which normal human emotion left me, to be replaced by a dark set of psychological tools that seemed far more appropriate to the task at hand. The shadow of my psyche now began to envelop me, providing the armour required to continue.

My keen interest in medical training became near maniacal. On every occasion where I wasn't otherwise occupied, I would organise realistic combat casualty scenarios, drilling my skills in assessing and treating gunshot and blast wounds into muscle memory. I inflicted the same brutal regimen on the medics under my command, often berating them when I perceived a less-than-perfect performance, reducing them to near tears on more than one occasion.

The autopsy report on Brett had not yet been provided, and I was plagued by the thought that I had missed something.

Training relentlessly provided not only a distraction, but also an opportunity to further sharpen my own skills and those of my medics. Underpinning my efforts was the hope that if one of my medics was unable to save a teammate in the future, they would at least know they had done all they possibly could, and they would not find themselves racked by the guilt I was experiencing. But while my intent was good, I failed to realise that I was taking my emotions out on my medics, and driving a wedge between myself and them.

One victim of my emotional vortex was Brad, the young commando medic who had competently managed the child with the gunshot wound on the final mission of my first tour. Brad was once again deployed, and during a high-fidelity casualty training with some US Navy SEAL medics, he had uncharacteristically quit mid-scenario owing to some technical issues with the training equipment, requesting we reset and start again.

I saw red. Expecting that he would improvise and continue despite the adversity, I perceived his quitting as akin to giving up on the resuscitation of a wounded comrade. In my frame of mind at the time, I regarded Brad as arrogant; it seemed to me that his confidence exceeded his competence. Whether that was true, or whether my own mental state was colouring my perception, I'm not sure. Either way, I wasn't going to tolerate that attitude from a medic under my command, and on conclusion of the training serial I called Brad into my office and ripped into him. He was visibly shaken at the time, but to his absolute credit he took the criticism on board and adjusted his attitude. He remains one of the best medics I ever had the privilege of serving alongside.

Not all medics who incurred my not-too-constructive criticisms responded in such a fashion, and during my SOCOMD service I was instrumental in crushing several special operations medics' career aspirations when they didn't meet my (possibly unnecessarily high) standards. Although I regret this now, at the time I didn't care. I had been given the responsibility of preparing medics for war and had now seen the dire consequences of failure in the role.

Many years later, another of my medics would admit that he frequently felt the urge to punch me in the face during this period.

Although training served its purpose, the best form of distraction for me was missions, and thankfully there were plenty going at the time to occupy my mind.

In 2011 the SOTG had struck up a relationship with a paramilitary branch of US Drug Enforcement Administration (DEA) known as foreign-deployed advisory and support teams, or FAST. The relationship benefitted both parties, with the DEA's counter-narcotic mandate bringing new targeting opportunities to the SOTG, and the SOTG contributing firepower and niche skill sets not integral to the FAST elements or their Afghan partner force. Further sweetening the relationship was the DEA's dedicated aviation assets, which consisted of US State Department-owned Russian Mil Mi-17 helicopters and Huey gunships, piloted by civilian contractors. Although closely resembling cowboys in appearance and actions, the State Department pilots and aircrew were, for the most part, highly experienced ex-military pilots as well as being great guys.

Fortunately for me, the FAST elements lacked higher medical capability, meaning I was included in a five-man special operations liaison element to support the DEA missions, two of which were planned to take place on 6 June 2011, just two weeks after we'd lost Brett.

'Women and children leaving the village to the south,' came the transmission through our earpieces, indicating what we had already sensed; things were about to erupt.

The first indication that we were not welcome guests in the village came in the form of a single shot that zipped into our position and punctured the tyre of an old truck parked in the middle of the bazaar. The crack of the round and the hiss of the tyre served as a warning that we should move to a slightly more protected area to continue rigging the significant pile of captured weapons and drugs for destruction. The layout of the village centre offered a multitude of fire lanes for surrounding enemy to shoot at us from, and within minutes we were receiving probing fire from several directions.

I made my way to one periphery of the village centre and joined a couple of our Afghan partner force soldiers. They gestured animatedly towards a compound series approximately 300 metres away.

Taking a stance behind an upright 44-gallon drum, I rested my rifle on the drum to stabilise my firing position and scanned the compound series through the magnified scope of my rifle. The reticle of my rifle scope moved up and down slowly with my breathing as I methodically moved my field of view between the doorways and windows in search of targets. As I watched, an armed insurgent darted out of one compound, headed to the next. *Crack, crack*. I let off two rounds, only to watch him reach his destination safely, my rounds splashing in the dirt short and to the left of my target. Aiming high and

230

right to compensate for distance and wind, I sent a further two rounds at the target building and watched them strike exactly where the insurgent had been. With a good idea how far to aim off, I continued to observe the target buildings for another opportunity to present. It was not long before that opportunity came.

As I watched intently, my eye was caught by movement on the compound roof. Focusing on that area, I could see what looked like a head popping up and down. The Huey gunships were doing low runs over the compounds, trying to find targets for themselves. Unsurprisingly, every time the bird went over the head I was watching would disappear below the roofline.

As I continued to scan the roof of the compound, the rate of insurgent fire into the centre of the village from the other side of town intensified. I could hear the suppressed weapons of our element firing in response, interspersed with the louder crack of the AK-47s of our Afghan partner force. Things were heating up.

Shortly thereafter a transmission came over our radios informing us that the Hueys were heading back to base to refuel and would then return to escort the Mi-17s on extraction from our current target and reinsertion onto our next job. With the birds gone, my insurgent friend made his move. As I continued to surveil the roofline, I noticed a figure intermittently exposing himself to the level of his mid-torso above the roof. Due to the orientation of the compound he was in, he was visible to my location but protected from the view of our main element located in the village centre. His movement suggested that he was climbing up and down a set of internal stairs leading up to the roof, pausing now and then to reach down, as if someone was handing things up to him. It soon became clear what was going on, as the unmistakable barrel and tripod of a machine gun appeared from below the roofline and the insurgent hastily lined it up to face our main element.

This time there was no hesitation; my intent was to take life. I took a sharp breath in, held it, and tightened the grip on my rifle. Aiming off the calculated distance high and right, I gently increased the pressure on my trigger until a single round was released with a suppressed crack. Continuing to hold my breath, I watched the insurgent through my scope, and a fraction of a second later I saw him recoil violently, falling backwards out of sight. Moments later the machine gun disappeared from its rooftop position, retrieved by someone in the compound.

I have no way of knowing whether I killed the man, or indeed if I even hit him; it may have been that a very near miss had scared him shitless and he'd retreated. But I do know that we didn't receive any further fire from that position.

Seconds after I took my shot, my little moment of jubilation was broken by an ear-piercing *crack, crack* from over my right shoulder. Lost in the moment, and focused down my rifle scope, I hadn't been aware of one of the partner force soldiers lining up his unsuppressed AK-47 directly over my shoulder. On seeing that I was having a go, he had decided to chime in with a few rounds as well. It frightened the bejesus out of me and I spun around, instinctively barking at the soldier, '*What the fuck, man?*'

The exact meaning of my words was lost on my non-English-speaking comrade, however he clearly picked up on the theme of my outburst and appeared to apologise sheepishly.

While I had been watching the enemy compound, our engineers had destroyed all the captured drugs and weapons from the village in a series of controlled explosions, and the time for extraction was fast approaching. The Huey gunships had returned from their refuel and were back overhead. The enemy fire remained consistent, and by that time was coming from all directions. We were completely surrounded by Taliban, who had established a perimeter around the village at a distance of several hundred metres.

The partner force soldiers and I were drawn back into the village centre; everyone had to be accounted for prior to extraction. A small element maintained our outer security, while the remainder of the clearance force consolidated in the cover of a series of mudbrick shops. To the rear of our position, a massive plume of black smoke billowed from a fuel depot that had ignited during the firefight. Immediately to our front was a dirt clearing, about the width of a football field, and surrounded by dirt berms and mud walls. The structures surrounding the clearing offered protection from the enemy firing positions, and for that reason it was chosen as our extraction landing zone. As the JTAC coordinated our pick-up, the air above our heads continued to snap and crackle with the sound of supersonic enemy rounds.

Extraction was to be in three aircraft loads, or chalks, and we organised ourselves into those groups as the first Mi-17 came into view on the horizon. Enemy fire intensified as it commenced its final approach, its right-hand-door gun crackling to life in response. The aircraft flared hard, sending a wave of dust and small rocks in our direction, and then landed in the designated field. The members of chalk one bolted through the dust and piled onto the waiting helicopter. The instant the last man boarded, it departed, drawing a crescendo of enemy fire that was once more reciprocated by the door gunners.

The second bird followed suit, spending a painfully long period of time on the ground before taking off without incident.

Our bird appeared from over the ridge line to our front and began its final approach to the landing zone. Peering up from my rifle scope, I could immediately see something was wrong. It was way too high and going too fast. I watched as the bird sailed straight over the landing zone and continued its descent towards an open field directly in front of a Taliban position. Under heavy fire, it landed in a completely exposed position, a sitting duck for the enemy. Like it or not, it was our ride, and our only option was to get on the thing as quickly as possible and get the fuck out of there.

The group of soldiers providing perimeter security had drawn back to our position at the last possible moment to extract with our chalk. They were clearly confused as to why our helicopter was not where it should be.

'PUSHING THAT WAY!' I yelled as they approached, gesturing in the direction where the helicopter had landed. Then I turned and headed down the side of the mudbrick shop which had been providing us cover and started running up the unprotected slope towards the Mi-17 – and the Taliban fighting position.

I could hear the firefight before I saw it. As I rounded the back of the shop, I looked ahead to see our guys engaging the enemy with large volumes of rifle fire and 40 mm grenades. All hell had broken loose. The Taliban, sensing a good opportunity to take down our helicopter, were jockeying for the best fighting positions in a cemetery up the hill.

A surge of adrenaline energised me, and my 50-kilogram combat load became as light as a feather. Ten or so guys from my chalk were in front of me as we scrambled to the bird, some of them pausing briefly to engage the enemy. Immediately in front of me was Mick, who had caught the shrapnel in his shin on the day we lost Brett, back on the job for the first time since. His injury had required significant surgery, and this affected the pace at which he could run. I closed in behind him as we raced towards the waiting helicopter. Three guys had taken a knee directly under the main rotor on the side of the massive aircraft facing the enemy, and were engaging as I approached. Running past the back of the bird, I joined them to have a ping myself. Immediately to my left was John, a DEA special agent who had become a good friend of mine.

I levelled my rifle at the insurgents and fired.

In that instant time slowed. My focus narrowed and my vision sharpened. Strangely, I was not aware of breathing hard, even though I had just run several hundred metres uphill with a 50-kilo load in 45-degree Celsius heat. My pack weighed nothing. Despite the deafening noise of the helicopter behind me and multiple guns – including the door gun of the Mi-17 – erupting, my world was silent. It was a surreal and very calming experience.

Crack, crack . . . Crack, crack. Spotting an insurgent on the edge of the cemetery, I engaged with four rounds, sending him scurrying for cover. More movement, this time from a position slightly to the right of the first insurgent, was met with another four rounds from my rifle. After another two rounds in the direction of the first guy, I was snapped out of my Zen-like state by a tap on the shoulder and a voice yelling at me that we had a casualty and I should get my arse on the helicopter.

I had been blissfully oblivious to the bullet that passed within inches of my left ear, ripped through the DEA special agent next to me and then slammed into the helicopter behind us. The second before he was shot, John had stood and turned towards the bird. The bullet that tore through his upper-left buttock and exited through the side of his left thigh would have struck him in the head had he not stood at that very moment.

While I had been focused on the insurgents darting between firing positions in the cemetery, John had been knocked to the ground a metre to my left by the enemy bullet and then dragged to the back of the helicopter by other members of the chalk.

I stood and turned in time to see John being unceremoniously shoved into the back of the bird. As I climbed into the helicopter behind him, one of our engineers and a shooter were already going to work on him. The engineer was in the process of removing a combat tourniquet from the front of John's body armour, for use if the wound was low enough on the thigh and bleeding arterially. The shooter was kneeling level with John's pelvis with a set of trauma shears drawn, and was industriously cutting away his bloodstained pants to expose the exact location of the wound. As he peeled them away, I could see the small entrance wound on John's buttock, but the exit wound wasn't immediately apparent. Unclipping my M4 from the sling on my body armour, I laid it down on the seat to my right and grabbed a pressure dressing out of my right thigh pocket. The shooter continued to expose the area around John's left buttock and upper thigh. The engineer, realising that the wound was too high for a tourniquet and that the bleeding was not arterial anyway, began inspecting the rest of John's body for additional injuries. I placed a hand on the back of the shooter's shoulder to get his attention, and he turned his head in acknowledgement.

'LET ME IN THERE!' I screamed over the noise of the helicopter and ongoing gunfire.

At that exact moment the bird lurched forward and up into the air. As we gained altitude the door gunner on the right-hand side of the aircraft got a clear bead on the enemy position and engaged with a sustained burst from his 7.62 mm machine gun.

The shooter shuffled to his left and I kneeled where he had been and continued to cut John's pants away. Using a gloved finger to swipe the blood away from the entrance wound, I established that there was no life-threatening bleeding and that a basic dressing would suffice.

My transition from the application of lethal force on the ground to the medical management of a casualty was seamless. It had become second nature, and rather than existing at opposite ends of a spectrum of behaviour, they had become adjacent.

I leaned forward to talk to John. 'HOW'S THE PAIN?' I yelled.

John, who was chewing away on a piece of gum, forced a smile. 'IT'S FINE,' he replied, giving me a thumbs-up.

I pushed a dressing against the entrance wound with one hand, while using my other to sweep for additional wounds down John's left buttock. Finding no additional blood on my glove after the sweep, I was reassured that he didn't have any other significant wounds in the region.

'ROLL BACK TOWARDS ME!' I yelled, gesturing with my hand for John to shift onto his back, thus wedging the dressing between the floor of the aircraft and his wound to apply pressure.

He winced in pain as he complied.

'HOW'S THE PAIN, JOHN?' I asked again. 'DO YOU WANT MORPHINE?'

'NO!' he responded through another forced smile, still chewing away furiously.

I felt a hand on my shoulder and turned to see another shooter yelling something at me that I didn't quite catch.

'WHAT?' I yelled back.

'WHAT PRIORITY?' the shooter repeated.

I realised that someone must have been transmitting the casualty's information back to base in order to prepare a medical response for his arrival.

'BRAVO!' I yelled back at the shooter over my shoulder. I had assessed that John's life was not in immediate danger, but at that point I was yet to find the exit wound. This meant the bullet might still be inside him, and I was concerned it might have tracked up into his abdomen, causing an internal bleed.

I turned back to John, who had once again moved onto his right side, and gestured again for him to roll onto his back to keep pressure on the dressing over his wound. I then checked the other side of his pelvis and groin, to exclude additional injuries, before reaching my hand up under the front plate of his body armour to palpate his abdomen. Watching his face, I saw him wince in pain as I pushed down on his lower abdomen. *Shit, that's not good*, I thought, my suspicion that he might have internal injuries increasing. Although he appeared to be fine, if he was bleeding internally he could deteriorate into shock at any time.

'FIVE MINUTES,' came the warning from the front of the helicopter and was echoed at a yell throughout the bird. There would be no time for further medical management of John, so I hastily packed up my kit to prepare for insertion on the second target. I had a brief discussion with Mick, who in running to the helicopter for extraction had ripped open his leg wound. He was sensibly opting to stay on the bird and not inserting with us on the second target. I quickly instructed him on what to do if John deteriorated, and then slung my medical pack onto my back and reattached my M4 to my sling. I leaned over John and held out a hand for a high-five, which he gave with a smile.

'THIRTY SECONDS.'

The bird flared over a green field of crops and touched down with pleasingly little dust. We leaped out of the back of the helicopter and ran out 20 metres before forming a perimeter and taking a knee.

The other two Mi-17s had landed just ahead of us, and as we exited our helicopter they were already climbing back into the sky. Our bird powered up behind us and took off, sending a blast of rotor wash in our direction and causing the waist-high crops to sway around us as we picked up and began to move towards the large bazaar that was our second target. I walked over to our chalk commander, Ray, who had seen me coming and stopped to let me catch up. I was laughing as I approached him.

'That was fucking hilarious, man,' Ray said by way of greeting; there was no sympathy among this crowd. Then, aware of the tactical situation and our lack of cover in the middle of the field, he added, 'We should probably get out of here.'

'Fuck me man – GSW buttock,' I said, using the acronym for gunshot wound.

'I thought he got shot in the fucking leg,' Ray said.

Then we switched back to business mode to begin the stomp towards the second target.

In single file, we moved out of the crops and onto a grass strip at the field's perimeter. As I walked, I reflected on the events of the past hour, feeling nothing but elation and pure professional satisfaction. The significance of having potentially shot another human didn't register on any emotional level. The medical mantra of *do no harm* didn't apply here; instead, part of me resented the fact that I had been unable to confirm what damage, if any, my bullet had done to the insurgent. In the years of reflection that would follow, I came to appreciate that uncertainty, preferring to think that I might not have hit the enemy fighter at all, but had merely given him a scare; that possibility would eventually bring me peace and closure. However, as we walked towards the second target of that day, I remained intent on both taking enemy life and preserving that of our own, a juxtaposition that was the practice of Voodoo Medicine.

The shooter in front of me changed out the magazine in his M4 for a full one, prompting me to do the same. It was go time.

XIII

ROWAN ROBINSON

WITHIN MINUTES OF INSERTION OUR CLEARANCE FORCE entered the main street of the bazaar that credible intelligence suggested contained a Taliban heroin storage facility, as well as multiple weapons caches.

Prior to our arrival, two other elements of commandos had been inserted on the second target. Their mission was to clear the marketplace, and then take up strategic blocking positions surrounding it, to suppress the enemy while our clearance force swept through. The bazaar was situated on a gradual slope that steepened into a series of high features on which one of our blocking elements was positioned. A young combat engineer named Rowan Robinson, who at age 23 was on his second special operations tour of Afghanistan, had led that particular element into location.

The blocking elements had been met with heavy enemy

resistance from the moment they inserted and had been forced to fight their way into their positions. The combat had resulted in most of the store owners from the bazaar locking up their shops and returning to the safety of their homes, rendering the market a ghost town by the time we made our way from the landing zone to the first of the shops.

The bottom section of the bazaar consisted of the local butchers' stands, with semi-putrid, flyblown meat sitting on filthy tables, shielded from the midday sun by rusted corrugated-iron sheets on flimsy stands. The whole area stank as we patrolled through it on our way to the heart of the marketplace.

It was the fixed structures of the mudbrick shops that interested us the most, as these would afford superior hiding places to harbour Taliban drugs and weapon caches – and the fact that the enemy had put up such opposition to our blocking elements suggested they did indeed have something to hide.

In a coordinated fashion we continued our search of the bazaar, using boltcutters to bust the padlocks off doors and systematically searching the shops for contraband. Acutely aware that the Taliban might have booby-trapped doors or items within the shops before leaving, engineers led our search teams into any suspect buildings and cleared any suspicious items before we handled them.

It wasn't long before we discovered why the Taliban was so resistant to coalition presence. In shop after shop our clearance forces uncovered enemy weapons of all varieties and sticky bags of wet opium, hidden behind false walls, under fake floors or locked in metal toolboxes.

A detailed search of a textiles shop found weapons – including AK-47s and a Russian Dragunov SVD semi-automatic sniper rifle – hidden inside the bolts of fabric. We even turned up an old World War II 'Grease Gun', an M3 submachine gun, a find so unique that we took it in turns to pose for photos with it.

Operators with wheelbarrows borrowed from a nearby hardware store moved up and down the main street collecting the drugs and weapons, and transporting them to a centralised point for photographing, documentation and then destruction.

From the centre of the marketplace, we could hear the ongoing firefights from both of our blocking forces as the enemy intermittently engaged them. The helicopters continued to prowl the skies above, swooping low over areas the gunfire was originating from to try to locate its origin.

As we progressed up the hill through the centre of the bazaar, we came across a shop unlike any of the others. The shop was two storeys and constructed of actual brick, as opposed to the mudbrick typical of the surrounding shops. It had thick glass windows set into the brick walls, with solid steel bars welded across the windows for added security. Approaching the fortified compound, one of the DEA special agents on the clearance force and I agreed that we might be about to hit the jackpot.

Entry into the shop proved difficult, with a heavy iron door locked by an uncharacteristically high-quality padlock, further increasing our anticipation of what might be inside. After several minutes of convincing the lock with a set of bolt-cutters, we finally gained entry into the shop. We were not disappointed.

Once the engineers had cleared the store for bombs, the DEA entered and I followed closely behind. An acrid chemical smell took my breath away and sent me into a coughing fit. Composing myself, I surveyed the shop. Stacked high in the far corner were 1-kilogram bags of heroin, wrapped neatly in silk and marked in red ink with the producer's stamp.

Scattered around the concreted floors were scales and counterweights to weigh the heroin, as well as quantities of the silk wrapping materials and the stamping equipment. It seemed our mission had interrupted the packaging of further bags, leaving the Taliban no option but to hurriedly abandon the shop, throwing a padlock on the door as they left.

A more thorough search of the room revealed huge wads of cash, both afghani and Pakistani rupees. Bingo! It was turning out to be an excellent day, and certainly the best haul of drugs and weapons since our joint operations with the DEA had commenced.

The bricks of heroin and wads of cash were counted and photographed before being taken out into the street and thrown onto a large pile, along with a couple of hundred kilograms of wet opium found in other compounds, before being doused in petrol and set alight. I stood and watched the flames engulf millions of dollars' worth of hard drugs, sending a massive dragon into the sky unchased.

We made our way up the hill to the base of the feature that our uppermost blocking force was positioned on. That point signified the limit of our planned exploitation, and we regrouped in a series of shops to destroy all the weapons we had found, and to plan our exfiltration back down the hill to an extraction site in a creek bed near our insertion point.

As we commenced our move, the blocking element on the high ground behind us was once again under enemy attack, returning fire with semi-automatic shots from suppressed M4s. The bazaar was still largely abandoned as we made our way back down the hill. A few shopkeepers had returned to their stores to assess any damage and reopen for business as usual. We passed the smouldering remains of the multi-million-dollar drug bonfire. The wet opium had liquefied in the fire and, mixing with dirt on the way, was running down the hill into a nearby rubbish-filled gutter. I suspected that the Taliban would likely recover what was left of the drug and process it anyway. I found myself wondering if the average heroin addict back home had any idea that what they were injecting into their veins had started life this way, or if they'd even care.

Hitting the creek line, we had started our march out of town to the extraction point when our radios crackled to life with a transmission from the blocking force on the high ground. The content of the message was hard to decipher over the sound of intense gunfire in the background, but what I did pick up was that they had sustained a CAT-A gunshot wound casualty in their position. Fuck – that was not good. They were more than a kilometre away, all uphill, and under heavy enemy fire.

Ray and I considered the best way to evacuate the casualty. A dedicated AME bird would take around 30 minutes to reach us, however one of the State Department Hueys supporting our mission was a combined gunship and casualty evacuation platform, with a minigun hanging out of the right side of the aircraft and a stretcher mounted directly behind the pilots. Complementing the pilots and door gunner was an ex-US special operations 18 Delta combat medic named Jack. I had met with him prior to the operation, and we'd had detailed discussions about evacuating casualties on the Huey.

Our extraction birds, with the Hueys in support, were due to be back on station in around fifteen minutes, and I suggested to Ray that I should make best pace to the casualty and then bring in to land the Huey fitted with the stretcher to evacuate the casualty back to TK. Ray agreed to the plan and, sending the remainder of the clearance force on to extract as planned, joined me in a mad dash back up the hill, through the centre of the bazaar, to the casualty location. Having just patrolled in the opposite direction down through the same route, we were confident that our security wasn't a great concern.

The run was exhausting, carrying 50 kilograms of equipment in the mid-afternoon summer heat of Afghanistan. A glance at Ray told me he felt the same, but there was no way either of us was going to slow down under the circumstances.

Reaching the base of the feature, I was completely spent and collapsed in the shade of a compound before retrieving a bottle of lukewarm water and draining it in seconds. A member of the blocking element had come down to guide us to the casualty, his greeting confirming I looked as bad as I felt. 'Hey, Doc, we can rest here for a bit if you like before I take you up.'

There was no way on earth I was going to put my personal comfort over the chance to get to the casualty sooner. 'Fuck that,' I replied. 'Where is he?'

We proceeded up the reverse slope of the feature – the one facing away from the enemy – before pausing and dropping to a crouch as we neared the top so as not to expose ourselves to the unfriendly fire that was cracking overhead.

I could hear the voices of the guys managing the casualty and, peering over the crest of the feature, I caught the occasional glimpse of the tops of their heads as they moved around in the trench they had been fighting from.

Trying to time my dash between enemy bullets, I stood up and scurried the 15 metres across the exposed top of the feature before dropping into the 1.5-metre-deep fighting trench. The trench system was no more than a metre wide at most and snaked around the top and forward slope of the feature, facing the village from which effective enemy fire was coming. The trenches had been carved out of hard rock, leaving jagged edges that ripped at the fabric of my pants as, in a hunched posture, I made my way to the wounded soldier. He was lying feet towards me with a shooter attending to his airway. There was no room on either side of the casualty to manoeuvre past, so placing one leg either side of his body I made my way up to his head end to start assessing him.

The first responders had cut his shirt and pants off and I could see no obvious injuries on the front of his body from the neck down. He had a small wound on his throat adjacent to his Adam's apple; I assumed this had been the start of an attempted surgical airway, or cricothyrotomy.

'Who had a go at the cric?' I asked the shooter looking after the casualty.

He explained that the wound was not an attempted airway, but was in fact where the casualty had been shot.

I reached around and swept my hand behind the casualty's head, neck and upper shoulders, palpating for an exit wound, but felt none, which suggested that the bullet had tracked down into his chest.

As I examined him, I noticed that he didn't appear to be showing any signs of life, with no response and no obvious breathing. It was close to the worst possible situation: stuck in a narrow fighting trench, facing a village full of Taliban engaging our position, with a critically injured casualty. It was hopeless trying to treat the casualty in the confines of the trench. We desperately needed to get him out of there and onto the evacuation helicopter, which by that time was back on station.

I spoke briefly with the shooter on the scene, requesting him to commence CPR while the move was being organised. Although the casualty was unconscious and not breathing I couldn't confirm that he was deceased in that setting, and I held the tiniest glimmer of hope that his injuries were surviv-able. The shooter leaned over the casualty from the head end and started chest compressions as I departed, taking the casualty's helmet and rifle with me. I returned to the point where I had entered the trench system and paused briefly to psych myself up for the mad dash back over the top of the feature to the safety of the reverse slope. Hauling myself up, I bolted, bracing for the enemy fire at my back as I ran, but it never came. I slipped back down the slope and slowed to a fast walk briefly, before a large explosion 50 metres to my front prompted me to break into a sprint again. Turning at a right angle, I scrambled for the nearest cover, suspecting that the explosion had been an enemy rocket or mortar. Strangely, other friendly elements on the reverse slope continued about their business casually, seeming highly amused by my panicked reaction. It turned out that the explosion had been a controlled blast to fell a tall tree in the clearance of a landing zone for the evacuation helicopter.

Minutes later, the Huey with Jack aboard descended on its final approach to the now-clear landing zone. As it touched down, I approached the bird from its front, holding my thumb up to check that the pilot had control of the rotor and was happy for me to come in under the disc. Getting a thumbs-up in reply, I made my way to the side of the bird where Jack was preparing to exit the helicopter and receive the casualty.

Assuming, foolishly, that him getting off implied that the aircraft was staying on the ground, I put the casualty's rifle and helmet, as well as my medical kit, onto the floor of the doorless machine, then Jack and I walked away to find a quieter place to discuss our response.

As we did, a stretcher team carrying the casualty crested the feature I had just descended and began making their way towards us. I was briefing Jack on my proposed management plan for the flight when the pitch of the Huey's engines changed, causing me to turn just in time to see it take to the sky with my medical kit and the casualty's rifle and helmet unsecured and placed precariously on its floor.

I stood gazing in disbelief at the departing bird; I now had no medical kit and a critically injured casualty was rapidly descending upon my position. I yelled at Jack to get the door gunner on the bird to secure the rifle, helmet and my kit, and for the pilots to bring the fucking helicopter back in for the casualty. Jack promptly established comms, advising the crew of the unsecured kit. The bird did a long banking turn and began its approach again. As it drew near, the stretcher team carrying the casualty arrived at the landing zone.

The casualty was a muscular, fit soldier and it had taken a considerable effort to get him out of the trench and to our position. Chest compressions continued, despite the soldier administering them being sandblasted by dust as the Huey landed.

I climbed aboard and assumed a standing position in the centre of the back of the aircraft. The stretcher on the bird was fitted immediately behind the pilots' seats, leaving little room between it and the central protuberance below the helicopter's rotor system. I wedged myself into the limited space and helped load the casualty, feet first, shuffling him onto the stretcher so that his waist was level with me and his head at arm's reach to my left.

Jack piled on after me and assumed a position at the casualty's head as we launched again, bound for the surgical hospital at TK.

On review once airborne, the casualty was still showing no signs of life. With Jack continuing chest compressions, I retrieved two large-gauge needles and inserted one in each side of the casualty's upper chest to relieve any trapped, pressurised air. Despite the intervention, his condition remained unchanged.

I took an oxygen cylinder out of my medical kit and, attaching a bag-valve-mask device, handed it to Jack to start breathing artificially for the casualty. As he did so, I took over chest compressions, leaning awkwardly to my left, attempting to centre my weight over the casualty's chest to maximise the effectiveness of my compressions.

After several cycles of CPR my next concern was attempting to stimulate the casualty's heart with a shot of adrenaline. As Jack took over the chest compressions once more, I took out my intraosseous drill and within seconds had established an access line into the bone marrow of the casualty's upper-left shin. I drew up a vial of adrenaline and pushed it straight through the cannula, then quickly hooked up a bag of intravenous fluids which would flow through the casualty's bone marrow and into his circulation. I then returned to the chest compressions, examining the casualty's face as I did so. His head had tilted slightly to the left, towards the cockpit, and a small trickle of blood was running from the corner of his mouth, causing me to rethink the security of his airway. The first responders on the hill had placed a rubber airway tube into the casualty's left nostril, which appeared to be moving good amounts of air with the pressure generated by chest compressions. My concern at that point was that blood from inside his mouth or airway could easily be tracking down into his lungs, and in effect be drowning him. Another possibility was that the blood was actually coming from his chest cavity, which would indicate that the bullet had passed down and likely damaged vital structures. Either way, I needed to secure his airway.

Retrieving a surgical airway kit from my medical pack, I prepared the equipment for the procedure. As Jack took over compressions, I leaned over him and felt through the bullet hole in the casualty's neck for the appropriate anatomy to insert the airway. The casualty's airway was undamaged at that level and, making a small nick with my scalpel, I gained entry into his windpipe, sliding an airway tube in without resistance.

I once again resumed chest compressions, by now growing exhausted from the effort of effective CPR in the confined space. As I continued pumping, bright red spurts of blood jetted out of the newly inserted surgical airway tube. Propelled by the wind from the rotor system through the open cabin of the aircraft, it sprayed the inside of the cockpit, covering the controls.

The volume of blood coming from the casualty's lungs indicated that his internal injuries were severe, and it was obvious to me that our efforts were almost certainly futile. But, ignoring this rational assessment, I continued with every ounce of energy remaining to attempt to support his failing heart, desperate not to lose another teammate.

The second we touched down at TK a stretcher team raced under the disc and whisked the casualty off towards a waiting ambulance, continuing to pump his chest as they ran. I watched from the back of the bird as the ambulance pulled away. With the helicopter still running on the airstrip, I tried to manoeuvre myself out of the small space I was in. My back muscles were locked up from the effort of performing CPR at such an awkward angle, and any attempt to straighten my posture sent my back into excruciating spasms. I climbed out of the bird, hunched over, then turned to survey the scene. It was truly horrible. Blood from the casualty had sprayed over all the gauges of the aircraft and the backs of both pilots' helmets. A smear mark ran across the inside of the right-hand windshield, where one of the pilots had wiped the blood away to be able to see through the glass on landing. Congealed blood coated the floor under the stretcher and, looking down, I saw my body armour, pants and boots were soaked through.

I steadied myself against the side of the aircraft and once again attempted to straighten my back, feeling an electric bolt of pain as my muscles further seized. I called to one of the pilots, asking whether the helicopter needed to leave, with the reply confirming that they planned to take off again immediately and head to the refuelling point on the other side of the base.

I hauled my medical kit and the casualty's equipment, including his body armour and rifle, off the helicopter and piled it on the ground. With Jack's assistance I moved the kit to the edge of the airstrip, then I collapsed on the ground next to it while Jack reboarded the aircraft and it departed.

As the noise of the helicopter subsided I sat there in silence, alone on the side of the hot, dusty airstrip, completely dejected. I knew that the casualty was dead. I replayed the events of the last hour in my mind and tried to make sense of how I should feel. The truth was I had absolutely no idea how I was meant to feel; I could find no benchmark in my mind against which to judge the situation. I thought about crying but couldn't. I felt numb.

Any attempt to move was met with immediate excruciating back spasms, so I sat there in a daze, covered in blood, for a good ten minutes. My trance-like state was broken by an Australian voice.

I hadn't noticed the soldier approaching. He had been waiting with a group of vehicles at the next flight line across to pick up our clearance element, which was due back from the job on the extraction helicopters I had been meant to return with. The soldier stood over me, shading me from the sun, and as I looked up to greet him I saw the shock register on his face as he noticed the amount of blood soaking both my clothing and the pile of equipment next to me.

'Are you all right, mate?' he asked with genuine concern in his voice.

I explained briefly what had happened as he helped me to my feet and then assisted in carrying the casualty's equipment the few hundred metres to the surgical hospital.

Crowds of medical staff and SOTG members were waiting outside the resuscitation room of the hospital, eagerly awaiting information. They all stared as I made my way into the waiting area and dropped my kit, slumping into a vacant chair. A couple of them came up and patted me on the back, but none spoke. I'm sure that my appearance told them I wouldn't have anything positive to report about the casualty, and they were no doubt holding out hope for a miracle. I could have gone in to see for myself how the resuscitation was going but I didn't; the thought of another back spasm was more than I could bear and, more significantly, I already knew the answer.

One of the hospital staff offered me a drink, which I declined, and then offered to get me some wipes to clean my face. I declined that too, but she brought them to me anyway, and I scrubbed the blood and dirt from my face. Once finished, I looked up and locked eyes with another American hospital staff member. He stared at me with a combination of terror and fascination on his face, apparently unable to look away, even when he must have known he should. It was a strange interaction, and one that left me feeling sorry for the guy; he couldn't have been more than eighteen years old.

Twenty minutes later a solemn-looking doctor emerged from the resuscitation room and confirmed that the casualty had been declared deceased. In the turmoil of the situation,

I had not paused to consider his identity; I had once again seen him simply as a series of medical issues needing attention. It was only after the terrible news of his passing had been delivered that the casualty registered as a person. One of our own. His name was Rowan Robinson, and he was the special operations engineer who had cleared the path for his blocking force to insert into their overwatch position that morning.

I had not known Rowan well, having only met him for the first time several months ago, and my interactions with him were no more than a nod of recognition in passing or in the mess hall. That said, I was able to tell a lot about Rowan by the nature of his injury and the circumstances under which it occurred. Rowan's primary role was to clear the path for his element to establish their position, which he had done that day, as always, with distinction. When the fighting started, he would have been well within his rights to stay concealed in the trench until required for another engineer function. But Rowan was clearly not that kind of guy, and despite being fully aware of the very real threat to his life, when he was hit he was facing the enemy, returning fire, fighting shoulder to shoulder with the shooters on either side of him. Rowan's actions, along with those of other members of the blocking force, ensured that the enemy was adequately suppressed to allow our clearance force to successfully complete our mission and extract from the target unopposed. Rowan lived, and ultimately died, selflessly ensuring the safety of others.

Sitting in the waiting area outside the resuscitation room, I watched the reactions of those around me. Some looked stunned, others angry, a couple cried. No-one knew exactly what to do. The option came to go into the resuscitation room and pay last respects to Rowan but I declined; I'm not sure why.

My back had loosened up slightly by that time and I picked up my kit and walked slowly back to my room, avoiding eye contact with anyone I passed, but feeling their eyes locked on me in my bloodied state.

Once back in my room, I removed my clothing and showered before making a pile of my boots, pants and shirt in the dirt out the back of the medical centre, dousing them in petrol and setting them ablaze.

I sat alone and watched the flames lick at the material of the clothes and melt the rubber soles of my boots into the dirt until all that was left was smouldering residue. I then tore apart my medical kit and scrubbed the blood from it and my body armour, before replacing my used medical stores and refurbishing my combat equipment, with the knowledge that it would all start again within days.

We farewelled Rowan in the same fashion that we had Brett Wood, with a small ceremony followed by a procession to a waiting aircraft, which then departed to a task group salute.

In a poignant tribute to our fallen brother, the State Department Hueys performed a 'missing man' flyover, in which a single aircraft broke away from their formation as they passed overhead. It was gut-wrenching to watch, and a tear threatened to escape my eye, but didn't.

Although he never said as much to my face, I would later learn that Jack had been quite critical of my insistence on attempting to resuscitate Rowan despite it being apparent that he was almost certainly dead before he was loaded on the helicopter. I later learned that the contamination of the helicopter with blood required it to be taken offline for a week while it was ripped apart for cleaning, grounding Jack and his team and temporarily reducing their element's capability. He was right, of course, but I didn't want to hear that truth at the time. I never spoke to him again.

John, the DEA special agent who had been shot in the buttock on the morning that Rowan was killed, turned up for a mission 36 hours later with his wound still very much open and his entire buttock black with bruising from the shockwave of the bullet ripping through it.

Somewhat surprised to see him at the pre-mission staging area for the job, I suggested that no regular doctor would ever allow him to return to work that soon.

'That's why *you're* my doc!' was his enthusiastic response.

He finished that day with a streak of blood down the back of his pants from where the wound had bled through its dressing, but he never uttered a word of complaint. He didn't miss a single mission on account of the wound, which I would clean and dress nightly. Due to his lack of appropriate rest, compounded by the unhygienic conditions, John's wound would become horribly infected, and a week later I was forced to lightly anaesthetise him to scrub the pus from it, and treat him with a course of intravenous antibiotics. Fortunately, the DEA required John in Kandahar for planning purposes shortly thereafter and he had some time out of the field to let the wound heal, which it did without complication.

I had worked with some hardened individuals, but up until then I had never seen anyone get shot and then turn up for work two days later; John had reset the bar for toughness in my opinion.

On a subsequent rotation John would be equalled for toughness by one of our own guys who sustained a similar wound and, rather than call in a medivac, chose to stay in the field for a further twelve hours to finish the job he and his team had started. The guy in question was Mark Donaldson, VC.

XIV

TODD LANGLEY

IT APPEARED TO BE OVER BEFORE IT HAD EVEN BEGUN. THE thick plumes of white smoke billowing from the aircraft's engines certainly indicated that something had malfunctioned as it started up. Disappointed, I dropped my pack on the airstrip; I had been looking forward to my first chance to ride in the intriguingly cool MV-22 Osprey.

No sooner had I dumped my pack than a loadmaster appeared on the back ramp of the offending machine. Watching the guy for confirmation that his aircraft had indeed shat itself, I was surprised to see him instead give the thumbs-up for us to board. It turned out that what I had interpreted as an engine fire was simply the routine start-up procedure for an Osprey. We were in business for our vehicle interdiction mission after all.

* * *

One of the critical enablers for the Australian SOTG to reach out and touch the Taliban in the far corners of its jurisdiction was aircraft, specifically helicopters. While the American aviation task group based at TK was very forthcoming in the provision of Black Hawks for troop lift purposes, a larger aircraft was required to deliver the full force of the SOTG's commando contingent. The US State Department Mi-17s had provided a solution for the DEA-led operations against narcotic-related targets, however those birds couldn't be used to insert onto targets not directly linked with the drug trade.

To fill the void, in mid-2011 a relationship was developed between the SOTG and the US Marine Aircraft Wing (MAW) stationed out of the British Camp Bastion in Helmand Province. The MAW primarily flew the herculean Sikorsky CH-53E Super Stallion and the tiltrotor MV-22 Ospreys, and seeing as these were the two aircraft featured in the *Transformers* movies, I was keen as mustard to work with them both.

In the early stages of the relationship with the MAW, they wouldn't come and pick us up from TK, requiring us to pre-position at Bastion the evening before jobs. We would then wait until the wee hours of the following morning before piling into Super Stallions and inserting onto our target. Everyone involved in that process quickly came to dread it.

The general routine would be to wake on the day before the planned job and go about pre-mission procedure as usual. Late in the afternoon, several lifts of C-130 Hercules aircraft would then transport our fully kitted-up element down to Bastion. Owing to the cramped nature of the seating in the back of Hercs, coupled with the requirement to wear full combat gear, helmets and rifles, we would be packed like sardines into the back of the planes. We would sit facing but slightly offset to the soldier opposite, his knee rammed into your groin, and your knee returning the favour to the next guy along. Late afternoon temperatures at that time of year remained in the high 30s, causing mutual sweat to develop between yourself and those on either side.

Further detracting from the experience was the requirement for the Hercules' loadmasters to do their pre-flight checks, which involved them moving up and down the passenger compartment and inspecting various bits and pieces above our heads with a torch. With no space left between us, the loadmaster would be forced to climb over our laps, like some form of human sheepdog, periodically propping immediately in front of seated members, meaning their sweaty, flight suit-clad balls were only inches from your face. To add to the fun, the Hercs would often have some form of fault requiring us to either sit in place while it was rectified or dismount the aircraft and do it all again an hour later when they had fixed the thing or replaced it with one that worked.

This was exactly what happened on 3 July 2011, with an aircraft malfunction causing a one-hour delay in our departure from TK for Bastion. The eventual flight was hot and uncomfortable, topped off by the pilot performing a nauseating corkscrew dive through the surface-to-air missile danger altitude band on descent into the British base.

It was just on dusk when we finally disembarked and made our way across the grimy airstrip crammed with Super Stallions and Ospreys to the hangar that would be our waiting point until it was time for insertion. The floodlit hangar was massive and served as a 24-hour-a-day aircraft maintenance depot for the Super Stallions. Several of the huge machines sat in various stages of disassembly, both in the hangar and immediately in front of it, with aircraft mechanics in grease-stained grey overalls, helmets, goggles and earmuffs clambering all over them. At any given point, one or more of the engines of the helicopters being serviced would be fired up and revved to redline, often for fifteen or twenty minutes at a time. Not only did this generate an ear-splitting noise, it also spat out fiery exhaust fumes to add to the already intolerably hot environment.

A small chow point for the aircraft mechanics was located at the edge of the airstrip and was stocked with a pitiful quantity of sickly processed muffins, stale chips and warm water. Come dinnertime, a few vats of fatty slop were wheeled in, and the mechanics downed their tools to eat. The leftover food was offered to our element. After eating half a plate of lukewarm brown-coloured mush, I scrounged around in a nearby industrial bin and salvaged a filthy discarded mattress. Positioning it in the shadow cast by a shipping crate, I lay down to rest. Insertion onto target was scheduled for 0200 hours the following morning, and having been up since 0800 I was keen to get some sleep before the job. But the combination of heat, noise, dust, light and excitement made sleep an impossibility. Sweat streamed down my forehead as I tossed and turned, turning the thick dust coating the mattress into mud. Midnight came and went, and then it was time to get up and gather for our final set of confirmatory orders. That done, I went back to my squalid mattress and lay down to contemplate the mission ahead.

As far as I understood, the job was another *kick the hornet's nest and see what happens* mission. We would be conducting a pre-dawn insertion of a large force into a known Taliban village and strong-holding our various elements in strategically located compounds to prepare for the day's fighting. It was anticipated that the Taliban would attempt to reinforce from another village a few kilometres away, and for that reason a five-man sniper detachment would be inserted onto a large feature overlooking the second village. The snipers would be dislocated from our main force by a distance of about 2 kilometres, and would be completely unreachable if they sustained a casualty.

I had felt a little uneasy about their isolation in the pre-mission planning, but the risk had been rationalised by the relative unlikelihood of them taking a hit, along with the fact that they had an extraordinarily competent combat first aider among their ranks, being the sniper who had assisted in the attempted resuscitation of Brett Wood.

The other medical elements on the ground for the mission would be Chris, the medic who had also been on the scene the day Brett was killed; an attitude-adjusted Brad with the commando platoons; and the Viking, who would be collocated with me.

The Viking, as his nickname suggests, was a 2-odd-metre-tall, 100-kilo medic of Nordic appearance, who looked like he would be more at home pillaging and plundering in medieval times than carrying an M4 on the modern-day battlefield. A paradox of a guy, the Viking had a very calm demeanour and was softly spoken, yet possessed a strong capacity for violence when the situation demanded it. He had been a role model to generations of junior special operations medical members, myself included, and it was excellent to have him by my side for that mission.

At long last we got the order to move out in our chalk groups to the waiting Super Stallions. It was just before 0200 hrs and I was dog-tired.

My kit was abnormally heavy due to three mortar rounds I was carrying for a mortar detachment coming along for the job. The only place that I could fit the high-explosive rounds had been on the outside of my pack, immediately next to my

600-litre oxygen cylinder. I gave a quick thought to the spectacular nature of the explosion that would ensue if the right kind of ordnance hit my pack, before pushing that thought to the back of my mind and making my way out onto the airstrip. The three Super Stallions for our insertion were just firing up as we approached them, and we paused briefly behind them before getting the thumbs-up from the loadmasters to proceed up the back ramps and into the aircraft.

Super Stallions were notorious for leaking fluid from the metres of exposed hydraulic lines running through them, and as I loaded onto the helicopter my feet slipped and skated on the saturated floor. The joke went that the only time you needed worry in the back of a Super Stallion was not when hydraulic fluid was dripping freely on you, but rather when it *stopped* dripping on you, the implication being that it had run dry.

I made my way towards the front of the bird and took a seat on the left-hand side, near the door gunner. A flight of stairs led up to the cockpit, with the two pilots sitting well above the passenger level and looking out through what seemed to be a disproportionately small series of windscreens for such a massive aircraft. The helicopter's array of digital controls glowed a dull green, and I watched as the pilots went through their pre-flight checks, tweaking dials and flipping switches. I tilted my head back and rested the back of my helmet against the side of the vibrating aircraft, closing my eyes. I was exhausted and we hadn't even taken off for insertion yet; it was going to be a long mission.

The bird picked up revs and began taxiing towards an appropriate location on the airstrip, before pausing briefly and then lurching vertically into the sky. It was an impressive sensation to feel a helicopter of that size lift off with such power, and as it did a trickle of hydraulic fluid ran off the front of my helmet and onto the right side of my face.

In the dimly lit passenger compartment I managed to get the attention of the loadmaster sitting directly across from me, and gestured towards the significant leak above my head. He climbed up, straddling me, to assess the offending pipe by torchlight. After a brief inspection, he pulled a rag from the pocket of his flight suit and tied it around the area of leaking pipe before giving me an enthusiastic thumbs-up, dismounting and resuming his seat. Problem solved. I figured that he would meet the same fiery fate as the rest of us if the helicopter ploughed in, so if he wasn't worried about the leaking pipe than I needn't be.

I closed my eyes again and drifted off to near-sleep before being roused by the familiar call: 'TEN MINUTES.'

I flipped my NVG down in front of my eyes, flicked them on, and commenced my pre-insertion ritual of donning my pack, tapping and slapping my M4, and sitting back on the edge of my seat, angled towards the rear of the bird.

The five- and three-minute warnings were screamed over the noise of the helicopter, and then finally, with the 30-second warning, the bird levelled out into a painfully slow descent for our insertion. My heart began to thump excitedly in my chest, my drug of choice coursing through my body and banishing my fatigue.

After what seemed like an eternity of slow descent, the wheels of the Super Stallion finally touched down. When it was my turn, I ran off the back ramp of the helicopter and followed my element out through the rotor wash and into the night.

The noise of the helicopters subsided into the distance and the night fell silent. We had been inserted a few kilometres from the target village, into a series of tiered fields of crops bordered by irrigation channels. Although it wasn't a particularly long insertion, I struggled over the uneven terrain under the weight of my pack. The target village was at a significantly higher altitude than TK and my breathing was uncomfortable as my lungs battled to extract the required oxygen from the thin air.

I had already been losing distance to the soldier in front of me when, failing to appropriately perceive depth under NVG, I misjudged a small jump over an irrigation channel. Pulled backwards by the weight of my pack I fell unceremoniously into the water. Landing with a splash on my right side my head was briefly submerged in the putrid water before I managed to right myself enough to get my face above the waterline. As I struggled against the weight of my pack to sit up, the soldier behind had to assist in hauling me out of the ditch.

Once back on my feet, and soaking wet, the very next obstacle was a 1.5-metre-high mud wall retaining the next tier of crops. The only way I could scale the wall with the weight of my load was to jump as high as I could, flop my torso up onto the obstacle, and then scramble with all four limbs to climb up. In the process, three of my spare rifle magazines fell from pouches on the front of my body armour and landed with a metallic clatter in the mud below. The noise caused the soldier in front of me to turn and stare at the spectacle that was me floundering around in the mud retrieving them. I was having a truly shit time.

Once I had recovered my muddy magazines and refurbished my kit, I proceeded without further incident to the compound that CHQ would be occupying for the day.

The Viking was there, and we had a laugh about my dreadful performance on the insertion. We chatted quietly with other members of our element, which included an engineer dog handler, who had brought along his explosive detection dog, Lucky, and another guy who had a megaphone for spruiking anti-Taliban propaganda to the villagers throughout the day. As we talked, the Viking excitedly proposed an alternative use for the device.

His idea, which he played out for us in interpretive dance, was to beatbox through the megaphone and dance on the rooftop of our compound to draw enemy fire, thus revealing the Taliban positions. For better or worse, the grainy green NVG image of the Viking in full combat order, gyrating his hips to a deplorable rendition of C+C Music Factory's 'Gonna Make You Sweat (Everybody Dance Now)', is my enduring memory of that compound on that particular morning.

Dawn broke to the anticipated probing enemy fire at our positions, as well as a series of sniper engagements from the overwatch positions. Communications with the snipers, as well as the periodic thumps of their rifles, indicated that the Taliban were indeed trying to reinforce from the second village, as expected.

The village we occupied was organised in roughly equal quadrants, with a large area of green belt located to one side. Our friendly elements occupied strategic positions in all four quadrants, with the CHQ group I was with being in a protected sector furthest from the green belt.

As the morning progressed, enemy fire intensified as Taliban located in the green belt developed a good idea of our disposition on the ground and began to focus their small-arms and RPG attacks. The sniper element up on the feature was also firing down into the second village increasingly regularly as armed targets presented. An AH-1W SuperCobra soared above, providing battlefield commentary and engaging enemy targets under the control of the JTACs on the ground. The mortar element with our group had established their tubes, and after orientating them towards a few predetermined likely targets were waiting for an invitation to the fight. The Viking and I were doing much the same, sitting and talking in the morning sun, which, given that I had been drenched during insertion, was most welcome. The guy with the megaphone was belting out his propaganda, with the occasional supersonic crack over our compound indicating that at least some members of the audience weren't buying his brand.

Despite sitting in the middle of a Taliban village, surrounded on three sides by enemy, the CHQ element was pretty much perfectly safe and I was getting a little bored. The day had started to heat up, and once I'd dried out I began chasing the shade around the compound rather than the sun. The adrenaline surge of insertion had well and truly worn off and I was coming down from my high, with the fatigue of 24 or so waking hours setting in.

With nothing much for us to do at that point, the Viking and I climbed up onto the roof of our compound and were talking with a pair of US Marines attached to our group for the operation when one of our element called, 'Hey, Doc, we've got a casualty.'

The Viking and I left the roof and moved back to the main courtyard of the compound. The ground force commander, his signaller and a JTAC were industriously conducting multiple parallel conversations on their radios with ground elements, aircraft and higher command. As we arrived, a long burst of automatic rifle fire could be heard from the vicinity of our sniper position.

Not wanting to interrupt, I approached the command group without speaking, and watched over the JTAC's shoulder as he scribbled out the detail coming through his radio earpiece. As the words materialised on his notepad, the gravity of the situation began to sink in. *CAT-A, GSW neck*. As he continued to write, other coded indicators that the casualty was one of our own, would require a stretcher, and that there were enemy in the area. I was close enough to hear directly the radio transmission coming from the sniper up on the feature that loomed over the village. In a calm voice, he was calling in a mortar fire mission pretty much on his own position.

It transpired that while the snipers had been busy engaging multiple targets in the second village, a Talib armed with an AK-47 had managed to slip away unnoticed and climb the feature our sniper element occupied. Getting within a few hundred metres of their position, the enemy fighter initiated on them. A bullet from his initial burst had struck one of the snipers in the neck, causing a shockwave that passed through his spinal cord and rendered him temporarily quadriplegic. Caught completely by surprise, the other member of the sniper pair had been required to simultaneously return fire at the enemy, apply first aid to his wounded mate and coordinate a mortar fire mission to neutralise the enemy. It was his calm voice that could be heard over the radio at our position.

The mortar team in our location was called to action, and within seconds had dialled their tubes onto the target and were pounding mortar rounds down range. The sound of the departing bombs was thunderous, causing me to clasp my hands over my ears. Over the racket of the mortar mission, the JTAC was calling the SuperCobra gunship onto the enemy position. Purposefully, the lethal machine sailed directly over our position. Following the trajectory of its fire, I watched as plumes of dust rose from the enemy position on the feature a couple of kilometres away.

The frustration of the situation started to set in. One of our guys was potentially mortally wounded on the feature right next to us and I had no way of helping him.

The Viking and I ran through the options. Getting there on foot would be impossible; we would be sitting ducks as we ascended the near vertical feature. But watching the Super-Cobra line up for another gun run, an idea occurred to us simultaneously: we could call it in to land and attach ourselves to the stub wings on the side of the bird to get a lift up onto the feature. We had both heard the story of a British special operations patrol which had allegedly done exactly that, using an Apache to get a wounded soldier out of a tight situation.

It was an unorthodox idea but the situation was dire. Between radio transmissions, I got the JTAC's attention and proposed the concept to him. The stupidity of my suggestion was reflected in the man's face. He held my gaze for several seconds without responding before turning his attention back to the transmissions coming through his radio.

In the commotion of the mortar mission, Lucky the bomb dog had got spooked and had hightailed it out of our compound. Through their scopes, a second sniper element on the feature behind us tracked the dog towards the centre of the village, where it was led into a compound by some local kids. Lucky was never seen again.

I was pacing furiously, ruminating on the situation, when word of a second casualty came over the net. The details were transmitted over the channel I was monitoring, so I received the information firsthand. It was another CAT-A casualty, this time with a gunshot wound to the head. The day had gone from routine to chaos in the space of ten minutes.

The second casualty was in the quadrant diagonally opposite our location and approximately 1 kilometre away.

We hastily assembled a QRF: a shooter to navigate us to the casualty; an engineer to clear the path as required; the company sergeant major, Mick, to provide command and control; and The Viking and myself as the medical response. Within a minute, our group had departed and we were weaving our way through the complex urban terrain towards the casualty.

The layout of the village dictated that we had to cross multiple fire lanes opening into the Taliban-inhabited green belt. Every mad dash across the exposed ground was met with sprays of AK-47 fire, most of which passed safely overhead, though the occasional burst kicked up dust fairies around our feet.

Nearing the casualty compound, the shooter leading us took a wrong turn. Realising his mistake very quickly, he paused at a five-way intersection to consult his map and GPS. The remainder of the group took up defensive positions in the directions of most likely threat, with the Viking looking over the shooter's shoulder down the alleyway to our front, and myself and the engineer backing up a small distance to cover the alleyway we had just emerged from. I was busy surveying my designated arc when the *whoosh* of an RPG zipped past low and fast to my rear and slammed into the side of a compound about 50 metres from our position. The rocket had been aimed at the shooter and the Viking, and had passed between them at about head height, missing them both by inches. Another two rockets came in quick succession, passing slightly high over our position and air-bursting at the end of their trajectory a safe distance away. Reorientated, the shooter picked up and led us the final few hundred metres to the casualty compound.

I entered the compound with purpose, expecting to find the casualty laid out on the ground with guys working on him, but instead was met by Scott, the bear-like shooter who had provided blood for Brett Wood, and no obvious sign of the casualty. Scott gave me a quick rundown of the casualty's injuries as we walked to the centre of the compound.

Confused, I interrupted him. 'Yeah, righto, but where the fuck is he?'

The wounded commando was still on the roof, Scott explained, and due to the intense fire that followed him being hit he was unable to be recovered. The rest of his team had been forced to jump off the roof to avoid being hit themselves. Any subsequent attempt to get to the casualty had been met with deadly accurate bursts of enemy fire.

I discussed the wounded soldier's injuries with the shooter who was right beside him when he was hit, and it didn't sound good.

The casualty was Sergeant Todd Langley, the very soldier who had bravely led our QRF to Brett Wood's position six weeks prior. He and his team had been fighting from the roof of their compound when he had been struck by an enemy bullet in the head.

A large bamboo ladder leading to the roof rested against the side of the compound's inner wall. Mick cautiously scaled the ladder to get a look at Todd's position, but was repelled by an enemy round that cracked within inches of his head, and he came back down the ladder at pace. The only way to recover Todd was going to be to blow a section of the roof from underneath.

Scott retrieved two explosive charges from his team and wired them into the thatched wooden structure that supported the underside of the mudbrick ceiling. Moving back a safe distance, he initiated the charges with a focused explosion that blew a clean hole in the roof. We then took the bamboo ladder and inserted it through the new hole, and I climbed up to get a look at Todd.

From what I had heard of his injury, I strongly suspected nothing could be done for him, but I wanted to make that call myself. As my head crested the rooftop, any hope of Todd's survival was extinguished. He was quite clearly dead.

His body lay about 3 metres from the hole in the roof and, attempting to recover him, I leaned forward, my right foot edging one rung further up the ladder. A second later a section of the low mudbrick lip forming the perimeter of the roof disintegrated to my immediate left, showering me with debris and sending me scrambling back down the ladder to the safety of the compound. The enemy had an excellent bead on the rooftop and was clearly intent on making the recovery of Todd's body as difficult as possible.

Accepting that we wouldn't be able to climb onto the roof to recover Todd, the Viking produced a length of tube tape from his pack and suggested that we could throw it through the hole we'd made and try to snag Todd and drag him towards us. To add weight to the tape, and increase our chances of snagging Todd's body, I pulled the head off a mattock I had found in the compound and the Viking attached it to the tape. He then took his turn to scale the ladder and proceeded to throw the tethered mattock head in Todd's direction. After several attempts, the mattock caught on Todd's clothing and the Viking was able to drag him close enough that he was able to reach out and grab Todd's left arm. Pulling him closer, the Viking removed the mattock head and attached the tube tape to Todd's left wrist before a well-aimed enemy bullet struck the roof directly in front of him, precipitating the Viking's rapid retreat down the ladder.

The loose end of the tube tape was dangling through the hole but, try as we might, we couldn't come up with a graceful solution to the problem of retrieving Todd, with our only safe option being to pull his body through the hole and control its descent from below as best as we could.

I climbed the ladder one final time to confirm that Todd was dead before we proceeded. He was much closer this time, and I was able to inspect his injuries and assess for any signs of life. There were none, and I was further convinced that not only was he gone but that his passing would have been instantaneous, with absolutely no pain or awareness. One moment Todd would have been doing what he loved and what he did best, the next he would have entered the Hall of Valhalla, without a split second to contemplate the transition. That thought comforted me a little as I made my way back down the ladder and cleared Todd's team from the room to prevent them from witnessing something that they needn't.

When only the three of us remained, Mick, the Viking and I set about piling mattresses and blankets we'd found in the compound under the hole in the roof to cushion Todd's fall. We agreed among ourselves that we would all look away as Todd came through the roof, and with that the Viking began pulling on the tube tape attached to Todd's wrist. I saw Mick turn away, but for some reason I didn't.

I watched as Todd's left arm and then his torso came into view. His body gained momentum as it emerged progressively through the hole in the roof, and then fell freely onto the pile of mattresses on the ground, slumping to rest lifelessly in an unnatural position. It was a ghastly thing to witness, and an image that stays with me to this day. The Viking, too, had failed to look away, and a discussion on the topic some years later revealed that, like me, he was still haunted by the image of Todd falling.

I withdrew a stethoscope and torch from my medical kit and went through the formal process of declaring Todd deceased, noting on a casualty card the exact time of the declaration and the GPS coordinates of our location.

We wrapped Todd with blankets and secured him to the bamboo ladder, which we would use as a stretcher to carry him off target that night. As if by fate, we found in the room a large piece of fabric with the Realtree camouflage pattern, a camo that Todd loved. We used it as the final wrapping material for his body. I hadn't seen Realtree fabric in any other Afghan compound before, and never saw it subsequently. It was meant to be.

While we were recovering Todd, a firefight had broken out in proximity to our compound. As the fighting gained momentum, two RPG rounds slammed directly into the outer wall of our compound in quick succession. Safe behind the thick mudbrick walls, we had gone about our business unperturbed, but as we exited the room from which we had recovered Todd a prodigious explosion erupted outside, the blast wave of which shook the earth and rocked the compound walls, sending hanging pot plants crashing to the ground and cloaking us in dust. Fearing that the blast represented an enemy attack immediately outside our compound, Scott and Mick set about organising a hasty defence, while seeking clarification as to the origin of the blast over the radio. We learned that the blast was a 2000-pound joint direct attack munition bomb, dropped from God-knows-what aircraft, that had detonated on an enemy target hundreds of metres from our position. Following the blast, all enemy fire ceased, presenting a good opportunity for our QRF group to start moving back through the village to our original position.

Our medical job done for the time being, we left Todd's body in the compound with his team members, and moved off once again under the lead of the shooter who had navigated us to the casualty compound. As we set off, an AME Black Hawk with the SuperCobra in chase flew overhead on their final approach to pick up the injured sniper from the over-watch position.

While we had been busy responding to Todd, the situation on the feature behind the village had been developing. The sniper team in overwatch had consisted of five members, broken into a sniper pair and a group of three, with about 80 metres separating the two elements. The casualty who sustained the gunshot wound to the neck had been one member of the sniper pair, leaving only his spotter to provide the immediate response. With fire from the helicopter gunships and the mortar mission suppressing the enemy, the remaining three snipers, including the combat first aider, were able to move to the casualty and provide additional assistance. By that time, the casualty had gone into shock and was drifting in and out of consciousness, desperately in need of intravenous fluids to bolster his failing blood pressure. The combat first aider was equal to the task and, after assessing and dressing the casualty's wounds, he rapidly established a drip and began infusing fluids. By the time the AME Black Hawk arrived, the casualty was fully conscious and was starting to get some sensation back in his limbs. The terrain prevented the AME bird from landing, so in an incredible display of flying skill the pilot held a precariously low hover over their position, allowing the snipers to heave their wounded brother onto the bird for extraction to the nearest surgical facility.

Back in the target village, our QRF opted to take a different route back through the village to avoid the fire lanes we had been forced to cross on the move to the casualty position. We zigged and zagged through the maze of compounds at a jogging pace, capitalising on the lull in the battle following the 2000-pounder.

Rounding one corner, we were met with the sight of a dead insurgent slumped over his AK-47 and leaning in a seated position up against a wall. One of our engineers was hunched over the corpse in the process of taking fingerprints, and he looked up briefly to greet us before returning to his work.

I assessed the dead enemy as I passed him. His blood-drenched shirt indicated that multiple gunshot wounds to the chest had been the cause of death. The terrain we were moving in suggested that the confrontation would have happened at very close range. Devoid of emotion, I considered the under-lying anatomy that the high-velocity rounds would have destroyed, concluding that catastrophic damage to his heart and lungs would have killed him quickly.

On our move back, we staged through the compound in which the platoon headquarters (PHQ) were located. Offering the verbal friendly force indicator as we approached, we made our way inside and dropped our packs.

The fighting in the village had flared up again, leading our QRF element to seek refuge in the PHQ compound rather than risk further movement back to our own position. With nothing specific to do other than wait for further casualties, the Viking and I wandered around the PHQ compound exploring the various rooms. We found a large, black silk Taliban banner, painted with gold Arabic script and pictures of AK-47s, and we posed for photos with it before continuing our exploration. Moving outside, we found a child's tricycle in the main courtyard, a slope with a single step in the centre of it. The two of us took it in turns to ride the tiny tricycle down the hill and over the step.

I had completely forgotten this, until discussing the day's events with the Viking several years later. The Viking produced some photos of me on the child's tricycle with my head thrown back, laughing hysterically like a crazed person might. Viewing the photos made me feel sick to the core at the disrespect it appeared to show towards Todd's death, which had occurred less than an hour before the photos were taken. Perhaps that was why I had pushed the memory out of my conscious thought in the years following. Analysing my behaviour with the benefit of hindsight, I can only conclude that it was some form of coping mechanism, and that I was avoiding contemplating the harsh reality that Todd was the third task group member lost in a short space of time, and I had been unable to save any of them.

We waited in the PHQ compound until a further lull in the battle, and then made our way back to our original compound unopposed. By that time it was late afternoon and the fighting subsided as dusk fell.

As we weren't extracting until 0200 hours the following morning, and had all been awake for around 30 hours, it was time to draw up a piquet roster and try to get some sleep. I pulled an early piquet, and once I'd completed it I dragged a dirty mattress from one of the rooms in the compound into the central courtyard area and collapsed onto it, falling instantly asleep.

A hand on my shoulder jolted me awake a few hours later, the shooter kneeling over me letting me know in a whisper that we would be moving out in twenty minutes. When the time came to extract, I watched the shadows of our element slink one by one out of the main door of the compound until it was my turn to move. As I flipped my NVG down in front of my eyes, the mount holding them to my helmet snapped clean off, leaving me with the pair of goggles in my hand, attached to my helmet by their lanyard only. *Fuck*. Retrieving some gaffer tape from my pack, I furiously wrapped layer after layer of the tape around the goggles and their mount, trying desperately to fix them in place. It worked, and I hastily donned my helmet again.

The shooter ahead was looking back at me as I began to move. It was the same guy who had been in front of me for my atrocious infiltration, where I had fallen into the irrigation ditch and then dropped my magazines; now he was witnessing another display of extreme cluster-fuckery. I waved at him to indicate that all was good, and he turned and moved off to catch up with the long line of special operators extending into the black night.

The goal was to exfiltrate silently and slip into the night, putting enough distance between us and the target village so that the first the Taliban would know of our exit would be the faint sound of helicopters in the distance.

The night was clear and the moon was yet to rise, giving us adequate darkness to depart the village unnoticed. Making our way back through the tiered crops at the edge of town, we traversed the irrigation channels, and then proceeded to skirt the base of a large feature. We paused at a pass between two peaks of the feature and waited for the element carrying Todd's body to catch up.

After three and a half painstaking hours, we arrived at our designated exfiltration area and fanned out into our respective helicopter loads. The birds were ushered in by a JTAC waving an infrared flashlight in a circular motion on the ground.

Despite a clearly marked landing zone, the pilot of our bird opted to land some 300 metres from our location, prompting a flat-out sprint to the aircraft. I made best pace down the slight decline, but I was struggling due to fatigue, which was compounded by the weight of my pack and the thin air of the high altitude. As I neared the helicopter my eyes were drawn to the heat signature coming from the engine exhaust, which appeared under NVG as a long green flame spewing from the bird. Hitting the rotor wash, I squinted against the debris being thrown around and bolted up the back ramp of the noisy machine, dumping my pack on the greasy floor and collapsing into a seat, completely spent. An agonising pain surged through my body, and as I gasped to catch my breath, I was overcome by the feeling that I might piss myself from the volume of lactic acid charging through me. Unable to flip my NVG up due to the metres of tape binding them to my helmet, I switched the goggles off and removed my helmet completely before cramming in a set of earplugs to drown the noise. I rested my head against the back of my seat, my breathing finally steadying as the helicopter took off to return us to base. Although the MAW wouldn't pick us up from TK at the start of missions, they would drop us back there after the job was done.

We touched down 40 minutes later. The Viking and I helped load Todd into a waiting Humvee ambulance for the short drive to the hospital where his body would be processed.

It was approaching 0400 hours, and only a skeleton crew was at the hospital to facilitate the X-rays and photographing of Todd's body. Unwrapping his lifeless form, we set about cleaning his face for members of the task group to pay their final respects. A member of the Australian Defence Force Investigation Service (ADFIS), who would ultimately take over responsibility for Todd's body, was standing respectfully in the back of the room. He was there, among other reasons, to ensure that no evidence was removed from Todd's body that might be relevant to the mandatory investigation into his death. With that in mind, I looked up to see if he was watching as I removed the velcro Australian national flag (ANF) and call sign patches that adorned the shoulders of Todd's uniform. The ADFIS rep was watching, and I saw him open his mouth to say something before stopping himself. I slipped the blood-soaked patches into my pocket.

By the time we had finished cleaning, X-raying and photographing Todd, dozens of task group members had gathered outside the resuscitation bay, and in ones and twos they started moving in to say their final goodbyes.

We had been required to use several loops of tube tape to secure Todd's body to the bamboo ladder, and during the stomp off target one of the loops of tape had chafed Todd's face, leaving an abrasion on his right cheek. One of the shooters filing through to say his goodbyes was greatly offended by this chafing, which he interpreted as a sign of disrespect for Todd, and he began to have a go at me verbally for it. I understood completely that it was his way of venting his grief and I just happened to be the immediate target. Without responding, I gathered my equipment, and made my way back to my room. Once there I dumped my kit and, rather than refurbish it, I set about scrubbing the blood from Todd's patches. The ANF patch cleaned up well, but I was unable to remove the stains from the call sign patch. I continued to scrub furiously, as if somehow getting all the blood out of the patch would have meant something.

It's possible that the significance of these patches might be lost on the civilian reader. While these pieces of embroidered material are probably worth only a dollar or two in monetary terms, they represent the nation that stands behind the soldier and which the soldier fights for, and the identity of that soldier within their team. The identity that the soldier is often fused with. The identity that would lay down their life for their fellow warrior, exactly as Todd had done.

My failure to adequately cleanse the symbol of Todd's identity left me distraught, and I hurled my plastic scrubbing brush across the room, where it shattered against the wall.

I showered and ate breakfast alone in the mess hall before refurbishing my kit and then crashing into an exhausted but uneasy sleep.

Once more the task group bid farewell to a fallen brother with the all-too-familiar ritual culminating in a slow march down to the airfield and the loading of Todd onto a Hercules that would take him home.

After standing at attention and saluting the departing aircraft, I approached Todd's best friend and presented him with Todd's call sign patch. I had rehearsed a small speech in my mind, but it came out nothing like I planned. The sentiment was there, however, and he hugged me in appreciation. Then, finding Todd's platoon commander, I gave him Todd's ANF patch with the suggestion that it might be returned to his wife.

The sniper who had been shot through the neck had undergone a series of scans and surgeries following his extraction and, considering the significance of his wound, made a remarkable early recovery.

The CT scan of his neck revealed that the bullet had passed within millimetres of his cervical spine, fracturing a small piece of bone from the back of one of his vertebrae before continuing straight through the location of his carotid artery and jugular veins, but by some miracle not disrupting the vessels.

He was returned to Australia to commence a long and painful road to rehabilitation. Not one to play the victim, in December 2013 the sniper accompanied His Royal Highness Prince Harry and a group of other injured veterans on a three-week, 200-mile trek through blizzard conditions to the South Pole as part of the Walking with the Wounded program. Since then he has gone from strength to strength, undertaking helicopter pilot and then instructor training, and gaining credentials to guide arctic treks himself.

XV

THE WAR GOES ON

WITNESSING THE LOSS OF THREE TASK GROUP MEMBERS IN the space of six weeks had a profound effect on the way I viewed my job. The exuberant attitude with which I had approached soldiering had vanished, replaced with a darker, meticulous and even further obsessive approach to medical planning for operations. I rarely slept, instead running the events surrounding the deaths through my mind, wondering how I could have done things differently. To counter my growing fatigue, I began to increase my caffeine intake and started taking regular doses of the thermogenic Hydroxycut. Although this kept me alert during the day, my use of stimulants further reduced my ability to sleep, so I started to pop pills for that as well. Starting with sedating antihistamines, and working my way up to sleeping pills prescribed by a coalition doctor on the base next door, I soon reached a point where

I was unable to sleep at all without pharmaceutical assistance. When I did manage to drop off, I suffered from intense nightmares, and so came to loathe sleep. To reduce the risk of bad dreams, I would stay up as late as I could, take a sleeping pill to knock me out, then set an alarm to wake me four or five hours later. That ensured I would get just enough sleep to function without entering the deeper stages of sleep where dreaming would occur.

During the day, I kept myself busy to take my mind off the deaths of the guys. I began pushing hard to get on every job I could, partly to distract myself, but also to ensure that I would be there if a further task group member got hit. I logged more and more time at the forward surgical team, responding to the endless stream of local nationals and coalition casualties coming through the facility, and helping to save countless lives but losing an equal number more. On some level, I saw the successful resuscitation of a young boy, brain on show and gut opened by an IED intended for our armoured vehicles, as equipoise for the infant girl I had failed to save on my first tour. It was as if there existed a set of divine scales, and were I only able to save more than I had lost, they would be balanced and my demons would rest. All the while the traumatic avalanche continued.

I stopped phoning home as regularly and increased my physical training, lifting heavy weights to the point where I could barely use my arms or walk without pain.

I found myself highly anxious and constantly angry.

Like many of the task group, I craved revenge on the enemy for killing our guys and felt pure hatred towards the Taliban. My role in performing the medical screening of detainees became increasingly difficult as I found myself detesting them, though as a doctor I was professionally obliged to remain neutral.

Towards the end of the rotation, I cut my hair into a mohawk and trimmed my beard to make myself look as mean as I could. With hindsight, I can see it was a physical expression of my emotional state at the time.

Further fuelling my anger were the ongoing mandatory investigations into the three deaths. High-ranking officers who had never spent a second in SOCOMD or Afghanistan, and who had certainly never seen combat, were sent over from Australia to pick apart every last detail of the events surrounding the deaths. It was the classic example of us having split seconds in which to act and them having all the time in the world and no context whatsoever to judge our actions. It pissed me off no end, and although I appreciated the necessity of the process, I resented it immensely.

I'm not sure if my internal state was outwardly obvious, or if the commanding officer of the task group was just a particularly insightful man, but several weeks after Todd's death the CO summoned me to his office and asked me how I was going, acknowledging that I must be harbouring a significant emotional burden. I did what every other task group member would have done under the circumstances and lied, telling him that I was perfectly fine, for fear of being left off jobs if I admitted otherwise.

The rotation drew to a close and my fury intensified. Towards the end of the tour even the most kinetic of jobs was doing little to satiate my desire for more.

Temporarily easing the tension, our final series of jobs for the tour finished with quite a comical interaction with a senior enlisted US Marine on an American base in southern Afghanistan.

Our last day of operations involved DEA-led daytime raids on two separate drug laboratories a short distance apart. As we inserted on the first target for the day, the Mi-17 I was on clipped its tail rotor on the ground before slamming down safely. A second bird in our packet had 'browned out' in the thick cloud of dust kicked up by its rotor wash as it neared the ground and dropped its front wheel into an unseen deep hole leading to a Karez system, trapping it in place.

Our aircraft was unscathed and able to extract us again when the time came, but the second bird was disabled by its crash. After completing our job, we left a security party with the busted helicopter and flew back to a nearby US Marine base to regroup and work out how to recover it.

The midday temperature was approaching 50 degrees on the ground, and after an hour of waiting on a scorching-hot airstrip, one of our guys somehow discovered that the base mess hall had a Gatorade slushy machine. It was shortly before lunch, and we figured that we could get into the mess, load up on slushies and be out again before the lunchtime crowd.

A group of five of us made a beeline for the mess and found the facility empty. We feverishly started packing every free pocket with beef jerky, chewing gum and chips, and took turns pouring all the large slushies we could carry to take back to our waiting team members.

I was standing at the machine, busy pouring my third slushy, and didn't notice when an extremely agitated US Marine sergeant major entered the mess and accosted one of the other guys. Hearing a commotion, I looked around to see my mate pointing in my direction and the irate marine storming towards me. Clutching three overflowing cups of slushy in my hands, my pockets brimming with stolen goodies, I waited. He propped inches in front of my face. He was slightly shorter than me but significantly broader across the shoulders. He had the textbook jarhead haircut: shaved bald on the sides and short and neat on top. His uniform was perfectly fitted and immaculately ironed. I, on the other hand, had a mohawk and an unkempt beard, and my ripped uniform was stained with sweat and coated with dust from the job that morning.

It transpired that the sergeant major had come to confirm that all was in order in the mess before lunch was served but had instead found our group tearing the place apart. He had approached the bloke closest to him and demanded to talk to the senior ranking member of the group. While I held no direct command over the other guys, owing to the fact I was a major that dubious honour fell to me. As we wore no rank on our uniforms, the marine reasonably deduced that he had interrupted a group of junior soldiers raiding the mess and he was out to set things straight. His face red with rage, he started on me.

'I AM SERGEANT MAJOR ANDERSON, AND THIS IS MY MESS,' he thundered.

'I'm Major Dan Pronk – it's nice to meet you,' I replied mildly.

It took a few seconds for the content of my words to register, with the marine's changing facial expression revealing the exact moment he realised he had just screamed in the face of someone who significantly outranked him. Still, the fact remained that I was making a prick of myself in his facility, so we reached a truce of sorts. He backed away from me slightly and offered an unconvincing apology for his outburst, which I graciously accepted while excusing myself and the other guys. We returned to the airstrip and distributed the stolen food and drinks as our broken helicopter was recovered from the field and a new one was flown in to allow us to prosecute our second target.

The second job for the day, and our final job for the rotation, was a hash-processing plant fully loaded with drugs as well as sophisticated equipment run by diesel generators to pack the hash into coffee wrappers for smuggling internationally. We took the required evidence from the laboratory, blew it sky high, then extracted unopposed just on dusk.

As our bird gained altitude away from the target site, I remember staring out the open back of the helicopter at the plume of smoke rising from the demolished compound against the orange glow cast by the sun setting over the mountains on the horizon. In that moment I felt a wave of relief wash over me: the tour was over, and we hadn't lost any further soldiers. For that brief period, in the cool air of the passenger compartment of the Mi-17, I felt peace for the first time in months.

Within two weeks of our final job I found myself sitting in the rooftop bar of a fancy hotel in Dubai having drinks with a group of commando mates. It was happy hour, and as such drinks were free and we could help ourselves to an array of spirits and mixers on a communal table.

Everyone in our group had been present for one or more of the three deaths on the rotation, and we were quietly debriefing the events among ourselves. Surrounding us were tables of expatriate civilian Australians who appeared fairly full of their own self-importance and whose glances in our direction suggested that they were somewhat put out by our presence in *their* bar.

Towards the end of happy hour the bartender called last drinks, and one member of our group poured himself a full tumbler of straight Scotch to keep him going for a while after the free drinks ended. A middle-aged woman who had been sitting nearby with her husband and teenage son was outraged by this. She approached our table and began berating us.

'How dare you people come in here and abuse the system by pouring full glasses of spirits,' she hissed.

I was in no mood for her attitude and without much thought erupted at her.

'Listen, lady, we've just come out of Afghanistan after six months of hard fighting in which we lost three good mates not much older than your son.' I gestured towards her table as I spoke. 'So why don't you fuck off back to your table and leave us alone?'

The lady promptly left. I watched out of the corner of my eye for a response from her husband, but thankfully for all involved there was none.

Shortly thereafter, the bartender announced it was closing time, and everyone started to clear the bar. Our group had got up to leave when the bartender approached our table.

'You blokes can stay, if you like. I'll leave the alcohol on the table so you can drink as much as you want. I'll just be out the back doing the dishes – let me know if you need anything else.'

I often reflect on that gesture and wonder what motivated the bartender. He couldn't possibly have understood what it meant to us on that night in Dubai. Being in that controlled environment with the group who had shared the experiences of our friends' deaths allowed us to commence the slow healing process. It was an opportunity that we would never have as a group again.

* * *

Less than a week after the bar incident, I was back in Australia. Having dropped my kit in Perth, I flew to Adelaide to reunite with my family. I was sitting with Kristy watching television while our two young sons slept in their rooms nearby. It was only then that I was finally able to let go of some of my emotional burden. I broke down and cried uncontrollably, swearing to Kristy that I would never return to Afghanistan.

On leave back in Australia, I tried to fit back into the life I'd once had, but I couldn't. To an outsider I would have looked like an ordinary family man, but on the inside I was spiralling down and inwards. My mind was churning with the events of the previous six months and guilt was welling inside me, not only for being unable to save the three guys, but also for surviving when they hadn't. I was drinking excessively to try to take the edge off my thoughts, and my restless sleep was regularly broken by vivid nightmares.

Had I known ten years earlier that my professional aspirations would lead to me feeling like this, I never would have chased them. I had got exactly what I thought I wanted, and it was awful.

As the weeks passed, however, slowly but surely, and with some significant input from an army psychologist, my demons retreated and my nightmares eased. I once more felt the itch to return to Afghanistan. I went back to work at the SASR but I was restless – and like all addicts, I began doing everything in my power to get another fix.

'I have platinum,' was what I thought the Papua New Guinean highlander whispered to me.

'What's that?'

'I have *platinum*,' he repeated, more loudly this time, surreptitiously offering me a glimpse of a stone in his hand impregnated with a glimmer of metal.

The trip to PNG had come at a welcome time, just as the army psychologist had been attempting to delve deep into my psyche and was threatening to make me do the hard but meaningful work to start processing my trauma. My preference was to shellac over my issues and focus on another distraction, and in the absence of an imminent deployment, this trip fit the bill nicely. Since returning from my second tour of Afghanistan and clearing a few weeks of leave, I had returned to work to support the 2011 mid-year SAS selection course, and was in PNG as medical support on the patrol course for the reinforcement cycle of the successful candidates. By that stage, my aspirations of rejoining a reinforcement cycle, and finally achieving my decade-long aspiration to qualify to wear the sandy beret, had been squashed. Circumstances had changed, and there was no longer an appetite for the unit to qualify support staff, slamming the door on me. While initially devastated, I was starting to see that it had been the wrong dream for me anyway. I had found my tribe, not in the beret-qualified operators of the SASR, but in the Voodoo Medics who supported them. They were my people, and acceptance into their fold was not contingent on the colour of my hat.

In PNG, my fellow SAS medics and I were conducting a remote medical clinic deep in the mountainous highlands of the country when I was approached by the man masquerading as a precious metal dealer. For all I knew it really was platinum, but after a further meeting with the man, followed by a few days of dreaming up schemes to import the metal to Australia and refine it, I realised that this fantastical retirement plan was not a goer. A geologist friend to whom I had sent an image of the metallic samples confirmed that what the man was pushing on us was not platinum at all. Ah well, the dream had been good while it lasted.

As the final months of 2011 drew to a close, I started to become acutely aware of missing home. I had been absent for the majority of both my sons' lives and was due back in Australia only a couple of months shy of Gilbert's first birthday.

We decided that Kristy, who had returned to Adelaide when I posted to SASR at the start of the year, would join me in Perth for the start of 2012. Accordingly, in between medical support requirements for patrol courses and medical clinics for the locals, I was contacting Defence Housing via a combination of satellite phone and a dodgy locally sourced mobile phone from PNG, attempting to secure appropriate accommodation in Perth for my little family on return.

Three-bedroom houses in Perth were in short supply at the time, and things were looking grim. But after dozens of phone calls, orchestrated during brief windows of opportunity in our schedule, I finally found the perfect place. As if by fate, a three-bedroom townhouse on the Swan River had unexpectedly become available immediately before one of my calls. Recognising the fortuitousness of the situation, I committed to the house immediately. I phoned Kristy with the good news and sent her an internet link to photos of our new family home. After reviewing the images, her frustrating response pinged on my mobile: *I'm not sure about the green carpet.*

* * *

I returned to Australia and was physically present for Christmas, New Year's and Gilbert's first birthday, if not psychologically all there. I found it difficult to connect with my family and looked around for distraction.

I decided that my vintage red Lamborghini in fact needed to be black, and that I would paint it myself. Disappearing into the garage for the entirety of my six weeks of accumulated leave, I wrestled every panel from the car, stripping off all evidence of red paint and priming it for replacement with black. After five weeks of dedicated effort, I had completed painting all the car's panels in a gloss black finish of surprising quality.

Then, with only days remaining before I was due back at work, I opted to add a final few coats of clear paint to really bring out some depth in the paint job. With no time to accommodate for error, I sprayed thick coats of clear paint onto the vintage panels, which immediately reacted with the underlying black paint, causing bubbling, and destroying my five weeks of hard work.

As disappointed as I was at the disastrous outcome, the weeks I'd spent in the shed had served its primary purpose of giving me time and space to process my thoughts; the paint on the car was very much a secondary agenda. I reassembled my dodgy-looking car and drove it back to work, much to the delight of my medics.

Within six months of devaluing my Lamborghini, I found myself back in Afghanistan and once again standing over the body of a dead friend. On 2 July 2012, SAS Sergeant Blaine Diddams had been mortally wounded by enemy small-arms fire in a contact for which he would be posthumously awarded the Medal for Gallantry. I had not been in the field for the event but was part of the resuscitation team at the American hospital he was evacuated to. From the moment Didds had been rushed through the doors of the hospital's emergency bay the situation had appeared bleak, and despite valiant resuscitation efforts, he was declared deceased shortly after his arrival.

As I was only in-country for a brief stint on that occasion, there was no opportunity to log the missions or time at the forward surgical team to try to balance my imaginary set of scales for Didds's loss. My next trip was in the pipeline, though, and the opportunity I craved would come sooner than expected.

XVI

CHASING THE DRAGON

THE EMAIL ON MY DEFENCE SECRET NETWORK ACCOUNT confirmed what I had already been told informally. My pending deployment, planned for early 2013, was being brought forward. My new deployment date was set for early December 2012. I couldn't wait to get back to Afghanistan, and the sooner the better; Kristy on the other hand, pregnant with our third son, was going to be furious!

We had made firm plans to return to Adelaide for the festive season, both to spend the holidays with Kristy's family and friends, and to choose the final fittings for a new house we were having built there, and which we hoped would one day become our family home.

That evening, after the kids were in bed, I set about breaking the news to Kristy. Doing my best to feign dismay, I explained that I was required back in Afghanistan earlier than expected, and I would miss another Christmas.

Kristy was having none of it. 'Just tell them you can't, and you'll deploy as planned in the New Year,' she said.

'Ah, it doesn't really work that way, babe,' I replied.

'You're not even going to try, are you?'

She was absolutely fucking correct that I wasn't going to try. Even if I felt it was remotely appropriate to request that my deployment date be bumped back, no part of me wanted to. Appeasing Kristy slightly was the fact that my new deployment dates gave me a much better chance of being home in time for the birth of our third child, anticipated in June 2013.

The weeks until deployment flew by, crammed with last-minute training and preparations. The photos tell me that I was present for Henk's fifth birthday, although my lack of memories of the event suggests that my mind was once again half a world away.

Thick snow cloaked the mountains of the TK bowl as I landed in Afghanistan in December 2012 for my fourth and final tour. In the last three years, I had spent more than thirteen months in this graveyard of empires, playing a mortal game. This tour would take that tally to eighteen months. By that time, the SOTG's role in the conflict had changed somewhat, and so had my attitude towards my role as RMO. While I still pushed hard to get on the jobs where I thought I could value-add, I began to eschew unnecessary risks. In the past, where I would have fought to be on *any* job, no matter how dislocated from the action, now I gave more thought to where I put myself and for what purpose. A fatalistic law of averages was at play in my mind: the more times I rolled the dice, the better my chance of being killed. In line with that, I tried to minimise the amount of helicopter flights I took. Of course, if there was a real-time AME mission going, I was on it, but if it was simply yet another training flight, I opted to stay on the ground. In my paranoid mind's eye I kept seeing the clichéd tear-jerking front-page newspaper article of my death, leaving behind a pregnant wife and two young sons. For this to happen on an unnecessary training flight would be tragically wasteful, though my fused identity remained completely willing to sacrifice my life on a real mission if required.

I also started to reduce my exposure to the trauma coming into the forward surgical team. As with the AME flights, if the FST needed an extra pair of hands I was there for them every time, but I no longer spent unnecessary spare time with them. I had seen enough dismembered bodies and dying kids to last a lifetime, and somewhere inside of me a psychological bucket was brimming full and threatening to overflow if I poured too much more trauma into it. On a not-yet-conscious level, I was recognising that this job I loved so much was destroying me.

The icy winter months had led to a drop in enemy activity and fewer missions than I was used to from my previous tours. By the time the weather started to warm up and the fighting season commenced in early 2013, the SOTG was well and truly working on its exit strategy from Afghanistan. As such, there was an increasing ratio of Afghan partner force soldiers on missions, with the goal of improving their operational independence from us. Increased partner force requirements made for fewer available seats on insertion platforms, which further diminished my opportunity to get outside the wire.

I spent my increased time on base focusing on the training of medics and the medical upskilling of the operators. Whereas previously I had egotistically considered myself, as a doctor, to be the most appropriate person to treat a combat casualty and ensure their survival, my cumulative experience was starting to tell me otherwise. A well-trained medic or operator could deal with the vast majority of immediately life-threatening wounds just as well as I could. Therefore, the best possible medical support outcome for the task group was not for me to be on every job but to improve the medical capability across the element. A sequence of incidents during the rotation validated that perspective beyond doubt.

The first incident occurred on a day when the task group had two simultaneous missions: one a seemingly high-risk night raid into Helmand to destroy what intelligence suggested was a Taliban strategic communications tower, and the other a more routine vehicle patrol south of TK. Having attended the planning groups for both missions, I opted to put myself on the night raid and allocated a medic to the vehicle patrol.

The night raid was a complete fizzer; the 'strategic communications tower' we had been sent to destroy turned out to be a tree. I was immensely grateful for the lack of action, as after trudging through shin-deep snow on insertion, and with my fingers numb from the sub-zero temperatures, I would have struggled to respond to combat casualties.

The vehicle patrol, on the other hand, was far more eventful, with an incident involving the Bushmaster the medic was travelling in rendering a commando critically injured. He quite possibly would have died if not for the rapid and decisive actions of that medic.

I was on the airstrip as the injured commando arrived via helicopter back at TK and followed him into the FST for emergency management. The initial clinical picture didn't look good, with the commando having no sensation from his shoulders down. X-rays confirmed our worst fears: he had sustained a severe fracture to his cervical spine, with the bone fragments all but severing his spinal cord. He remained fully conscious throughout the investigations, and I watched on as the young man before us suffered the devastating realisation that he had been rendered quadriplegic. True to the nature of SOTG members, he had been manning the back gun of his Bushmaster, helping to defend his convoy, when tragedy struck.

A second incident that further reinforced my investment in medical training for the task group came on a DEA-led night raid against a Taliban heroin laboratory.

The raid force had managed to gain entry into the lab unopposed and were in the process of gathering evidence, and rigging the structure with explosives for destruction, when an Afghan partner force soldier stood on a pressure plate that initiated a large IED hidden high in one of the compound walls. The ensuing blast tore through one task group member, critically injuring him, while several others were left with severe concussions and shrapnel wounds.

I was safe and sound back at base at the time of the blast and followed proceedings via the radio transmissions coming from the field.

Upon initial review of the casualty, the treating medic found no signs of life. Suspecting a punctured lung resulting in a life-threatening build-up of pressurised air in the casualty's chest, the medic immediately intervened with the swift insertion of a needle through the chest wall. A hiss of escaping air was heard, decompressing the casualty's chest cavity and allowing his collapsing lungs to re-expand and his heart to pump blood once more. With signs of life returning, and suspecting internal bleeding, the medic proceeded to administer the blood clot-stabilising drug tranexamic acid to help stem any internal blood loss. To the best of my knowledge, that was the first time TXA had ever been used in the field by an Australian medic, and subsequent investigations on the casualty revealed that he did in fact have a life-threatening internal bleed. There is no question that the timely interventions performed on that night saved the life of the injured commando.

At the time when both the spinally injured commando and the IED blast victim were being managed in the field, I was left pacing around the regimental aid post in TK, infuriated that I wasn't out on the ground managing the casualties myself. On reflection, though, it was for the best. The treating medics did an outstanding job, validating their own training and building real-time confidence in their own abilities. At the time when I left SOCOMD, the experience of those two medics remained within the command to help shape generations to come. I realise now that one's contribution to an organisation is more accurately measured by what they have left behind rather than what they achieved while they were there.

Within weeks of our task group member's IED strike, our Afghan partner force element had one of their own. They had been conducting an operation to diffuse a device that had been found in TK and reported to the authorities by someone claiming to be a local shop owner. Unbeknown to the partner force, the IED was a trap set by the Taliban and the bomb was detonated the moment the Afghan soldiers drew close, shredding their patrol and immediately killing the four closest to the blast.

The bodies of the dead soldiers were returned to our RAP to be prepared for transport back to their respective home villages. Coalition aircraft had been organised to move the remains, and part of the clearance required for the bodies to fly involved making sure that they didn't contain any unexploded ordnance. This meant the remains needed to be X-rayed, which I organised through the commander of the American hospital on the camp next door.

A kind and highly experienced American naval surgeon, the commander of the hospital had been a US Marine corpsman in Vietnam before studying medicine and rising through the ranks to his current position. He watched on as another SOTG medic and I commenced the ghastly task of laying out the bodies for X-ray. The dead soldiers' dismembered remains had arrived in multiple deliveries; even then, they were incomplete. Heads and limbs were missing, and I had to interrupt my work several times to step away from the revolting scene and breathe in air less tainted by the stench of the remains. The commander appeared particularly repulsed; as soon as he had set us up with everything we needed, he politely but hurriedly excused himself and left. I found his reaction unusual for a man of his experience.

A couple of weeks later I caught up with the hospital commander over cigars around a firepit out the back of his facility. In a quiet voice, so as not to reach the ears of his subordinates nearby, he raised the topic of his hasty departure from the scene of the body processing. In a roundabout way, he tried to warn me of the consequences of career-long exposure to such scenes. No matter how tough you think you are, he seemed to be saying, these experiences would have an effect.

Although I had already discovered some chinks in my own mental armour, the full weight of the commander's words would not register until years later.

While they were fewer and further between than previous tours, I did launch on a couple of dozen missions during my final deployment, firing my rifle in anger on a handful of them, and patching up the wounded as required.

Things had changed. While I still enjoyed the job, much of my passion for the role had waned, leaving me little more than a combat doctor automaton. With hindsight, I was burning out.

Towards the end of my tour, Camp Russell, the home of the SOTG, was being physically dismantled in preparation for withdrawal, and the purposeful atmosphere of the base was being lost in the process.

For a variety of reasons – one of them being the impending birth of my third son – I was happy when my deployment drew to a close and it was time to leave TK for the final time.

On the day I left Afghanistan, one of the last people I bid farewell to was Cam Baird. A highly respected commando and true warrior, Cam had been awarded the Medal for Gallantry for his conduct in action some years prior on a mission during which one of his teammates had been killed. After a brief chat I shook his hand, telling him to stay safe and keep his head down, and with that I departed Camp Russell and boarded a C-130 Hercules for my final flight out of country.

XVII

GETTING OFF
THE TRAIN

'IT'S TIME,' KRISTY SAID QUIETLY, SO AS NOT TO WAKE THE hours-old infant nestled against her chest.

I knew she was right.

While I had selfishly pursued my career aspirations with scant regard for Kristy's opinion, there was one point I had consistently reinforced with her, knowing that she appreciated the magnitude of the decision I was empowering her to make. I had always promised that on the day she told me to discharge from the army, I would listen. That day arrived on the same day as our third son, Toby: 6 June 2013, exactly two years after Rowan Robinson's death.

Over Oreo McFlurry ice creams in a Perth hospital room, the decision was made, and upon my return to work the following week I handed in my discharge paperwork. I would finish up the year at SASR, and then early in 2014 would be posted against a supernumerary position at a regular army medical unit in Adelaide while I cleared my accumulated months of leave and worked out what would come next.

Although I was comfortable with the decision to discharge, I fell into my usual restless and guilty post-deployment routine, although this time it felt different: I had an ominous feeling that something dreadful was going to happen back in Afghanistan. I found myself compulsively checking the internet news first thing every morning and then multiple times during the day. A little over a month after my return to Australia I found the article that I had been searching for: Corporal Cameron Baird, the commando I had spoken with during my last moments in Afghanistan, had been killed by small-arms fire in a violent gunfight with a determined and well-armed Taliban force.

Cam had been manoeuvring his element towards the location of a severely wounded teammate, and had repeatedly drawn enemy fire while systematically neutralising the Taliban threat in the village. He was killed on his third attempt to gain entry into an enemy compound, the first two attempts being aborted due to weapon failure and the exhaustion of his ammunition supply. For his valour, Cam posthumously became the hundredth Australian recipient of the Victoria Cross.

Reading the news of Cam's death saddened me deeply – not only for the loss of another soldier of his calibre, but also because it came at a time when withdrawal from Afghanistan was impending. None of that would have mattered to Cam, of course; whether it was the first or last day of a war, I guarantee he would have fought with the same ferocity.

* * *

306

My final major commitment with SASR was a hostage-recovery training exercise held on an island in the Torres Strait. Launching out of a military base near the northern tip of Queensland, our fighting force was to project forward by both boat and helicopter to rescue two simulated hostages from separate compounds on the island. Being a complex and dangerous mission profile, I had formulated a comprehensive medical support plan that involved myself and another medic inserting with the tactical headquarters element. After briefing it to the CO, it was swiftly dismissed in favour of taking two more operators instead, with the medical support for the mission being a single SAS medic attached to one of the assault elements.

I was relegated to the sidelines to watch as the sole medic for the job was notionally killed by a paint round to the face as his element approached their target compound. A communication issue then led to one of the hostages being mistaken for enemy and shot multiple times in the chest and abdomen, with zero dedicated medical support remaining on the ground to respond. I was apoplectic, but optimistic that the after-action review (AAR) would provide a good opportunity to reflect on the casualties and the lack of medical support.

After waiting patiently for the medical section of the AAR to be delivered, when the time came the casualties were glossed over, with no mention of medical response. I simply could not believe it. After more than a decade of combat operations claiming the lives of dozens of Australian special operations soldiers, it seemed as though medical support was not being taken seriously. I was making the mistake of taking it personally, and with hindsight what happened next was the first overt indicator that I was burnt out.

Interrupting the delivery of the AAR, and in front of a hangar full of senior-ranking military officers and government agents, I demanded a response from the SAS troop commander about his medical management of the casualties. I was inappropriate and rude, and my outburst was regrettable, but at the time it felt justified.

After a couple of minutes of petty back and forth between myself and the troop commander, I was unceremoniously shut down by the unit CO. Seething, I raised the issue with the troop commander again the second the AAR concluded. What I was failing to realise was that there was nothing personal about the CO's decision not to implement my medical support plan; he had simply chosen to allocate more operators to the limited space on the insertion platforms to maximise the chance of mission success, as opposed to taking along additional medical support as an insurance policy. On operations, he had the unenviable burden of knowing such a decision might lead to the preventable deaths of his men, but ultimately mission success had to take priority. I had been deeply affected by my experiences of watching soldiers die on the battlefield and could only see things from that perspective. I returned to Perth bitter and resentful and began counting days until my discharge from the SAS Regiment.

Then, in mid-December, it all came to an abrupt end. The occasion of my departure from the SASR was marked with a totally underwhelming informal gathering at the officers' mess, where thirteen years of heart and soul, blood, sweat and sacrifice was distilled into a three-minute speech by the commanding officer. The CO presented me with a pair of engraved whisky tumblers and then, with a handshake, I was farewelled from the unit and I was once again on the outside. The SOCOMD train sped away from the station and I was left standing on the platform, alone.

That was, of course, exactly as it should have been. The

emotionless machine that is SOCOMD has to keep churning; there is no time to stop and reminisce about former members.

The following day I was one of a group of SASR soldiers who were honoured in an investiture ceremony at Government House in Perth. I had been awarded a Commendation for Distinguished Service for my second tour of Afghanistan some eighteen months earlier, but owing to subsequent deployments had not been able to attend a ceremony to receive the award. My medal was the lowest on the list of those presented that day, but it was the greatest privilege to stand among such an esteemed group of SAS soldiers, receiving awards including the Medal for Gallantry and the Order of Australia.

One of the Medal for Gallantry recipients was Sergeant Blaine Diddams, who had been killed in action in the contact for which he was awarded the medal, and whose body I had stood over in the faraway resuscitation room the year before. The sight of his teenage son striding confidently onto the stage to receive the medal on his dad's behalf filled me with both pride and sorrow. But for little more than dumb luck, that could have easily been my son on the stage receiving a medal on my behalf.

A week after the investiture ceremony I drove into work to pick up my personal belongings only to find that my swipe card access had been deactivated. The slot in SASR's manning spreadsheet marked 'RMO' had been filled with another name and I had been wiped from the system. The guard at the front gate approached me with suspicion as I repeatedly swiped my card in an attempt to get it working. He ushered me into the car park outside the base and then escorted me to the guardroom. Fortunately, I knew the soldier on duty that day and was granted a few hours of base access to pick up my gear.

As I was cleaning out my desk and locker, a group of operators came into the medical centre to pick up some supplies for a short-notice deployment. I knew one of the guys well, and he appeared happy to see me.

'Hey, Doc, are you on this gig as well?' he asked.

'Nah, mate, I'm out of the unit,' I replied. 'I'm just picking up my kit.'

The operator's demeanour changed dramatically. I might as well have told the guy that I had terminal cancer. He shook my hand and offered his condolences, before going back about his business as if I wasn't even there. Once again, I understood the situation perfectly: either you're in or you're out, and I was out. I would probably have reacted in a similar manner if I had been in the operator's position.

I finished clearing out all my personal belongings from the medical centre and left Campbell Barracks for the final time. I watched the boom gate lower in my rear-view mirror, signifying my departure from Voodoo Medicine and the start of my transition back to normal society, back to the person I was before joining the army. Or so I thought.

The honeymoon period of civilian life was as wonderful as it was fleeting. We packed up our family and moved back to Kristy's home town of Adelaide, where we could rely on a support network to help with our young family. The option remained open to stay in the army and, likewise, job prospects as a civilian doctor were good and would see my pay rise significantly from my military wage. Topping it all off, I had accumulated almost a year of leave, meaning I could ease into my new life without financial hardship. The stress and frustration of my final months with SASR immediately lifted, and I was happy to be out of the unit. On paper, things were looking good.

But before long the honeymoon was over. Slowly at first, and despite my best efforts to ignore them, the cravings began to return – except for the first time in five years I had no access to my drug of addiction. I had left special operations and the bridge back to my role as a combat doctor had been burned behind me.

As I was yet to fully discharge from the army, I was required to turn up to my local unit once in a while, mostly for administrative functions. Even those brief interactions made it abundantly clear that I couldn't get my fix there. I had travelled so far down the special operations rabbit hole that I could never go back to the regular army. On top of that, I had spent the last few years of my service actively avoiding promotion in order to stay operational and thus had lost my provisional rank of major. This meant I was once more a captain, the same rank I had held on the day I graduated medical school a decade before and professionally years behind my army doctor peers.

Although being on extended paid leave, until my discharge was complete I needed to maintain my currency in basic fitness assessments and shooting. Accordingly, on allocated days I would shave, iron a uniform and dutifully present to the relevant base to complete the assessment required. To everyone I interacted with, I appeared as a junior captain army doctor and was rightly treated as such. Embarrassingly, my ego did not respond well to this, causing resentment, as if I were owed some form of special consideration.

The realisation that I had no future back in the regular army struck me during a weapons currency shoot at a simulated firing range.

With all the safety and procedure of a live-fire shoot, we had taken our prone positions behind the simulated weapons to fire laser beams at targets on a screen to our front. Under the command of a crusty, middle-aged civilian male instructor in a booth behind us, I had taken up my rifle, loaded it with a magazine and taken aim. When the command to fire came, I steadied my breathing, fixed the reticle of my scope on the target and squeezed the trigger. Nothing happened. With those to my left and right firing away, I tried again. Nothing. As I rolled over to raise my arm and inform the instructor that my weapon wasn't working, the causative issue became immediately apparent. The rolling movement caused my improperly inserted magazine to fall from my rifle and clatter to the floor. The instructor exploded, giving me a blast about how in combat that could have resulted in death, and admonishing me for failing to perform correct weapon handling drills when the rifle hadn't fired. He was right on both counts, and for all I knew he was a combat veteran himself, but I was in no frame of mind for his opinion. The dropping of my magazine struck me as hilarious and I laughed accordingly, before picking it up, shoving it into my rifle and hastily cracking off the requisite rounds to complete the shoot with ample accuracy to pass. At the time I was oblivious to just how much my attitude stank.

The instructor bailed me up after the shoot and offered me a further piece of his mind. It took all my discipline not to tell him to fuck off.

My only way forward was as a civilian, but I had no idea how to be one – and what's more, I had no desire to be one. Through my army indoctrination I had subconsciously, and ignorantly, been programmed to see civilians as inferior to military. Yet now I again was one.

I had lost both my identity and my purpose. In my mind I had become irrelevant and inconsequential. After the experiences I'd had in uniform, the world around me seemed shallow and preoccupied with minutiae. I craved the understanding and acceptance of my former tribe, but I had abandoned them. They had remained on the SOCOMD train, and I had chosen to get off. There was no going back and seemingly no way forward.

I attempted to adapt to civilian life, and for brief periods I even convinced myself that I was succeeding. At every school drop-off and soccer practice I studied those around me, looking for cues as to who I was meant to be, but it was futile. I felt a cavernous divide between myself and society, and I could see no way to traverse the divide.

My demons once again began to stir. Without the constant distraction of special operations to occupy my thoughts, memories that had been hidden away in dark recesses of my mind bubbled to the surface. The fear that had been lacking on my combat operations now found me, gripping me at inappropriate times, such as when in crowded shopping centres. The anxiety of sitting in a restaurant with my back to the entrance was intolerable, and I instinctively found myself scanning for threats where I knew there were none, avoiding eye contact with strangers and fixating instead on what their hands were doing.

A rage welled inside of me, and even with regular sessions of lifting weights until I collapsed from exhaustion and punching a bag until my knuckles bled it did not abate.

My nightmares returned, graphic dreams of my family dying, often in a submerging car as I frantically tried to undo their seatbelts against the rapidly rising water level. On one occasion I found myself standing helplessly on the pavement below a skyscraper watching my family members jump off one by one, impacting on the concrete in front of me. The images of the many mutilated women and children I had seen enabled my sleeping brain to formulate a vivid depiction of the carnage before a return to consciousness mercifully ripped me away and back to my sweat-soaked sheets. My ever-increasing attempts to outrun my demons or drown them in alcohol proved ineffective.

As a doctor, I of course recognised the symptoms of post-traumatic stress, yet I was not ready, or perhaps unwilling, to accept the diagnosis.

The eventual catalyst to seek help came in the form of a violent vomiting episode precipitated by the smell of raw pork. Reluctantly, and prompted primarily by Kristy's concerns, I attended a single counselling session with a Veterans' Affairs psychologist. After I'd given a brief overview of my cumulative experiences and symptoms, the psychologist appeared pre-occupied with establishing a formal diagnosis of PTSD, and the session concluded with the goal of having me reviewed by a psychiatrist, and the mention of medications and pensions. Although I now realise that what I heard was not necessarily what was actually said, either way I never went back. What I had wanted was tools, not medications. I wanted a roadmap back to a place of purpose and self-respect, not a diagnosis. I set about finding that myself.

My medical mind was bewildered as to how I had managed to continue to function at the elite level required of me when I was a combat doctor, while now, when I'd never been safer, I was coming apart at the psychological seams. What meta-phoric armour had been stripped from me when I took my literal armour off for the last time? That question would orientate me on a path of discovery, eventually leading not only to recovery from my traumatic experiences but to growth. To becoming a better version of myself *because* of the trauma. The answer to that question was resilience. But that was all still to come.

My eventual return to work as a civilian fly-in, fly-out doctor on a mine site did little to re-establish my sense of self-worth. Once again, it was my ego that prevented the progress I might otherwise have made through that job. Embarrassingly, I can see now that I continued to feel that I was owed something, as if some of the respect I had earned in the military should translate across to my new role. I failed to see that in this context I was the new guy, and I needed to earn that respect. Instead, I let the experience fuel my bitterness and resentment towards civilians.

It was not just the lack of respect that bothered me; I found the new role profoundly unstimulating. Gone were the high-stakes, complex environments I thrived in, replaced with routine medicals and the rehabilitation of injured miners. That said, the doctors and nurses I worked with were a fantastic bunch, and I was able to regain a small degree of self-worth through training the mine site paramedics in emergency first response. Despite this, I had all but given up on ever reintegrating with normal society and instead learned to mimic others to facilitate smooth social interactions. I drank more. Things worsened.

As I spiralled downwards, the opportunity that would prove to be my turning point presented around eighteen months post-discharge, in the form of a lifeline offered to me by a mate called Gog.

Gog was the doctor who had supported my selection course; the one who had urged me to get in the ambulance when he could see my body was failing on the final day. He had served as an Army Reserve doctor with SASR, and over my years with the unit I had got to know him well, even spending time on deployment together in Afghanistan. Gog was working as the medical director for a small hospital in regional Queensland, and his deputy had left the position on short notice. Although I wasn't necessarily the most qualified doctor for the role, Gog could see that I was struggling and he offered me the job.

Seeing no real future in my mine site job, and somewhat on a whim, Kristy and I pulled our kids out of their schools mid-year and moved halfway across the country to start again in Queensland.

The improvement was near immediate. The sense of purpose I had been lacking since discharge returned, and the pace of the role left me with little time to dwell on the negatives of past events. I was once again part of a small, high-performance team. The learning curve was steep, but I was well supported. I thrived. The medical skills I had honed during my military years, which had ultimately failed to save my mates, were now being employed in the emergency department with life-saving results. A glint of silver lining started to emerge from the black cloud that had been darkening my psychological skies.

The on-call roster for the job allowed scant room for drinking, and my desire to numb myself in this way was dropping off anyway. It was a crutch I was requiring less and less, replaced by far more adaptive coping strategies.

'STAND CLEAR . . . SHOCKING,' came Gog's stern voice over the alarms of the various machines in the resuscitation bay screaming at us that the patient's heart had clicked into a lethal rhythm. As drilled, I stood well clear of the bed on which the patient's pale, lifeless form lay, holding my hands up for Gog to see I was safe. Gog turned back to the defibrillator and hit the shock button, sending a bolt of lightning down the cables attached to the pads on the patient's chest, causing his entire torso to contract violently. A second later I returned to perform chest compressions, hunched over the patient, pumping hard, focusing intently on the position of my hands and the rate and depth of my compressions. Such was my state of concentration, I missed Gog's second call to stand clear, and only registered that another lightning bolt was inbound when the word 'SHOCKING' triggered a primal reaction deep in my brain. Gog had been performing a protocol in which three rapid consecutive shocks were given, as was indicated in the setting of a witnessed cardiac arrest. I had failed to register this fact and had defaulted to the protocol of recommencing compressions immediately after defibrillation.

It was as if time slowed. With Gog's warning I looked up to see his head turn from the defibrillator at the exact moment he pressed the button to deliver the second shock. He had rightly assumed that he would find me still a step back from the bed, my hands in the air. Our eyes met and Gog's facial expression began to morph as he realised I had failed to stand clear, and that a shock of electricity was headed my way. My reaction time was never going to be equal to the task, and as I began to retract my hands from the patient's chest they explosively recoiled with the assistance of a couple of hundred joules of energy to help them along.

The soundtrack for the moment of stunned comprehension that followed was the rhythmical metronome of the patient's heartbeat, now returned to normal. We had saved his life.

My arms hurt for a few days following that event, and my right hand wasn't its usual self, causing my already messy doctor's writing to deteriorate into hieroglyphics. I also had our facility's resuscitation protocols reinforced to me in no uncertain terms. But none of that mattered. The guy we had saved was in his early 50s and he had a wife and three teenage kids. A few days of discomfort was irrelevant. The professional satisfaction of having been able to save his life was immense, and with every successful resuscitation I was beginning to self-actualise once more.

It felt great to be working alongside Gog in the emergency setting, and some of the skills we had sharpened together in the forward surgical team in TK in 2009 came in incredibly handy now.

In one such instance, a patient had been delivered to our emergency department via ambulance with lights and sirens blazing, and with blood gushing from a severe laceration across their neck. The situation was dire, and on inspection the cut had severed multiple major blood vessels and opened the patient's windpipe at the level of the throat. Our small facility was ill-equipped to deal with injuries of this magnitude, but using techniques more often seen on the battlefield than in the regions of Queensland, we managed to secure the patient's airway and stem the bleeding sufficiently to buy time to pile him back into the ambulance and make best speed to the surgical hospital 40 minutes up the road.

Thankfully the patient was able to receive the specialist vascular reconstructive surgery he required, but unfortunately some of the techniques Gog and I had used to stabilise the casualty were subsequently brought into question. It was the Gerber incident all over again, and I strongly suspect that if the patient had died at our facility, the prevailing opinion would have been that there was little that could have been done and the injuries were not survivable. In the event, an investigation determined we had acted appropriately, and a letter of recognition for our efforts followed some time later.

'Don't wait for me, Dad. If you have to go sooner, you go.'

My dying father mumbled a semi-coherent acknowledgement down the phone line. It would be the last time I heard his voice.

It was early April 2017 and I was in the middle of a block of six days working in the emergency department. I planned to make the seven-hour drive to my dad's bedside on my next lot of days off, so as not to inconvenience the other doctors by taking leave at short notice.

The profoundly erroneous decision I was making, and why it was so effortless for me to make it, didn't register until several years later.

Just as it had been so easy for me to decide to leave the dying infant in regional Afghanistan almost a decade earlier, I was once again driven by a disproportionate sense of dedication to the mission and a glorified view of my own importance to it. I had found my new tribe and a new mission, and was clinging to both in the hope they would provide me a new identity and, with it, new self-worth. I was beginning to feel consequential once more and feared that abandoning my team, even for a few days, might compromise that.

Having been indoctrinated in an environment of mission primacy, and programmed with the willingness to die in the line of my work, the thought of leaving at a moment's notice to be at my dad's bedside was unthinkable; indeed, I didn't even consider it. I would finish my block of shifts and then, if Dad was still alive when I had days off, I would see him.

He wasn't.

Only 36 hours after I'd last spoken to Dad, I received the phone call from my brother Ben to let me know he had passed away. I took that call in the same location I had spoken to Dad from: the ambulance bay of the emergency department. After learning of my dad's death, I hung up and finished my shift.

I used my days off to attend my dad's funeral instead. It was a wonderful celebration of his life, attended by many of Dad's lifelong army mates. Out of respect for his contribution to the corps, a contingent of senior army aviation officers and soldiers in their finest dress uniforms not only attended, but organised a missing man flyover with a formation of my dad's beloved Kiowa helicopters. On cue, as we accompanied Dad's casket from the funeral parlour, the formation of birds flew low overhead, a single aircraft poignantly breaking off in recognition of the departed aviator we were farewelling. When I think of that moment now, tears well in my eyes and a ball of emotion builds in my chest. At the time, however, my eyes were dry.

Without resentment, I blame the army for my failing to see my dad one last time before he passed, for not having been there by his bedside at the time, and for not being capable of grieving as a son should at his funeral. Having seen the worst of deaths on the battlefield, where young soldiers were taken before their time, the loss of a 71-year-old who had lived a full life didn't strike me as sad. I had been recalibrated by the intensity of my experiences in Afghanistan, robbed of the perspective required to fathom the significance of losing Dad. I was still trapped in a mindset that prioritised the mission above all else.

While I was still years away from grasping the sadness of Dad's death, what I was beginning to appreciate during my time in Queensland was all I had missed in the early years of Henk and Gil's lives. My preoccupation with work and the richness of my army experiences around the times of their births and in their early childhood meant I hadn't appreciated the wonder of those years. I'd had no idea what I had been missing.

Being present for Toby's infancy opened my eyes. I experienced all the ups and downs – the first steps and first words, the crying, coughs, croups and crappy nappies – and began to understand for the first time the visceral experience that is parenthood. My guilt at having missed many of those moments with Henk and Gil was quickly superseded by a deep commitment to being the best parent I could from that time on. I would never get the lost time back, but I was determined not to lose any more.

It was around the time of my dad's passing that I took up something I had never done before. I began to meditate. Starting with ten minutes most days, my practice quickly became habitual, and my sessions increased. The clarity of thought that came with meditation was amazing. Through the application of non-judgement, I began to loosen my grip on many of the hot coals I had been holding, coming to realise that my guilt served no purpose, and that those we'd lost would not want me to feel that way. When I really explored my feelings, I was confronted by the discovery that much of my guilt stemmed from *not* feeling guilt about certain situations that I perceived a normal person should have felt guilty for.

Ultimately, we had all done the very best job we could under the circumstances, and no amount of revisiting events was going to alter the outcome. Instead of dwelling on the past to keep the memories of the dead alive, I would use their memory as fuel to live my best life, a life they would be proud of. I would spend more time with my kids because Todd could not. I would invest more in my relationship with my wife because Brett could not. I would phone my mum more often because Rowan could not.

It did of course occur to me that this epiphany was nothing more than denial, a convenient excuse to stop my memories from haunting me. Perhaps it was. But it likewise occurred to me that there was no other tenable option; that the downward and inward spiral of negative rumination had to be broken by whatever means possible or self-destruction was the inevitable outcome.

Towards the end of 2017 my contract in Queensland was coming to an end, and Kristy and I started planning a return to Adelaide. While working as a deputy medical superintendent at the hospital I'd also completed an MBA, and my experience and qualification secured me a position as medical director with the South Australian Prison Health Service.

The role was fascinating, and it provided me with my first real insight into the criminal underbelly of society, and specifically the health issues that face them. Concerns seldom seen in middle-class society – such as heroin addiction and hepatitis infections – are rife in the prison community, as are many other forms of substance abuse and mental health diagnoses. I soon discovered not only my ignorance of this disenfranchised population but also my pre-existing, subconscious stigmatisation of prisoners. The more I interacted with the incarcerated population, the clearer it became that, for the most part, they were good people who had been dealt a terrible hand of cards.

Time and time again, I read reports of prisoners having been born to drug-addicted mothers and absent fathers, having been beaten and abused throughout their childhood, and having bounced between foster homes while their parents did jail time. The predictable teenage pattern of drug and alcohol abuse, violence and crime would then follow, resulting in their own incarceration.

It was incredible how much a small gesture of human decency could mean to a prisoner, and it was a privilege to be able to offer that regularly in my new role.

My time in the prison health system also served to further reinforce the gratitude seeded in me by my time in Afghanistan. Not only am I incredibly thankful to be living in a country like Australia, I now appreciate too the good fortune of being born to parents who wanted and loved me, and who weren't struggling with the demons of addiction or poverty.

My phone had been set to silent as I chaired the clinical governance committee meeting, but its vibration alerted me to an incoming message. I snuck a covert glance at the text from Kristy.

Henk's dislocated his finger at school – can you put it back in?

My initial inclination to dismiss this diagnosis as a gross exaggeration of the injury was immediately overruled by the image that followed the message. There was Henk, looking surprisingly pleased with himself given the circumstances, holding up his left hand to reveal a little finger bent outwards at a right angle. Without hesitation, I rose and declared that I needed to leave, handing over responsibility for the meeting to the deputy chair. I wasn't asking; I was telling.

While that decision might seem intuitive to other parents, for me it represented a pivotal moment. It was the first time since discharge from the army that I had prioritised family over work, and I had done it instinctively.

I didn't end up cranking Henk's finger back into alignment myself, but I was with him every step of the way as the emergency department crew at the local hospital did. It just so happened to be the same hospital at which I had trained in myself, and the exact ED where I had worked as a junior doctor fifteen years before.

When his little digit once again looked somewhat like a finger, Henk and I stopped for KFC on the way home to round out the experience. It was wonderful.

As interesting as my role with prison health was, after three years I began to stagnate. I had become comfortable and was getting restless. It was time for a new challenge.

Since completing an entrepreneurship subject for my MBA, I had been dipping my toe in the waters of small business and start-ups. I was surprised to learn that the thrill of entrepreneurial ventures came close to replicating the buzz I had experienced in special operations. While being vastly different domains, the underlying psychology of special operations and small business struck me as remarkably similar. Both involve small teams of highly motivated individuals, united and driven by an ambitious goal, with a decent probability of failure. Both require high risk tolerance and the ability to pivot and adapt in response to an evolving environment.

One of the companies I had become involved with was the medical equipment, training and services company TacMed Australia. Jeremy, a former special forces medic and Medal of Gallantry winner, had founded the venture, and Adam (another ex-special forces medic) and I were helping him to build the business.

In 2021, TacMed was offered the medical support contract for the reality TV series *SAS Australia*, and a doctor was required. Although I probably could have negotiated leave from my job to cover the commitment, I knew deep down that I had to take the leap from prison health. So I used the opportunity to jump, resigning from my position with few plans beyond the three-week TV gig. It was equal parts exciting and terrifying to know that I would have to sink or swim again professionally, with multiple mortgages and three sets of private school fees to pay.

I recovered my old MultiCam uniforms from a trunk in the shed to wear on the show, and found that while they still fit me, they seemed to have shrunk around the waist and mid-section, while at the same time stretched in the bicep and chest regions. An effect of those harsh Adelaide summers, no doubt!

Having completed SAS selection myself, and having supported multiple courses since, I was initially dubious as to whether the TV show could replicate the real thing. But I was pleasantly surprised. Behind the theatricality that is a necessary element of TV beats the heart of a proper military selection course. As the course progressed and recruit numbers were whittled down through voluntary withdrawals and injuries, I saw the exact same trend emerge that I had previously observed on military courses. Irrespective of gender, size, age or background, there were those who possessed the grit to knuckle down and endure what others couldn't, to keep pushing beyond their physical and psychological limits, despite knowing that immediate relief was available to them if they quit. Further adding to my respect for the recruits on *SAS Australia* was the fact that, unlike their military counterparts, there was no career path at the end of the suffering. They were taking time out of their lives, and for some risking their very livelihood, to test themselves. Those who made it to the end of the course epitomised resilience.

Resilience was a concept I had become increasingly interested in since my discharge from the army and my subsequent mental health wobbles. It had sustained me during my service, and if I had possessed it once, I was sure I could do so again. The keys, I became convinced, were to first define resilience, and then to break it down to its constituent components and rebuild it.

In search of answers, I began to journal and blog in a quest to decipher all the events of my military service, and scour the relevant scientific literature to codify them using a psychological lens. It was early in this process that I uncovered some musings on the deaths of Brett, Rowan and Todd that I had written as a cathartic exercise on the recommendation of an army psychologist at my post-deployment screen in 2011. Those scribbles would form the eventual skeleton of this book.

It wasn't long before I found an audience for my blogs and social media posts. Unsurprisingly, other veterans were negotiating the same dark path, and I began to receive regular messages from others around the globe letting me know that what I was saying was resonating. This encouragement inspired me to compile some of my reflections and lessons learned, and in 2019 I self-published a short book titled *Average 70kg Dickhead*. It developed an unexpected cult following, selling thousands of copies.

I also began to team up with Ben occasionally to deliver presentations on leadership and resilience to military and government groups. By that time, Ben had completed his terminal army posting as the commanding officer of the SAS Regiment, completed an MBA and started a consultancy firm with another ex-SAS squadron commander and MBA grad, Tim Curtis.

Before long the three of us started to come together regularly to ponder the concept of resilience based not only on our own personal experiences in and out of uniform, but also through reflections on those we knew who had faced adversity and reacted in vastly different ways, ranging from thriving to suicide. We started to wonder why it was that most people would wait for a stress event to overwhelm them before consciously doing something to help themselves. We thought there must be a better way. We felt that heeding the advice of Marcus Aurelius to 'get active in your own rescue' and consciously build resilience as a matter of habit was a preferable approach.

With the backing of a federal government research grant, and partnered with the University of Western Australia, we developed and scientifically validated a model of building resilience that was multifactorial, dynamic and modifiable. We called it the Resilience Shield and wrote a book with that title detailing the model and how it can be applied. Within months of release in August 2021, *The Resilience Shield* hit the best-seller list.

When I told Kristy that the book had become a bestseller, she responded: 'That's great news!' and then added, 'I think we'll have the leftover chicken for dinner.' While Kristy has always been my rock, no-one would ever accuse her of being my cheerleader. I wouldn't have it any other way.

EPILOGUE

For quite some time after my discharge, I assumed that part of me had died on the battlefields of Afghanistan; that I was broken, no longer complete. As time passed, however, I began to consider things in a different light. Perhaps, rather than a part of me having died, a part of me had been born, or a dormant part of me had awoken. Maybe the person I had become was who I had been all along, but I hadn't had the opportunity to reveal him. Maybe rather than being broken I had become more complete.

Psychiatrist Carl Jung, the founder of analytical psychology, spoke of the unconscious negative aspects of our personality, which most of us choose to ignore and deny, as our shadow, and he theorised that it might provide a direct link back to one's primitive animal instincts. It is these facets of our personalities that might enable us to kill another human, or to witness human suffering on mass, without overwhelming psychological cost. Clinical psychologist Jordan Peterson provides a contemporary elaboration on Jung's shadow, referring to our inner *monster*, which he encourages us to become, and then tame.

There is no question that during my time in Afghanistan I stepped through my shadow and embodied my inner monster. I learned things about myself that I would never have known had I not gone to war.

I now know that I can run towards the sound of gunfire instead of away from it. I know I am capable of employing lethal force against someone I don't hate, and saving the life of someone I don't like. I know that when called on to risk my own life to save another, I can answer, and that even when my body and mind are broken, I can endure. I have pushed and pushed the envelope of what I believed to be my physical and psychological limits, and watched it bend every time. I have evolved.

Just as a piece of meat, once cooked, cannot return to its raw state no matter how much it is cooled, I can never return to my former self. I realise now that should not be the goal; that my trajectory back to normal society will never converge but will, rather, run parallel. There is no bridge back, and that's okay.

The goal now, as Peterson proposes, is to keep my monster tame rather than attempt to kill him off. Whereas his presence once terrified me, it now reassures me. I know he is there, ready and eager to step up if ever called upon again. Equally, I know he is subordinate to my conscious mind now, and that the likelihood of him taking control by coup is low.

The larger part of me hopes I will never see him again, but like any rehabilitated addict who still aches for the familiar sting of the needle and rush of the drug, another part of me still craves the darkness of my shadow, the weight of an M4 in my monster's hands and the thrill of loading into an insertion bird to be delivered deep into enemy territory. If I close my eyes and imagine that scenario, my heart still quickens. My subconscious mind still occasionally takes me there in my dreams, but I am fortunate to no longer be plagued by nightmares. My war dreams are now positive experiences in which my weapon never jams and no good guys ever die.

Once buckled by my trauma, I have now grown because of it. I revel in the routine, mundane tasks that used to bore me. The range of fresh produce at the supermarket takes my mind back to the Afghan bazaars with their decaying fruit and rotting, flyblown meat. Seeing my sons play, I am reminded of the countless broken, and dead, Afghan children I encountered over the years. I am truly grateful for all I used to take for granted. My blinkers are off, and for the first time in my life I feel I can truly see what has been right there in front of me all along.

My time with SOCOMD taught me many things, but above all else it has taught me that I have absolutely no excuses in life. I fear that, as a society, we tend to look for excuses to account for mediocrity. We are too comfortable.

I have seen operators who have been shot, blown up, drowned and busted in the worst conceivable ways go on to return to the highest levels of soldiering. I've stood in a pub and watched Damien Thomlinson, a commando who lost both of his legs in an IED blast in Afghanistan, walk casually past the disabled toilet on his prosthetics to take a piss at the urinal with the rest of us. I've been on the ground in Afghanistan as a sniper was rendered temporarily quadriplegic by a bullet passing through his neck, and then watched from a distance as he raced on foot to the South Pole and learned to fly helicopters.

I have a bulged spinal disc, my ears sometimes ring, my right knee will never be the same and my psychological demons still stir occasionally, but apart from that I am unscathed. I have no excuses.

Nowadays, when I speak with medics who have not been to war, and watch their eyes light up with enthusiasm at the prospect of combat and treating war wounds at the point of injury, I wish that I could tell them. To convey what it is truly like, and make them understand that they should be careful what they wish for. I can't, of course; they can't be told just as I couldn't have been told. They need to live it, to feel it and to smell it themselves to truly comprehend. While I wouldn't wish that experience on those young medics, my heart is gladdened by the fact that they exist and that they too will be there when their fellow operator needs them most. They are the future of the capability I loved so dearly, and I know they will wear the medic callsign with all the allegorical pride and burden that comes with it.

In a podcast interview around the time of finishing this book I was asked whether, knowing everything I know now, I would do it all again. After a moment of contemplation, my answer was a resounding *fucking oath*. In spite of all the highs and lows of my time with SOCOMD, it has unquestionably provided me with the richest experiences of my life to date. When all is said and done, I will not die wondering, and my place shall never be with those cold and timid souls who know neither victory nor defeat.

ACKNOWLEDGEMENTS

KRISTY – THANK YOU FOR BEING THE SUPERGLUE THAT'S HELD not only me, but our family, together throughout this crazy rollercoaster ride. You're one in a million and it's you who should be wearing a chest full of medals.

Henk, Gil and Toby – It's the greatest privilege to be your dad and to get to share my life with you. I hope this book helps to explain why I'm missing from a lot of the photos of your early years, and perhaps why I get a little anxious when you point Nerf guns at my face.

Dad – It was one of your dying wishes to see this book published, and we finally did it! I will forever remember the encouragement you provided on this project. The hardcopy early draft of this manuscript that bears your handwritten comments is a cherished possession and gave me guidance from beyond the grave for the final version. I miss you, mate.

Mum – It's only now that I feel I truly appreciate the role you played in raising Ben and me with dad away so often. You, too, are superglue. Thanks for being an ongoing sounding board and friend.

Ben – You're the very reason this all came to be. Had it not been for your drive and dogged determination to reach the pinnacle of soldiering, I would have never had my eyes opened to the path I followed. You're the best big bro a little bro could hope for.

To the families of Brett, Rowan, Todd and Blaine. I cannot imagine the pain of your loss. There's rarely a day that passes when I don't think of you, and I wish you nothing but the best in continuing to heal.

To the men and women that I had the privilege to serve alongside. There are thousands of you spread across many units and multiple nations, and all of you have played a role in this story. I truly hope you have all been able to make sense of your military experiences and grow from them. Thank you for whatever part, big or small, you played in shaping my experience.

Gog – Who could have possibly known how our lives would intersect as you stood over my depleted form on the final day of selection? Thank you for your faith in me as a doctor, for your professional mentorship, and mostly for your ongoing friendship to me and my family.

Tom – Thank you for your friendship, mentorship, and encouragement on not only this project, but in general. I look forward to many more deep discussions over whisky together.

Ange, Luke and Tori – You're my trusted panel of proof-readers, and your feedback was the fuel that kept this project going through the periods of doubt and fear. Thank you.

Marty – The stars truly aligned for me to be able to follow in your footsteps as a special operations doctor. Thank you for your courage in pushing the boundaries and redefining the role of doctors in forward support to combat operations. The grace and humour that you did it with made it seem effortless, however I of course know it wasn't. Please don't ever write a book of your own, as by comparison it will diminish my career into insignificance!

Jim – You're one of a kind and rightly hold legendary status among the Voodoo Medic community. Seldom have I seen such selfless contribution to a cause. The training you provided allowed me and others to approach the most horrendous of traumas with confidence and has unquestionably saved the lives of many. In my opinion you are a true unsung hero of Australian special operations medical capability. Stay powerful!

To Jez, Adam, Davs, and the team at TacMed Australia – What a privilege it is to be a part of the company's amazing journey. It's healing for my soul to be able to continue to engage with my fellow Voodoo Medics.

Mr Richard Villar – Never has such a small interaction had such a massive impact on my life. That single email you sent me on 4 March 2003 was like rocket fuel for my motivation. Receiving words of encouragement from someone who had lived the life I aspired to somehow gave me the permission to dare to try. Thank you.

To the men and women of our police forces, ambulance services, fire brigades, correctional facilities, emergency departments, intelligence services, and other first-response organisations, thank you for what you do for our community. The burden that you shoulder while wearing your respective uniforms is significant and I fear often goes largely unrecognised and unappreciated.

Last, but most certainly not least, to Alex Lloyd, Belinda Huang and the team at Pan Macmillan – It's been an absolute pleasure to work with you on this book. The way you have taken the original manuscript and guided it to its final form is little short of magic. Thank you for your sage advice, infinite patience, and the wonderful energy you have brought to the project.

MORE FROM DR DAN PRONK

The Resilience Shield
Dr Dan Pronk, Ben Pronk DSC and Tim Curtis

Life is hard. Rocketing rates of physical and mental health issues are testimony to the immense pressures of our complex world. So how do we become tough and adaptable to face life's challenges?

The Resilience Shield provides that defence. In their ground-breaking guide to overcoming adversity, Australian SAS veterans Dr Dan Pronk, Ben Pronk DSC and Tim Curtis take you behind the scenes of special operations missions, into the boardrooms of leading companies and through the depths of contemporary research in order to demystify and define resilience. Through lessons learned in and out of uniform, they've come to understand the critical components of resilience and how it can be developed in anyone – including you.

The Resilience Shield explores the hard-won resilience secrets of elite soldiers and the latest thinking on mental and physical wellbeing. This book will equip you with an arsenal of practical tools for you to start making immediate improvements in your life that are attainable and sustainable.

Let's build your shield!

'a powerful text that will benefit any reader'
DR RICHARD HARRIS SC, OAM

'informative and enlightening . . . compelling lessons and advice'
THE HON JULIE BISHOP

'Clear, approachable insights into resilience'
MERRICK WATTS

'A blend of raw experience and impeccable science . . . a brilliant guidebook for our times'
HUGH MACKAY AO